CONTENTS

KV-026-278

PUBLISHED

Iane Austen: *Emma*

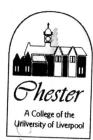
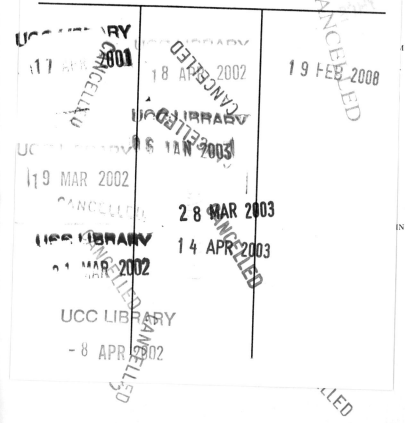

Shakespeare: *Henry IV Parts I and II* G..K. HUNTER
Shakespeare: *Henry V* MICHAEL QUINN
Shakespeare: *Julius Caesar* PETER URE
Shakespeare: *King Lear* FRANK KERMODE
Shakespeare: *Macbeth* JOHN WAIN
Shakespeare: *Measure for Measure* G.K. STEAD
Shakespeare: *The Merchant of Venice* JOHN WILDERS
Shakespeare: *'Much Ado About Nothing' and 'As You Like It'* JOHN RUSSELL BROWN
Shakespeare: *Othello* JOHN WAIN
Shakespeare: *Richard II* NICHOLAS BROOKE
Shakespeare: *The Sonnets* PETER JONES
Shakespeare: *The Tempest* D.J. PALMER
Shakespeare: *Troilus and Cressida* PRISCILLA MARTIN
Shakespeare: *Twelfth Night* D.J. PALMER
Shakespeare: *The Winter's Tale* KENNETH MUIR
Shelley: *Shorter Poems and Lyrics* PATRICK SWINDEN
Spenser: *The Faerie Queene* PETER BAYLEY
Swift: *Gulliver's Travels* RICHARD GRAVIL
Tennyson: *In Memoriam* JOHN DIXON HUNT
Thackeray: *Vanity Fair* ARTHUR POLLARD
Webster: *'The White Devil' and 'The Duchess of Malfi'* R.V. HOLDSWORTH
Wilde: *Comedies* WILLIAM TYDEMAN
Virginia Woolf: *To the Lighthouse* MORRIS BEJA
Wordsworth: *Lyrical Ballads* ALUN R. JONES AND WILLIAM TYDEMAN
Wordsworth: *The Prelude* W.J. HARVEY AND RICHARD GRAVIL
Yeats: *Last Poems* JON STALLWORTHY

Drama Criticism: Developments since Ibsen ARNOLD P. HINCHLIFFE
Poetry of the First World War DOMINIC HIBBERD
Tragedy: Developments in Criticism R.P. DRAPER
The English Novel: Developments in Criticism since Henry James STEPHEN HAZELL
The Romantic Imagination JOHN SPENCER HILL

TITLES IN PREPARATION INCLUDE

Defoe: *'Robinson Crusoe' and 'Moll Flanders'* PATRICK LYONS
T.S. Eliot: *Plays* ARNOLD P. HINCHLIFFE
Henry James: *'Washington Square' and 'Portrait of a Lady'* ALAN SHELSTON
O'Casey: *'Juno and the Paycock', 'The Plough and the Stars' & 'The Shadow of a Gunman'* RONALD AYLING
Trollope: *The Barsetshire Novels* T. BAREHAM
Keats: *Narrative Poems* JOHN SPENCER HILL
Shakespeare: *A Midsummer Night's Dream* ANTONY W. PRICE
Yeats: *Poems, 1919–35* ELIZABETH CULLINGFORD
The 'Auden Group' Poets RONALD CARTER
Post-Fifties Poets: Gunn, Hughes, Larkin & R.S. Thomas A.E. DYSON

Poetry Criticism: Developments since the Symbolists A.E. DYSON
Comedy: Developments in Criticism DAVID PALMER
The Language of Literature NORMAN PAGE
Medieval English Drama PETER HAPPÉ
Elizabethan Lyric and Narrative Poetry GERALD HAMMOND
The Pastoral Mode BRYAN LOUGHREY
The Gothick Novel VICTOR SAGE

Shelley

Shorter Poems and Lyrics

A CASEBOOK

EDITED BY

PATRICK SWINDEN

M

First edition 1976
Reprinted 1983

Published by
THE MACMILLAN PRESS LTD
London and Basingstoke
Companies and representatives throughout the world

ISBN 0 333 18248 0 (paper cover)

Printed in Hong Kong

ACKNOWLEDGEMENTS

The editor and publishers wish to thank the following who have kindly given permission for the use of copyright material: Judith Chernaik, 'The Magic Circle: Poems to Jane Williams' in *The Lyrics of Shelley*, 1972, by permission of the author; Donald Davie, 'Shelley's Urbanity' from *Purity of Diction in English Verse*, 1952, by permission of Routledge & Kegan Paul Ltd; T. S. Eliot, extract from 'A Note on Richard Crashaw' from *For Lancelot Andrewes*, 1928, and extract from 'Shelley and Keats' from *The Use of Poetry and the Use of Criticism*, 1933, reprinted by permission of Faber & Faber Ltd; David V. Erdman, extract from 'Reading Shelley' in *Essays in Criticism*, 1954, by permission of the author and editors of *Essays in Criticism*; John Holloway, extract from the Introduction to *Selected Poems of P. B. Shelley*, 1960, by permission of Heinemann Educational Books Ltd; Ralph Houston, 'Shelley and the Principle of Association' from *Essays in Criticism*, 1953, by permission of the editors of *Essays in Criticism*; Edward B. Hungerford, 'Shelley's *Adonais*' in *Shores of Darkness*, 1941, by permission of Columbia University Press; Israel James Kapstein, 'The Meaning of Shelley's "Mont Blanc"' from *PMLA*, LXII (1947), by permission of the author and the Modern Language Association of America; F. H. Ludlam, 'The Meteorology of Shelley's Ode', by permission of the author; Geoffrey Matthews, 'Shelley's Grasp upon the Actual' in *Essays in Criticism*, 1954, by permission of the author and the editors of *Essays in Criticism*, and 'Shelley's Lyrics' from *The Morality of Art: Essays Presented to G. Wilson Knight by his Colleagues and Friends*, 1969, by permission of the author, editor and Routledge & Kegan Paul Ltd; W. Milgate, extract from 'Reading Shelley' in *Essays in Criticism*, 1954, by permission of the editors of *Essays in Criticism*; Valerie Pitt, extract from

'Reading Shelley' in *Essays in Criticism*, 1954, by permission of
the author and editors of *Essays in Criticism*; F. R. Pottle, 'The
Case of Shelley', by permission of the author and the Modern
Language Association of America; Patrick Swinden, 'The
"Ode to the West Wind" ' revised, first published in *Critical
Survey*, 1973; Allen Tate, extract from 'Understanding Modern
Poetry' reprinted from *Essays of Four Decades* by permission of
the author and The Swallow Press Inc., Chicago.

GENERAL EDITOR'S PREFACE

Each of this series of Casebooks concerns either one well-known and influential work of literature or two or three closely linked works. The main section consists of critical readings, mostly modern, brought together from journals and books. A selection of reviews and comments by the author's contemporaries is also included, and sometimes comments from the author himself. The Editor's Introduction charts the reputation of the work from its first appearance until the present time.

The critical forum is a place of vigorous conflict and disagreement, but there is nothing in this to cause dismay. What is attested is the complexity of human experience and the richness of literature, not any chaos or relativity of taste. A critic is better seen, no doubt, as an explorer than as an 'authority', but explorers ought to be, and usually are, well equipped. The effect of good criticism is to convince us of what C. S. Lewis called 'the enormous extension of our being which we owe to authors'. A Casebook will be justified if it helps to promote the same end.

A single volume can represent no more than a small selection of critical opinions. Some critics have been excluded for reasons of space, and it is hoped that readers will follow up the further suggestions in the Select Bibliography. Other contributions have been severed from their original context, to which some readers may wish to return. Indeed, if they take a hint from the critics represented here, they certainly will.

A. E. Dyson

INTRODUCTION

I have divided this Casebook into three parts, of which the first will do duty for the conventional introduction to members of this series. Professor Pottle's review of Shelley criticism was first published in *PMLA* in 1952. Eight years later he revised his essay when it was reprinted in M. H. Abrams's *English Romantic Poetry*. In one version or the other it has often been anthologised and is clearly a thoughtful and comprehensive account of the problems of evaluation raised by Shelley's poetry. These problems are considered both as they appeared from the vantage point of the 1950s, and as they have been understood during the 130 years that have elapsed since Shelley's death in 1822. For this reason, I reprint the essay as a substitute for a longer introduction of my own. By doing so I allow myself more space to explain the rationale behind the selection of extracts from full essays that this anthology comprises.

Several presumptions have influenced my selection of material. The first is that Shelley is among the finest lyrical poets in the language. This is not the place to explain my reasons for saying so. I have included an essay of my own which I hope will go some way towards justifying my opinion. In any case, most of the essays printed below have been chosen with a view to reinforcing it.

Second, there is a very powerful body of critical opinion that has thought otherwise, indeed that has believed Shelley's poetry to be ruined by sloppy thinking, vaguely enthusiastic expression and an insufficiently close correlation between thought and imaginative expression – in other words that the gap between thought and expression is so wide that all the poetry manages to do is to expose the poverty of the one and the looseness of the

other. This way of thinking is most often, and rightly, associated
with the names of Eliot, Leavis and Tate. I have reprinted the
relevant passages from Eliot and Tate, together with one or two
other essays which seem to be pushing in the same direction.
(It was not possible to include material by Leavis in this
selection.[1]) On the other hand I have sought to redress the
balance by including as many good essays as I can find by
critics who admire Shelley. I have to say that these are few and
far between. Nevertheless, since Pottle's 1960 revision of his
essay there have been signs that a serious attempt to rescue
Shelley from the most serious charges of emotional self-indulgence and verbal imprecision has got under way. This has involved the admission that much of the early poetry, up to the
spring of 1819 when the first three acts of *Prometheus Unbound*
were written, is worthless – except as a record of technical
experiment and discovery; also that discriminations still have
to be made among the large body of work written between
Spring 1819 and July 1822. Nevertheless, during those last
three years of his life Shelley composed a great deal of remarkable poetry, much of it lyrical (even where the lyric stanzas
proper are incorporated in a narrative or dramatic framework,
as in *Prometheus* and *Hellas*), much of it refuting the charges
brought against Shelley's poetry in general by the Eliot/Leavis
argument. John Holloway's selection of poems, with its polemical introduction (reprinted below) and excellent notes, was a
popular sign that the defence of Shelley had got off the ground;
and Judith Chernaik's recent edition of the lyrics, with its long
introductory chapters on the various groups of short poems,
comes near to completing the work. Wasserman's enormous
critical reading of the poetry gathers together and enlarges
material published in different format over the previous twenty
years. Since its strengths are mainly to do with the evolution of
Shelley's philosophical system and the bearing of that system
on the structure of his long poems, it was difficult to make use
of his book in an anthology of this kind. In my judgement, the
best contemporary critic of Shelley is G. M. Matthews. His

brilliant essay on the lyrics brings me to my third presupposition about Shelley's poetry.

This is that it is a pity earlier Shelley criticism did not take account of the fact that most of the lyrics were not published in Shelley's lifetime (and therefore may not have been intended for publication at all – certainly not in the form we know) and that even among those that were, knowledge of context may be all-important. Matthews's interpretation of *The Indian Serenade* and Chernaik's comments on the 'social context' of some of the very late short poems show how important this might be. Undoubtedly a great deal of damage has been done to Shelley by a modern critical theory of poetry which insists on the integrity and self-sufficiency of the isolated poem, especially the lyrical poem. Where the context of the poem is removed by circumstances of publication, and a consequent misunderstanding of Shelley's intentions arises, the correct interpretation of the poem is seriously put at risk; and this can bring with it those accusations of uncritical self-indulgence which, when the facts *about the poem* are fully ascertained, are often seen to be beside the point. This is not to say that sometimes Shelley doesn't unwittingly expose himself to these accusations. But where, for example, the speaker of the poem and the (narrative or dramatic) situation from within which it is spoken are not understood, it is unlikely the reader will grasp the poem's intention. It is then even less likely the reader will be in a position to judge whether or not that intention has been adequately realised.

There are one or two further points I would like to make about the composition of this anthology. There are very few nineteenth-century reviews and essays. Originally it was intended to include more of these but when it became clear to me that the objections to Shelley made by Eliot, Leavis and others must be met, and met as fully as possible, it became clear also that, for the most part, criticism of Shelley in the nineteenth century would have to be sacrificed in the interest of critical rigour and responsibility. The fact is that contemporary reviews

of Shelley's work are almost entirely worthless. I had toyed
with the idea of offering Wilson's (or Lockhart's?) anonymous
review of *Alastor* in *Blackwood's* (vi, November 1819, 153–4) as
an example of hysterical defence of Shelley (against the
Quarterly). But I decided that this, along with other, usually
negative, criticism has only an historical interest and must be
set aside. The volume on Shelley criticism in Routledge's
'Critical Heritage' series will surely meet this need in the event
of its being strongly felt.[2] I have chosen to publish only those
articles which contribute intelligently to the argument about
Shelley, and for that reason the nineteenth century does not
feature significantly in my selection.

On the other hand there is a very good essay by Leslie
Stephen in *Hours in a Library*, first published in 1879. Its title,
'Godwin and Shelley', indicates the problem. Much of the best
material on Shelley before the 1920s and 1930s is either on his
thought or on the longer poems. In other words, it concentrates
on those areas that have nothing to do with our present purpose,
which is to ascertain the value of Shelley's shorter poems and
lyrics by paying careful attention to details of their language
and context. This explains the omission of essays by Stephen,
Lewes and Masson in the nineteenth century, and C. S. Lewis,
Carlos Baker and D. J. Hughes more recently. But I have not
restricted my choice unduly by abiding by the most rigorous
interpretation of the phrase 'shorter poems'. As a rough rule of
thumb I have assumed that a shorter poem means a poem of
less than 500 lines (which just lets *Adonais* in and *Epipsychidion*
and *The Triumph of Life* out). No essay has been included which
concentrates attention on a poem of more than that size. But
I have included essays which take their examples incidentally
from longer poems (among others) provided that these do not
represent a significant proportion of the whole and that information acquired from a consideration of the passages quoted
is helpful to the reader whose interest is in the lyrics. In the
third section, of full-length modern essays, all the writing is
explicitly and exclusively on the lyrics and shorter poems.

The form of this Casebook is even more than usual one of a
debate. Unlike in the '30s and '40s it is now much more a debate
between equally competent and well-informed critics of Shelley.
This being the case, I have tried to provide equal space for
both sides of the argument in what I suppose is the historical
section of the anthology. Thereafter, in Part Three, I have
inclined the balance towards a defence of Shelley. There is
an element of editorial partiality in this, but I suppose no one
will come to a book of this kind who does not possess some
slight predisposition to see Shelley vindicated, or at least a
readiness to examine the grounds on which other readers have
sought to vindicate him.

PATRICK SWINDEN

NOTES

1. Dr Leavis has not agreed to republication of his essay on
Shelley in the present Casebook. This is doubly unfortunate on
account of both its intrinsic merit and the crucial position it occupies
in the history of Shelley criticism. Because it is of such considerable
importance I shall summarise its main conclusions here, and advise
the reader to consult the details in chapter 6 of *Revaluation* (London,
1936) pp. 203–32.

Dr Leavis's judgement of Shelley is based principally on his
reading of five poems. The last two of these, *The Cenci* and *The Triumph
of Life*, need not concern us since they are dramatic and narrative
poems which fall outside our brief. In any case Leavis's denigration
of Shelley arises out of his reading of three shorter poems: *Ode to the
West Wind*, *Mont Blanc* and the lyric *When the lamp is shattered*. His
painstaking analysis of these poems discloses a vagueness and gener-
ality in Shelley's handling of imagery and a naïve insistence on
spontaneity (in *West Wind*); confusion of the metaphysical and the
actual, the real and the imagined (in *Mont Blanc*); and 'radical dis-
abilities and perversions, such as call for moral comment' (in *When
the lamp is shattered*). The 'sentimental commonplaces' of this last
poem are the expression of a self-regarding pathos which Leavis finds
in most of Shelley's work. It depends on an abnegation of critical

intelligence and issues in a surrender to inspiration conceived in the most trivial and emotionally self-indulgent terms:

> The antipathy of his sensibility to any ploy of the critical mind, the uncongeniality of intelligence to inspiration, these clearly go in Shelley, not merely with a capacity for momentary self-deceptions and insincerities, but with a radical lack of self-knowledge.

> This immaturity is particularly impressive in Shelley's writing about love, which is characterised by a highly generalised and effusive altruism coexisting with blindness to the claims, even to the separate existence of the beloved object.

The more one reads this section of the essay, the more Shelley sounds like Othello as Leavis describes him in his essay on 'Diabolic Intellect and the Noble Hero'. This might suggest a predisposition in Leavis's critical work, even a need, to expose a certain kind of self-deception which he associates with excessive idealism, ardour, a complex blend of egoism and self-transcending aspiration from which Shelley is certainly not immune, but with which not all readers will be so savagely unsympathetic as Leavis appears to be. Of course the grounds of his disapproval are in the textual criticism of the poems, which the reader is advised to consult. My own hope is that some of the essays in this present volume, particularly perhaps those by Holloway and Matthews, will persuade readers of Shelley that much of this criticism is misdirected (Leavis's grasp of Shelley's intentions is itself sometimes faulty, because his own hold on objects is weaker than Shelley's) and that when it is not misdirected it is often intemperate.

   2. Or see N. I. White, in Bibliography.

PART ONE

Shelley and the Critics

Frederick A. Pottle

THE CASE OF SHELLEY (1960)

The case of Shelley requires us to come to grips with the problem posed by the decline of a first-rate reputation. It would be easier to discuss if it followed a more conventional formula; if, for example, it were true to say that Shelley was ignored in his lifetime, idolized by the Victorians, and not seriously attacked till the New Critics took him in hand. As a matter of fact, he was not ignored in his lifetime, and some extremely able depreciation of his poetry appeared in the Victorian era. The critics of the period 1814–22 paid a surprising amount of attention to him, generally concurring in the verdict that he was a poet of great but misguided powers.[1] This attitude did not give way to one of complete approval, but continued to characterize much of the most respected criticism of the century down almost to its end. The classic statement of the position is perhaps that of Wordsworth, made only five years after Shelley's death: 'Shelley is one of the best *artists* of us all: I mean in workmanship of style.'[2] This is high praise from a man whose praise in such matters counts, but it is far from being unmixed praise. By saying *artist* rather than *poet*, and by emphasizing the word, Wordsworth meant to qualify: Shelley, he is saying, was a very able craftsman but he chose to write about the wrong things. Matthew Arnold and Leslie Stephen disagreed about the nature of Wordsworth's virtues but they were essentially in agreement as to the nature of Shelley's defects. Those defects, they said, were unreality and unsubstantiality. To Arnold, Shelley was a beautiful *and ineffectual* angel; to Stephen, Shelley's poetry was too often the rainbow-coloured mist into which the stagnant pool of Godwin's paradoxes had been transmuted.[3] Poe,

Melville, George Henry Lewes, Swinburne and Francis
Thompson were ardent Shelleyans, Browning an ardent
Shelleyan who later admitted some qualifications. Lamb,
Hazlitt, Carlyle, Kingsley and Mark Twain were violent anti-
Shelleyans; the admiration of Emerson, Tennyson and William
Morris was less than hearty.[4] During this time, generally speaking, the objections to Shelley's subject-matter shade off from
loathing to unexcited disapproval or to the mere recognition of
a limitation; while at the same time the emotions roused by his
personality can be seen generally changing from hatred to
affection, or at least to respect. To the earliest critics Shelley
was a monster of immorality and impiety; to the later (even to
many who did not care much for his poetry) he was an angel,
a pure unearthly spirit. And a remarkable paradox emerges:
though respected critics continually reiterate their lack of full
satisfaction with the subject-matter of Shelley's poems, it is
conceded as a matter of course everywhere in England and
America, long before the end of the century, that he is one of
the greatest English poets.

But not quite like the others in that company. From the first
appearance of Shelley's poems down at least to the year 1917
(and I can hardly have been the last to experience it) his poems
had a unique power to intoxicate and to enthral sensitive young
men and women, to operate upon them with the force of a
sudden conversion. And this power of conversion had un-
pleasant consequences. Many people, as the range of their
literary experience widened, grew ashamed of the extravagance
of their youthful discipleship and transferred their disgust to the
poetry that had caused it. Others never did extend their range
much but remained one-poet men all their lives. The Shelleyans
have included an alarming number of crackpots, cranks, fana-
tics and bores. A discouraging amount of the writing on Shelley
at all periods has been polemical: violently for or violently
against. . . .

The period from about 1895 to 1920 marked the highest
point of the tide of Shelley's reputation. The problem of belief

became a great deal less troublesome. Two of the most distinguished practitioners of literature during that time, Hardy and
Shaw, were out-and-out Shelleyans: men who not only respected Shelley's art but who also found his ideas congenial. Shaw's
religion, in fact, was by his own confession derived in large part
from Shelley, and it resembled Shelley's closely. Yeats in his
first period was a committed Shelleyan, regarding *Prometheus
Unbound* as 'a sacred book' and *A Defence of Poetry* as 'the pro-
foundest essay on the foundation of poetry in English'.[5] Some
of the best academic critics of the time, for example, Bradley
and Elton, wrote sympathetically and persuasively of the
positive virtues of Shelley's poetry, without more qualification
than is to be expected in any serious and patient evaluation.
The consensus of this late-Victorian or late-Romantic criticism
was that Shelley's minor works were his major works; that
admirable as his longer works may be, they show his limitations
in a way that his lyrics do not; that Shelley was England's
greatest lyric poet.

The rise of the New Humanists marked the turn of the tide.
Paul Elmer More's essay on Shelley appeared in 1910, but it is
my impression that the water-line did not begin visibly to re-
treat until the publication of Irving Babbitt's *Rousseau and
Romanticism* in 1919. From that time to this the reputation of
Shelley has continued steadily to ebb.

I wish I knew whether the assault of the New Humanists
really had anything in common with that of the New Critics.
I should rather guess that it had little more than the fact that
T. S. Eliot was educated at Harvard in the prime of Irving
Babbitt, and that Eliot admired the work of Paul Elmer More.
The New Humanists were not practitioners of any literature
except the literature of criticism; they were academics, and
their attack was essentially moralistic. Though their standards
of value were somewhat different from Arnold's, their methods
were similar. The New Criticism is something very different.
Like Wordsworth's prefaces, it is essentially the manifesto of a
new idiom in poetry; it has its origin in the works of practitioners

like Pound, Eliot, the later Yeats, Ransom, Tate and Warren. It will be sufficient for the purposes of this paper to say that the New Humanists' attack on Shelley, though it was vigorously continued and has not yet ceased, soon merged with and became trifling in comparison with the attack of those younger contemporary practitioners of literature who devote themselves also to criticism, and of critics who followed their lead.

It is very important to realize that the present revolt from Shelley was not academic in origin, but was a revolt of practitioners of literature. It is not necessary to name the significant modern writers who are anti-Shelleyan; one had better save time and say that they all are. And the more significant modern academic criticism, as I have said, took its lead from the practitioners, and is remarkably like that of the practitioners. Brooks and Leavis are in substantial agreement on the subject of Shelley with Ransom, Tate and Warren. Indeed, the central modern critical document on Shelley may be taken to be Leavis's essay in *Revaluation*.

Because modern criticism is so polemical, it is not easy to discover what it really wants to do with Shelley. One distinguished modern practitioner of whom I asked the question told me with warmth that he wished Shelley to be completely forgotten and as soon as possible; but he added that he knew he was unfair. Another, whom I charged with disliking Shelley, replied, 'I like Shelley very much when he will behave himself.' The second statement is probably the more candid, and indicates a wish on the part of modern critics, not to eliminate Shelley utterly from the roll of English poets, but to reduce his stature, to turn him from a major into a minor poet. And they are not content, as the nineteenth century was, to rest their case for this depreciation on the truth and seriousness of his substance and matter. When Mr Eliot invoked the Arnoldian formula, saying that he could 'only regret that Shelley did not live to put his poetic gifts, which were certainly of the first order, at the service of more tenable beliefs', Dr Leavis rebuked him rather sharply.[6] Modern critics repudiate the dualism of the nineteenth century and test all poetry by a unitary standard. They may be diametrically opposed in their basic positions, some asserting that the aesthetic value of a poem is a function of its moral and theological soundness, others that when the beliefs of a poet are properly ordered in a poem, the question of their truth or falsity outside the poem does not rise, but the practical result is the same. One no longer says that a man is a great artist but lacking in wisdom. To Dr Leavis or Mr Tate, Shelley is not a great artist dealing with an unfortunate subject-matter; he is a bungler, a bad craftsman, and *therefore* a bad poet. This, in spite of the confusing survivals of older oppositions that turn up in the New Criticism, is something new. Our survey of Shelley's reputation has given reason to suppose that a poet can withstand a good deal of attack on the soundness of his ideas so long as a majority of the people who read him find aesthetic value of a high order in his poetry. But if a majority of the people who read him get little aesthetic value from him, his reputation is certainly going to be scaled down. . . .

Modern criticism maintains that . . . Shelley is a bad poet. He is sentimental: that is, he calls for a greater display of emotion than the modern reader feels to be warranted by the occasion. He employs pronounced, intoxicating, hypnotic rhythms that seem to be trying to sweep the reader into hasty emotional commitments. He seldom uses a firmly held, developed image, but pours out a flood of images which one must grasp momentarily in one aspect and then release. He is fond of figures within figures. He imposes his will on the object of experience: he does not explore 'reality', he flies away from it. He seldom takes a gross, palpable, near-at-hand object from the world of ordinary perception and holds it for contemplation: his gaze goes up to the sky, he starts with objects that are just on the verge of becoming invisible or inaudible or intangible and he strains away even from these. He exhibits dissociation of sensibility: though he is even too much aware of the disgusting, the ugly, the painful and the horrible, he puts all the beauty into one poem and all the ugliness into another, or he sorts them out in different portions of the same poem. He luxuriates in emotion. He embarrasses the reader by representing himself as weak, frail, bowed, bleeding, fainting and dying. . . .

The judgment of modern criticism on Shelley, though valid and permanently valid, is not exclusively valid. It does not impair in the least the validity of the serious criticism that preceded it. And it will not prevent Shelley from returning to very high general esteem. I do not see how any one could read carefully the great critical essays on Shelley from Bagehot's in 1856 to Grierson's in 1946 and still predict that the history of Shelley's reputation will be like Cowley's. It will probably be much more like Pope's. Though the Romantics and the Victorians steadily depreciated Pope and even went so far as to call him no poet at all, they continued to accord him practically the status of a major poet by showing that they were unable to ignore and forget him. By shifting the area of their attention, they were even able to read him. Though they were repelled by the satires and the *Essay on Man*, they found they could enjoy *The Rape of the Lock*, *Eloisa to Abelard* and the *Elegy to the Memory of an Unfortunate Lady*. Shelley will not be dropped from the academic curriculum, but he will probably occupy a less prominent place there than he now does, and he will be represented by different assignments. It will be possible, even in Shelley, to find some poems congenial to the modern temper. *Mont Blanc*, with its extended image, will be preferred to the *Ode to a Skylark*. Dr Leavis has also said a good word for *The Mask of Anarchy*. Mr Eliot, whose pronouncements on Shelley since 1933 have been generally respectful, has high praise for *The Triumph of Life*.[7]

Are we then to conclude that whatever is is right, that the experiential method merely describes the vicissitudes of reputation but never submits any critical practice to judgment? By no means. I believe that modern criticism is doing very well, but I think it could be improved and still remain true to itself.

I have no right to demand of those modern critics who are genuinely and thoughtfully absolutist that they accede to the views I am here setting forth. My views and theirs are radically incompatible. We must simply say to each other, 'Our disagreement is fundamental.' But I cannot escape the feeling that the majority of the New Critics are anything but consistent and clear-headed absolutists. It appears to me that they constantly make statements which indicate that the real cast of their thought is, like mine, subjective and experiential, and that therefore their absolutism is arbitrary and illogical. I do not think that many of them, if they forced themselves to think that far back, could tolerate the stark rationalism of the *a priori* position which they would see that their absolutism assumes. It appears to me that their absolutism is a prejudice; that it springs in part from the very human but unregenerate passion we all have for bullying other people, in larger part from not having recognized the fact that one can make real judgments without making absolute judgments; that a judgment may be firm, unqualified and valid without being absolutely so.

Let me illustrate. An observer on the ground, standing at the right place, will announce that the track of a bomb falling from a plane is a parabola. If another person *standing at that same point* says it is something else, he is simply wrong. But if an observer *in the plane* says that the track is a straight line, he is not wrong. In relation to the plane the track *is* a straight line. This observer's report has the same standing as that of the first observer on the ground.

I sincerely believe that many of our modern critics would not only be more comfortable, they would be a good deal more persuasive on a basis of reasoned relativism than they are on their present basis of uneasy and dogmatic absolutism. A critic who changed his base would not have to alter his critical standards in the least. He would merely give up the attempt to identify – I am partly quoting, partly paraphrasing a recent pronouncement of Mr T. S. Eliot[8] – what is best for his own time with what is best universally and always; he would stop pretending to erect a theory good for all time upon his perception of what is needed for the present. It is a necessary and laudable task to show the limitations of Shelley's poetry by measuring it against modern sensibility. But (I should maintain) it is equally necessary and laudable to expose the limitations of modern sensibility by measuring it against Shelley's poetry.

I wish modern criticism to continue to judge literature firmly by modern standards, but if it could find ways to be less polemic, it would go down better with me, and I think it would read better a hundred years from now. It is true that our present-day critics are no more arrogant than Wordsworth and no more spiteful than Swinburne, but I should like Wordsworth's criticism better if he had not been so arrogant and Swinburne's better if he had not been so spiteful. The battle, though not over, is clearly won. Is it not possible now to relax, to be candid, to stop sneering and snarling? Is it not possible for the New Critics to admit a little *pietas*? Would it not be more seemly for critics who occupy prominent positions as professors of English to stop using the term 'professor' merely as one of abuse?

For it must be clear to any fair-minded observer that modern criticism of Shelley is not completely candid. The critics are still making a case. They are suppressing much that could be said for his poetry on their own grounds. They are practicing, and encouraging others to practice, a kind of reading of him which they would brand as superficial if applied to Donne or Yeats.

I wish modern criticism would spend less time in prescription and more in calm, patient, neutral description. Though our judgments of the value of Shelley's poems are bound to vary widely and unpredictably, all critics of all periods ought ideally to be able to *describe* his poems in the same way: ought to be able to say, 'The structure of thought of this poem is so-and-so', or, 'The metaphors of this poem are such-and-such'. Actually, after a thorough-going shift in sensibility, critics manhandle and misread poems because, since they dislike them, they do not approach them with patience and good will.[9] We can now see how clumsy and obtuse the Victorians often were in reading Pope: they speak glibly of the lack of distinction in his ideas without bothering to understand them, and they misread his figures. We cannot blame them for not liking Pope better, but it does seem as though they could have described him more accurately. Wordsworth says that you must love a poet before he will seem worthy of your love. It is so; and love is a thing that cannot be commanded. Respect, however, can, and respect will go a long way. One can, and should, conclude that a poet is worthy of respect when one finds that a good many respectable critics have respected him and still do respect him. All accomplished poetry requires close reading and Shelley's is especially difficult. The danger the New Critics run is that of not taking Shelley seriously enough.

A critic who calls Shelley careless should be very careful to make sure he has understood him. It is true that Shelley is more careless than Wordsworth or Milton, but he is less careless than Keats or Shakespeare. Shelley appears to have been quite innocent of any instruction in English grammar: he writes just as he talked and his conversational tradition (Eton), though good, was not at all points identical with the formal written standard. Consequently his poetry anywhere may make the verb agree in number with the nearest noun rather than with the actual subject; like Byron he is capable of sentences that never conclude. His larger compositions show occasional patches that read like improvisations that he never went back to finish. But these sketchy or unfinished areas are generally peripheral; they seldom affect the main design. On the whole he deserved Wordsworth's tribute to his craftsmanship. What modern critics call carelessness in Shelley is more often the highly adroit and skilful writing of a kind of poetry which they do not understand because they do not like that kind of poetry.

The New Critics show a remarkable want of delicacy of touch in handling Shelley, and they too often misread the poems they condemn. The tactic of bringing up *Romeo and Juliet* to demolish *The Indian Serenade* is a good deal like training a sixteen-inch gun on a cat-boat. The poem was never meant to compete in that class. It is playful and extravagant; it is a

dramatic poem; it follows a well-known convention. One is not
to assume that the person speaking is really fainting or failing
or dying or even that he thinks he is; he is a young man (an
East-Indian young man, at that) singing a serenade. Faced with
a witty seventeenth-century love-poem of extravagant compliment, the modern critic knows just how to handle it; faced with
Romantic extravagance, he loses all lightness of touch and
becomes priggish and solemn.

Or take Dr Leavis's contention that Shelley's metaphors
sprout other metaphors that are suggested merely by the *words*
he has just used. 'What,' says he, referring to the opening lines
of the second stanza of the *Ode to the West Wind*, 'are those
"tangled boughs of Heaven and Ocean"? They stand for nothing that Shelley could have pointed to in the scene before
him; the "boughs", it is plain, have grown out of the "leaves"
in the previous line . . .' Because things cannot be given precise
and limited location by a gesture of the forefinger, it does not
follow that they are non-existent. Clouds, it is true, have no
visible means of support, but they are actually just as much
subject to gravity as leaves are. If they 'hang' high in the
heavens, forming a solid and relatively stationary canopy, it is
because they are being held there by a tangle of sunbeams, air
and water vapor ('Ocean'). A critic who believes that it is bad
poetic practice to cite transparent and diffused substances as
parts of a visual image will undoubtedly find a great deal to
object to in Shelley, for this is one of Shelley's favorite devices.
But it is the old and familiar objection of vaporousness or
'abstraction', not verbalism. That Shelley puts figures inside
figures is certainly true. It may well be that in the debased
Shelleyan tradition of the end of the nineteenth century and the
beginning of the twentieth the secondary figures have only a
verbal existence. I doubt if that ever happens with Shelley. At
any rate, before I said so in any particular case, I should expect
to have to approach him with good will and to spend as much
time on the poem in question as I would on one by Donne or
T. S. Eliot.

A final instance. Both Dr Leavis and Mr Tate have subjected *When the lamp is shattered* to extended destructive analysis. Both have misread the basic figures of the poem. Dr Leavis calls the first two lines a sentimental banality, an emotional *cliché*:

> When the lamp is shattered
> The light in the dust lies dead.

The figure, at least, is not a *cliché*; it is a brilliant one that I do not remember ever having seen in any other poem. Dr Leavis must have read the second line as 'The light lies dead in the dust', and have taken this to be a pretentious and ultimately dishonest way of stating the commonplace that light cannot survive its source. But Shelley has not inverted the word order: he wants the words to be read just as he wrote them. His figure (see the following one of the rainbow) deals with reflected or refracted light. In a room which is lighted by a lamp, some of the light of which you are aware comes directly from the lamp to your eyes, some is reflected from walls, ceiling and floor. The direct rays Shelley might have called 'the light in the lamp'; the reflected light he calls 'the light in the dust'. What he is saying is not something so obvious as that when the lamp is broken the light goes out; it is that when the lamp goes out, the walls and floor of the room don't go on shining with a luminescence of their own. The point of this appears in the second stanza, where he applies the figure. The 'light in the lamp' is the love of the spirit, the 'light in the dust' is the love of the flesh. But when the light of the spirit goes out, the 'light in the dust' does *not* go out; it shines on with a mournful vitality of its own. Love goes, lust remains. When we come to 'heart' in the second stanza we see the reason for both the 'dust' and the 'lies dead' of the first. A heart *is* 'dust'; it could in literal fact 'lie dead'. When Shelley applies the expression figuratively to light, he is deliberately and purposefully anticipating. This is what Professor Wimsatt, in his useful analysis of the nature of Romantic imagery, has called the importation of the tenor into the vehicle.[10]

Mr Tate[11] confines his strictures to the last (the fourth) stanza
of the poem, but that stanza cannot be discussed apart from the
preceding one:

> When hearts have once mingled   17
> Love first leaves the well-built nest;
>   The weak one is singled
> To endure what it once possessed.
>   O Love! who bewailest
> The frailty of all things here,
>   Why choose you the frailest
> For your cradle, your home and your bier?
>
>   Its passions will rock thee   25
> As the storms rock the ravens on high;
>   Bright reason will mock thee,
> Like the sun from a wintry sky.
>   From thy nest every rafter
> Will rot, and thine eagle home
>   Leave thee naked to laughter,
> When leaves fall and cold winds come.

Mr Tate identifies 'Its' of line 25 with 'Love's', makes 'thee' a
human lover (a woman), and says that the ravens in line 26 are
eagles in line 30. It is quite certain, I think, that the antecedent
of 'Its' is 'the frailest [heart]' of line 23, and 'thee' is Love. The
poem is a bitter or ironic contrary to *Music, when soft voices die*,
which Shelley had written in the previous year. The 'argument'
of the concluding stanza is that as soon as lovers have enjoyed
each other, they always fall out of love, but unfortunately not
at the same time. The weaker of the two (man or woman) goes
on loving after the stronger has been released. This hopeless
persistence of love on one side causes love generally to seem
unreasonable and ridiculous. The ultimate tenor is stated only
in the three spaced terms: 'passions', 'reason' and 'laughter'.
Lines 18–24 adopt and develop as vehicle the old conceit that
when a man and a woman are in love, it is because the god of

Love is nesting in their hearts;[12] while in the concluding stanza, this conceit in turn becomes tenor to a vehicle of a nesting raven. Line 17 is the most troublesome of the poem, and perhaps should not be defended. Having committed himself, contrary to his general practice, to an elaborate extended figure, it may be thought that it was bad judgment on Shelley's part to lead into it by another heart figure which appears to be radically incompatible. The difficulty, I think, here as elsewhere in Shelley, is caused by telescoping of syntax. Lines 17–18, if one spelled out the mental connections one needs to make if one is to read the passage with the right tone, might run something like this: 'When hearts have once mingled [and separated again into the usual divided state which we express by calling them nests of the god of Love], Love first leaves the well-built nest.' The effect of the syntactical fusion on me, at least, is to reduce line 17 to the status of dead metaphor or ironic *cliché*, which is perhaps just what was intended: 'When hearts have once mingled [as one reads in sentimental poems, including my own].' But past that snag, the rest seems to me reasonably clear sailing. The poet addresses the god of Love: 'You are always complaining about human frailty, but if what you want is stability, why do you choose the frailer of two hearts to come to first and to linger in longest? You are supposed to be a noble creature, and your nest is supposed to be an eagle home; why, then, choose something much more like a raven's nest? [In Shelley's day the English raven commonly nested near the top of a tall tree; the golden eagle – the eagle *par excellence* – always built its nest on a cliff.] The passions of the frailer heart will rock you as rudely as the storm winds rock the ravens in their nest. Just as the raven, if it stays in the nest after the leaves fall, will be exposed to the bright cold sun and biting winds of winter, so, if you linger in the frail heart, you will be exposed to rational mockery and to laughter.' There are two parallel series of four terms each: on the one side, Love, frail heart, mocking reason, laughter; on the other, raven, nest in a deciduous tree, winter sun, cold winds. 'Eagle home' in line 30 I take to be bitterly ironic.

Mr Tate cites the 'confusion' of line 31: 'Are we to suppose that the other birds come by and mock the raven (eagle), or are we to shift the field of imagery and see "thee" as a woman?' This implies a rule that there shall never be any crossing-over of tenor into vehicle: extended similes must always run either a, b, c, d as w, x, y, z, or a as w, b as x, c as y, d as z. 'Laughter' in line 31 is mere carelessness: the figure demands 'sun and wind'. That Shelley constantly flashes back and forth between tenor and vehicle is undoubted, but I should agree with Professor Wimsatt (who of course does not guarantee this particular instance) that such practice is not carelessness but a brilliant extension of poetic possibilities.

I am not under the illusion that I have gone very far towards proving *When the lamp is shattered* to be a good poem. I have no conviction that if Dr Leavis and Mr Tate accepted my reading of it they would like it any better. I doubt whether any person of advanced modern sensibility can like it very much. But I should like to think that I could make any patient and candid modern reader agree that it is a respectable poem.

I do not expect to reverse the decline in Shelley's reputation, though I confidently predict that that decline will one day be reversed. I do own my hope of persuading some of our modern critics to extend their present, very narrow choice of judgments. A mature and complete criticism needs more verdicts than stark 'Good' and 'Bad'. It needs to recognize degrees of goodness and badness. Particularly, it needs to be able to discriminate poems that have seldom or never been found good by any recorded serious set of standards – metaphysical, neo-classical, romantic, present-day – from poems that have been emphatically declared good by a long line of respectable critics. Evaluation that confines itself to the sharp delineation of the present perspective is no doubt our first need, but it is only half of criticism.

SOURCE: Extracts from '*The Case of Shelley*', *English Romantic Poets*, ed. M. H. Abrams (New York and London, 1960) pp.

289–90, 293–5, 297, 298–306; revised version of essay first published in *PMLA*, LXVII (1952).

NOTES

[Notes retained from the original text are here renumbered]

1. See Newman I. White, ed., *The Unextinguished Hearth* (Durham, N.C., 1938).

2. An oral judgment recorded by his biographer, Christopher Wordsworth, in 1827. See Markham L. Peacock, Jr, ed., *The Critical Opinions of William Wordsworth* (Baltimore, 1950), under *Shelley* and *Byron*.

3. Matthew Arnold, concluding paragraphs of 'Byron' and 'Shelley', in *Essays in Criticism, Second Series*; Sir Leslie Stephen, 'Godwin and Shelley', in *Hours in a Library*. The judgments were first published in 1881 and 1879 respectively.

4. Most of this material is conveniently collected in Newman I. White's *Shelley* (New York, 1940), especially in II 389–418.

5. W. B. Yeats, 'The Philosophy of Shelley's Poetry', in *Ideas of Good and Evil* (London, 1903) pp. 91, 93, 110–11.

6. T. S. Eliot, 'Shelley and Keats', in *The Use of Poetry and the Use of Criticism* (Cambridge, Mass., 1933) p. 88; F. R. Leavis, 'Shelley', in *Revaluation* (London, 1936).

7. T. S. Eliot, 'Talk on Dante', *Kenyon Review*, XIV (1952) 178–88. Mr Donald Davie's essay, 'Shelley's Urbanity', in *English Romantic Poets*, ed. M. H. Abrams (New York and London, 1960), first published in 1952 [and reprinted below, pp. 78–100 – Ed.], furnishes other choices.

8. T. S. Eliot, Preface to Leone Vivante's *English Poetry and Its Contribution to Knowledge of a Creative Principle* (London, 1950).

9. 'Our "Neo-classic" age is repeating those feats of its predecessor which we least applaud. It is showing a fascinating versatility in travesty. And the poets of the "Romantic" period provide for it what Shakespeare, Milton and Donne were to the early eighteenth-century grammarians and emendators – effigies to be shot at because what they represent is no longer understood' (Ivor A. Richards, *Coleridge on Imagination*, London, 1950, p. 196).

10. William K. Wimsatt, 'The Structure of Romantic Nature

Imagery', in *English Romantic Poets*, ed. M. H. Abrams (New York and London, 1960) pp. 24 ff.

11. Allen Tate, 'Understanding Modern Poetry', in *On the Limits of Poetry* (New York, 1948) p. 126.

12. Mr Tate approves of this conceit as it appears in Guido Guinizelli: 'Al cor gentil ripara sempre Amore/Come alla selva augello in la vedura' (*Ibid.*, p. 78).

PART TWO

General Opinions and Criticism 1820–1960

Anonymous (*1820*)

'BABYLONISH JARGON':

... We shall not follow the long accounts of the hero's tortures, nor the longer rhapsodies about the blissful effects of his restoration; but produce a few of the brilliant emanations of the mind modified on the study of *extraordinary* intellects. The play opens with a speech of several pages, very argutely delivered by Signior Prometheus, from an icy rock in the Indian Caucacus, to which he is 'nailed' by *chains* of 'burning cold'. He invokes all the elements, *seriatim*, to inform him what it was he originally said against Jupiter to provoke his ire; and, among the rest,

> Ye icy Springs, *stagnant* with wrinkling frost,
> Which *vibrated* to hear me: and then *crept*
> *Shuddering* through India.
> And ye, *swift* Whirlwinds, who, on *poised* wings
> Hung *mute* and *moveless* o'er yon hushed abyss,
> As thunder, *louder* than your own, made rock
> The orbed world.

This first extract will let our readers into the chief secret of Mr Shelley's poetry; which is merely opposition of words, phrases and sentiments, so violent as to be utter nonsense: *ex. gr.* the vibration of stagnant springs, and their creeping shuddering; – the swift moveless (*i.e.* motionless) whirlwinds, on poised wings, which hung mute over a hushed abyss as thunder louder than their own! In the same strain, Prometheus, who ought to have been called Sphynx, when answered in a *whisper*, says,

> Tis scarce like sound: it tingles thro' the frame
> As lightning tingles, *hovering ere it strike.*

Common bards would have thought the tingling **was felt**
when it struck, and not before, – when it was hovering **too,** of
all things for lightning to be guilty of! A 'melancholy voice'
now enters into the dialogue, and turns out to be 'the Earth'.
'Melancholy Voice' tells a melancholy story, about the time –

> When plague had fallen on man, and beast, and worm
> And Famine;

She also advises her son Prometheus to use a spell, –

> . . . So the revenge

> Of the Supreme may sweep thro' vacant shades,
> As rainy wind thro' the abandoned *gate*
> Of a fallen *palace.*

Mr Shelley's buildings, having still gates to them! Then the
Furies are sent to give the sturdy Titan a taste of their office;
and they hold as odd a colloquy with him, as ever we read.
The first tells him,

> Thou thinkest we will rend thee bone from bone,
> And nerve from nerve, working like fire within:

The second,

> Dost imagine
> We will but laugh into thy lidless eyes?

And *the third*, more funnily inclined than her worthy sisters –

> Thou think'st we will live thro' thee
> Like animal life, and though we can obscure not
> The soul which burns within, that we will dwell
> Beside it, like a vain loud multitude
> Vexing the self-content of wisest men –

This is a pozer! and only paralleled by the speech of the 'Sixth Spirit', of a lot of these beings, which arrive after the Furies. She, for these spirits are feminine, says,

Ah, sister! *desolation* is a *delicate thing;*
It walks not on the earth, it floats not on the air,
But treads with *silent footsteps*, and fans with silent wing
The tender hopes which in their hearts the best and
                                            gentlest bear;
Who, soothed to false repose by the fanning plumes above,
And the *music-stirring motion* of its soft and busy *feet*,
Dream visions of aerial joy, and call the monster Love,
And wake, and find the shadow pain.

The glimpses of meaning which we have here, are soon smothered by contradictory terms and metaphor carried to excess. There is another part of Mr Shelley's art of poetry, which deserves notice; it is his fancy, that by bestowing *colouring* epithets on every thing he mentions, he thereby renders his diction and descriptions vividly poetical. Some of this will appear hereafter; but we shall select one passage, as illustrative of the ridiculous extent to which the folly is wrought.

Asia is longing for her sister's annual visit; and after talking of Spring clothing with *golden* clouds the desert of life, she goes on:

This is the season, this the day, the hour;
At sunrise thou shouldst come, sweet sister mine,
Too long desired, too long delaying, come!
How like death-worms the wingless moments crawl!
The point of one *white* star is quivering still
Deep in the *orange* light of widening morn
Beyond the *purple* mountains: thro' a chasm
Of wind-divided mist the *darker* lake
Reflects it: now it wanes: it gleams again
As the waves fade, and as the burning threads

Of woven cloud unravel in *pale* air:
'Tis lost! and thro' yon peaks of cloudlike snow
The *roseate* sun-light quivers: hear I not
The Æolian music of her *sea-green* plumes
Winnowing the *crimson* dawn?

Here in seventeen lines, we have no fewer than seven positive
colours, and nearly as many shades; not to insist upon the everlasting confusion of this rainbow landscape, with *white* stars
quivering in the *orange* light, beyond *purple* mountains; of *fading
waves*, and clouds made of *burning threads*, which *unravel* in the
pale air; of cloudlike snow through which *roseate* sun-light also
quivers, and *sea-green* plumes winnowing *crimson* dawn. Surely,
the author looks at nature through a prism instead of spectacles.
Next to his colorific powers, we may rank the author's talent
for manufacturing 'villainous compounds'. *Ecce signum*, of a
Mist.

Beneath is a wide plain of billowy mist,
As a *lake*, paving in the morning sky,
With azure waves which *burst* in *silver* light,
Some Indian vale. Behold it, rolling on
Under the curdling winds, and *islanding*
The *peak* whereon we stand, *midway, around,*
Encinctured by the *dark* and *blooming* forests,
Dim *twilight-lawns*, and *stream-illumined* caves,
And *wind-enchanted* shapes of wandering mist;
And far on high the keen *sky-cleaving* mountains
From icy spires of sun-like radiance fling
The dawn, as lifted Ocean's dazzling spray,
From some Atlantic islet scattered up,
Spangles the wind with *lamp-like water-drops.*
The vale is girdled with their walls, a howl
Of cataracts from their *thaw-cloven* ravines
Satiates the listening wind, continuous, vast,
Awful as silence.

This is really like Sir Sidney Smith's plan to teach morality to Musselmans by scraps of the Koran in kaleidoscopes – only that each scrap has a meaning; Mr Shelley's lines none.

We now come to a part which quite throws Milton into the shade, with his 'darkness visible'; and as Mr Shelley professes to admire that poet, we cannot but suspect that he prides himself on having out-done him. Only listen to Panthea's description of Demogorgon. This lady, whose mind is evidently unsettled, exclaims,

> I see a *mighty darkness*
> Filling the seat of power, and *rays of gloom*
> Dart round, as *light* from the *meridian sun,*
> *Ungazed upon* and *shapeless* –

We yield ourselves, miserable hum-drum devils that we are, to this high imaginative faculty of the modern muse. We acknowledge that hyperbola, extravagance and irreconcileable terms may be poetry. We admit that common sense has nothing to do with 'the beautiful idealisms' of Mr Shelley. And we only add, that if this be genuine inspiration, and not the grossest absurdity, then is farce sublime, and maniacal raving the perfection of reasoning: then were all the bards of other times, Homer, Virgil, Horace, drivellers; for their foundations were laid no lower than the capacities of the herd of mankind; and even their noblest elevations were susceptible of appreciation by the very multitude among the Greeks and Romans.

We shall be very concise with what remains: Prometheus, according to Mr Percy Bysshe Shelley –

Gave man speech, and *speech created thought* – which is exactly, in our opinion, the cart creating the horse; the sign creating the inn; the effect creating the cause. No wonder that when such a master gave lessons in *astronomy*, he did it thus –

He taught the *implicated orbits woven*

> *Of the wide-wandering stars;* and how the sun
> Changes his *lair*, and by what *secret spell*

The pale moon is transformed, when *her broad eye*
Gazes not on the *interlunar sea.*

This, Promethean, beats all the systems of astronomy with
which we are acquainted: Shakespeare, it was said, 'exhausted
worlds and then imagined new'; but he never imagined aught
so new as this. Newton was a wonderful philosopher; but, for
the view of the heavenly bodies, Shelley double distances him.
And not merely in the preceding, but in the following improved
edition of his astronomical notions, he describes –

A sphere, which is as many thousand spheres,
Solid as crystal, yet through all its mass
Flow, as through empty space, music and light:
Ten thousand orbs involving and involved,
Purple and azure, white, green, and golden,
Sphere within sphere; and every space between
Peopled with unimaginable shapes,
Such as ghosts dream dwell in the lampless deep,
Yet each inter-transpicuous, and they whirl
Over each other with a thousand motions,
Upon a thousand sightless axles spinning,
And with the force of self-destroying swiftness,
Intensely, slowly, solemnly roll on,
Kindling with mingled sounds, and many tones,
Intelligible words and music wild.
With mighty whirl the multitudinous orb
Grinds the bright brook into an azure mist
Of elemental subtlety, like light;
And the wild odour of the forest flowers,
The music of the living grass and air,
The emerald light of leaf-entangled beams
Round its intense yet self-conflicting speed,
Seem kneaded into one aerial mass
Which drowns the sense.

Did ever the walls of Bedlam display more insane stuff than this?

When our worthy old pagan acquaintance, Jupiter, is disposed of, his sinking to the 'void abyss' is thus pourtrayed by his son Apollo –

> An eagle so caught in some bursting cloud
> On Caucasus, his *thunder-baffled wings*
> *Entangled in the whirlwind! &c.*

An' these extracts do not entitle the author to a cell, clean straw, bread and water, a strait waistcoat and phlebotomy, there is no madness in scribbling. It is hardly requisite to adduce a sample of the adjectives in this poem to prove the writer's condign abhorrence of any relation between that part of speech and substantives: sleep-unsheltered hours; gentle darkness; horny eyes; keen faint eyes; faint wings; fading waves; crawling glaciers, toads, agony, time, &c.; belated and noontide plumes; milky arms, many-folded mountains; a lake-surrounding flute; veiled lightening asleep (as well as hovering); unbewailing flowers; odour-faded blooms; semi-vital worms; windless pools, windless abodes and windless air; unerasing waves; unpavilioned skies; rivetted wounds; and void abysms, are parcel of the Babylonish jargon which is found in every wearisome page of this tissue of insufferable buffoonery. After our quotations, we need not say that the verse is without measure, proportions or elegance; that the similes are numberless and utterly inapplicable; and that the instances of ludicrous nonsense are not fewer than the pages of the Drama. Should examples be demanded, the following, additional, are brief. Of the heroic line: –

> Ah me! alas, pain, pain ever, for ever –

Of the simile: –

> We will entangle buds and flowers and beams
> Which twinkle on the fountain's brim, and make

Strange combinations out of common things,
Like human babes in their brief innocence. –

Of the pure nonsensical: –

> Our *feet* now, every *palm*,
> Are *sandelled* with *calm*,
> And the *dew* of our wings is a rain of balm;
> And *beyond* our eyes,
> The human love lies
> Which makes all it gazes on paradise.

> We'll pass the eyes
> Of the starry skies
> Into the hoar deep to *colonise*:
> Death, Chaos, and Night,
> From the sound of our flight,
> Shall flee, like mist from a tempest's might.

> And Earth, Air, and Light,
> And the Spirit of Night,
> Which drives round the stars in their fiery flight;
> And Love, Thought, and Breath,
> The powers that quell Death,
> Wherever we soar shall assemble beneath.

> And our singing shall *build*
> In the *void's loose field*,
> A world for the Spirit of Wisdom to *wield*;
> We will take our plan
> From the new world of man,
> And our work shall be called the Promethean.

Alas, gentle reader! for poor Tom, whom the foul fiend hath (thus) led o'er bog and quagmire; and blisse thee from whirle-windes, starre-blasting and taking. Would that Mr Shelley made it his study, like this his prototype.

How to prevent the fiend, and to kill vermin.

Poor Tom's affected want of wits is inferior to Shelley's genuine wandering with his 'father of the hours' and 'mother of the months'; and his dialogue of ten pages between *The Earth* and *The Moon*, assuredly the most arrant and gravest burlesque that it ever entered into the heart of man to conceive. We cannot resist its opening

> *The Earth.*   The joy, the triumph, the delight, the
>   madness!
> The boundless, overflowing, bursting gladness,
> The vapourous exultation not to be confined!
>   Ha! ha! the animation of delight
>   Which wraps me, like an atmosphere of light,
> And bears me as a cloud is borne by its own wind.
> *The Moon.*   Brother mine, calm wanderer,
>   Happy globe of land and air,
> Some Spirit is darted like a beam from thee,
>   Which penetrates my frozen frame,
>   And passes with the warmth of flame,
> With love, and odour, and deep melody
>   Through me, through me!
> *The Earth.*   Ha! ha! the caverns of my hollow mountains,
> My cloven fire-crags, sound exulting fountains
> Laugh with a vast and inextinguishable laughter,
>   The oceans, and the deserts, and the abysses,
>   And the deep air's unmeasured wildernesses,
> Answer from all their clouds and billows, echoing after.

This is but the first of the ten pages: the sequel, though it may seem impossible to sustain such 'exquisite fooling', does not fall off. But we shall waste our own and our readers' time no longer. We have but to repeat, that when the finest specimens of inspired composition may be derived from the white-washed walls of St Lukes or Hoxton, the author of *Prometheus Unbound*, being himself among these bound writers, and chained like his subject, will have a chance of classing with foremost poets of the place.

SOURCE: Extracts from unsigned review of *Prometheus Unbound*, *The Literary Gazette*, 9 September, 1820; reprinted in N. I. White, *The Unextinguished Hearth* (1938, 1968).

W. S. Walker (*1821*)

INTRINSICALLY UNINTELLIGIBLE

A great lawyer of the present day is said to boast of practising three different modes of writing: one which any body can read; another which only himself can read; and a third, which neither he nor any body else can read. So Mr Shelley may plume himself upon writing in three different styles: one which can be generally understood; another which can be understood only by the author; and a third which is absolutely and intrinsically unintelligible. Whatever his command may be of the first and second of these styles, this volume is a most satisfactory testimonial of his proficiency in the last.

If we might venture to express a general opinion of what far surpasses our comprehension, we should compare the poems contained in this volume to the visions of gay colours mingled with darkness, which often in childhood, when we shut our eyes, seem to revolve at an immense distance around us. In Mr Shelley's poetry all is brilliance, vacuity and confusion. We are dazzled by the multitude of words which sound as if they denoted something very grand or splendid: fragments of images pass in crowds before us; but when the procession has gone by, and the tumult of it is over, not a trace of it remains upon the memory. The mind, fatigued and perplexed, is mortified by the consciousness that its labour has not been rewarded by the acquisition of a single distinct conception; the ear, too, is dissatisfied: for the rhythm of the verse is often harsh and unmusical; and both the ear and the understanding are disgusted by new and uncouth words, and by the awkward and intricate construction of the sentences.

The predominating characteristic of Mr Shelley's poetry, however, is its frequent and total want of meaning. Far be it from us to call for strict reasoning, or the precision of logical deductions, in poetry; but we have a right to demand clear, distinct conceptions. . . . Upon a question of mere beauty, there may be a difference of taste. . . . But the question of meaning, or no meaning, is a matter of fact on which common sense, with common attention, is adequate to decide; and the decision to which we may come will not be impugned, whatever be the want of taste, or insensibility to poetical excellence, which it may please Mr Shelley, or any of his coterie, to impute to us. . . .

The want of meaning in Mr Shelley's poetry takes different shapes. Sometimes it is impossible to attach any signification to his words; sometimes they hover on the verge between meaning and no meaning, so that a meaning may be obscurely conjectured by the reader, though none is expressed by the writer; and sometimes they convey ideas, which, taken separately, are sufficiently clear, but, when connected, are altogether incongruous. We shall begin with a passage which exhibits in some parts the first species of nonsense, and in others the third.

> Lovely apparitions, dim at first,
> Then radiant, as the mind arising bright
> From the embrace of beauty, whence the forms
> Of which these are the phantoms, casts on them
> The gathered rays which are reality,
> Shall visit us, the immortal progeny
> Of painting, sculpture, and wrapt poesy,
> And arts, tho' unimagined, yet to be.

The verses are very sonorous; and so many fine words are played off upon us, such as, 'painting', 'sculpture', 'poesy', 'phantoms', 'radiance', 'the embrace of beauty', 'immortal progeny', &c. that a careless reader, influenced by his habit of associating such phrases with lofty or agreeable ideas, may possibly have his fancy tickled into a transient feeling of satisfaction. But let any man try to ascertain what is really said, and he will immediately discover the imposition that has been practised. From beauty, or the embrace of beauty (we know not which, for ambiguity of phrase is a very frequent companion of nonsense), certain forms proceed: of these forms there are phantoms; these phantoms are dim; but the mind arises from the embrace of beauty, and casts on them the gathered rays which are reality; they are then baptized by the name of the immortal progeny of the arts, and in that character proceed to visit Prometheus. This *galimatias* (for it goes beyond simple nonsense) is rivalled by the following description of something that is done by a cloud.

> I am the daughter of earth and water,
>   And the nursling of the sky;
> I pass through the pores of the oceans and shores,
>   I change, but I cannot die.
> For after the rain, when with never a stain
>   The pavilion of heaven is bare,
> And the winds and sunbeams with their convex gleams,
>   Build up the blue dome of air.

I silently laugh at my own cenotaph,
    And out of the caverns of rain,
Like a child from the womb, like a ghost from the tomb,
    I arise and unbuild it again.

There is a love-sick lady who 'dwells under the glaucous caverns of ocean', and 'wears the shadow of Prometheus' soul', without which (she declares) she cannot 'go to sleep'. The rest of her story is utterly incomprehensible; we therefore pass on to the *debut* of the Spirit of the earth.

And from the other opening in the wood
Rushes, with loud and whirlwind harmony,
A sphere, which is as many thousand spheres,
Solid as crystal, yet through all its mass
Flow, as through empty space, music and light:
Ten thousand orbs involving and involved,
Purple and azure, white, green, and golden,
Sphere within sphere; and every space between
Peopled with unimaginable shapes.
Such as ghosts dream dwell in the lampless deep,
Yet each inter-transpicuous, and they whirl
Over each other with a thousand motions,
Upon a thousand sightless axles spinning,
And with the force of self-destroying swiftness,
Intensely, slowly, solemnly, roll on,
Kindling with mingled sounds, and many tones,
Intelligible words and music wild.
With mighty whirl the multitudinous orb
Grinds the bright brook into an azure mist
Of elemental subtlety, like light;
And the wild odour of the forest flowers,
The music of the living grass and air,
The emerald light of leaf-entangled beams
Round its intense yet self-conflicting speed,
Seemed kneaded into one aerial mass
Which drowns the sense.

We have neither leisure nor room to develop all the absurdities
here accumulated, in defiance of common sense, and even of
grammar; whirlwind harmony, a solid sphere which is as many
thousand spheres, and contains ten thousand orbs or spheres,
with inter-transpicuous spaces between them, whirling over
each other on a thousand sightless (alias invisible) axles; self-
destroying swiftness; intelligible words and wild music, kindled
by the said sphere, which also grinds a bright brook into an
azure mist of elemental subtlety; odour, music and light,
kneaded into one aerial mass, and the sense drowned by it!

Oh quanta species! et cerebrum non habet.

One of the personages in the Prometheus is Demogorgon.
As he is the only agent in the whole drama, and effects the only
change of situation and feeling which befalls the other personages; and as he is likewise employed to sing or say divers
hymns, we have endeavoured to find some intelligible account
of him. The following is the most perspicuous which we have
been able to discover: –

> . . . A mighty power, which is as darkness,
> Is rising out of earth, and from the sky,
> Is showered like the night, and from within the air
> Bursts, *like eclipse which had been gathered up*
> *Into the pores of sun-light.*

Love, as might be expected, is made to perform a variety of
very extraordinary functions. It fills 'the void annihilation of a
sceptred curse'; and, not to mention the other purposes to
which it is applied, it is in the following lines dissolved in air
and sun-light, and then folded around the world.

> . . . The impalpable thin air,
> And the all circling sun-light were transformed,
> As if the sense of love dissolved in them,
> Had folded itself around the sphered world.

Metaphors and similes can scarcely be regarded as ornaments of Mr Shelley's compositions; for his poetry is in general a mere jumble of words and heterogeneous ideas, connected by slight and accidental associations, among which it is impossible to distinguish the principal object from the accessory. In illustrating the incoherency which prevails in his metaphors as well as in the other ingredients of his verses, we shall take our first example, not from that great storehouse of the obscure and the unintelligible – the Prometheus, but from the opening of a poem, entitled, *A Vision of the Sea*, which we have often heard praised as a splendid work of imagination.

> . . . The rags of the sail
> Are flickering in ribbons within the fierce gale:
> From the stark night of vapours the dim rain is driven,
> And when lightning is loosed, like a deluge from heaven,
> She sees the black trunks of the water-spouts spin,
> And bend, as if heaven was raining in,
> Which they seemed to sustain with their terrible mass
> As if ocean had sunk from beneath them: they pass
> To their graves in the deep with an earthquake of sound,
> And the waves and the thunders made silent around
> Leave the wind to its echo.

At present we say nothing of the cumbrous and uncouth style of these verses, nor do we ask who this 'she' is, who sees the water-spouts; but the funeral of the water-spouts is curious enough: 'They pass to their graves with an earthquake of sound.' The sound of an earthquake is intelligible, and we suspect that this is what Mr Shelley meant to say: but an earthquake of sound is as difficult to comprehend as a cannon of sound, or a fiddle of sound. The same vision presents us with a battle between a tiger and a sea-snake; of course we have –

> . . . The whirl and the splash
> As of some hideous engine, whose brazen teeth smash
> The thin winds and soft waves into thunder; the screams

And hissing crawl fast o'er the smooth ocean streams,
Each sound like a centipede.

The comparison of a sound to a centipede would be no small
addition to a cabinet of poetical monstrosities: but it sinks into
tame common-place before the engine, whose brazen teeth
pound thin winds and soft waves into thunder.

Sometimes Mr Shelley's love of the unintelligible yields to his
preference for the disgusting and the impious. Thus the bodies
of the dead sailors are thrown out of the ship:

And the sharks and the dog-fish their grave-clothes
unbound,
And were glutted, like Jews, with this manna rained down
From God on their wilderness.

Asia turns her soul into an enchanted boat, in which she
performs a wonderful voyage. . . . [Quotes Act III, Scene v,
lines 73–94.]

The following comparison of a poet to a cameleon has no
more meaning than the jingling of the bells of a fool's cap, and
far less music.

Poets are on this cold earth,
As camelions might be,
Hidden from their earthly birth
In a cage beneath the sea;
Where light is camelions change:
Where love is not, poets do:
Fame is love disguised; if few
Find either never think it strange
That poet's range.

Sometimes to the charms of nonsense those of doggrel are
added. This is the conclusion of a song of certain beings, who
are called 'Spirits of the human minds':

And Earth, Air, and Light,
And the Spirit of Might,
Which drives round the stars in their fiery flight;
And Love, Thought, and Breath,
The powers that quell Death,
Wherever we soar shall assemble beneath.
And our singing shall build
In the void's loose field
A world for the Spirit of Wisdom to wield;
We will take our plan
From the new world of man,
And our work shall be called the Promethean.

Another characteristic trait of Mr Shelley's poetry is, that in his descriptions he never describes the thing directly, but transfers it to the properties of something which he conceives to resemble it by language which is to be taken partly in a metaphorical meaning, and partly in no meaning at all. The whole of a long poem, in three parts, called *The Sensitive Plant*, the object of which we cannot discover, is an instance of this. The first part is devoted to the description of the plants. The sensitive plant takes the lead:

No flower ever trembled and panted with bliss,
In the garden, the field, or the wilderness,
Like the doe in the noon-tide with love's sweet want,
As the companionless sensitive plant.

Next come the snow-drop and the violet:

And their breath was mixed with fresh odour, sent
From the turf, *like the voice and the instrument!*

The rose, too,

Unveiled the depth of her glowing breast,
Till, fold after fold, *to the fainting air*
The soul of her beauty and love lay bare.

The hyacinth is described in terms still more quaint and
affected:

> The hyacinth, purple, and white, and blue,
> Which flung from *its bells a sweet peal anew*,
> Of music so delicate, soft, and intense,
> It was felt like an odour within the sense.

It is worth while to observe the train of thought in this stanza.
The bells of the flower occur to the poet's mind; but ought not
bells to ring a peal? Accordingly, by a metamorphosis of the
odour, the bells of the hyacinth are supposed to do so: the
fragrance of the flower is first converted into a peal of music,
and then the peal of music is in the last line transformed back
into an odour. These are the tricks of a mere poetical harlequin,
amusing himself with

> The clock-work tintinnabulum of rhyme.

In short, it is not too much to affirm, that in the whole volume
there is not one original image of nature, one simple expression
of human feeling, or one new association of the appearances of
the moral with those of the material world. . . .

SOURCE: Extract from unsigned review of *Prometheus Unbound*,
in *The Quarterly Review*, XXVI (October 1821).

William Hazlitt (1824)

'VOLUNTARY INFLICTIONS, MOODS OF MIND'

Mr Shelley's style is to poetry what astrology is to natural
science – a passionate dream, a straining after impossibilities, a

record of fond conjectures, a confused embodying of vague abstractions, – a fever of the soul, thirsting and craving after what it cannot have, indulging its love of power and novelty at the expense of truth and nature, associating ideas by contraries, and wasting great powers by their application to unattainable objects.

Poetry, we grant, creates a world of its own; but it creates it out of existing materials. Mr Shelley is the maker of his own poetry – out of nothing. Not that he is deficient in the true sources of strength and beauty, if he had given himself fair play (the volume before us, as well as his other productions, contains many proofs to the contrary): But, in him, fancy, will, caprice, predominated over and absorbed the natural influences of things; and he had no respect for any poetry that did not strain the intellect as well as fire the imagination – and was not sublimed into a high spirit of metaphysical philosophy. Instead of giving a language to thought, or lending the heart a tongue, he utters dark sayings, and deals in allegories and riddles. His Muse offers her services to clothe shadowy doubts and inscrutable difficulties in a robe of glittering words, and to turn nature into a brilliant paradox. We thank him – but we must be excused. Where we see the dazzling beacon-lights streaming over the darkness of the abyss, we dread the quicksands and the rocks below. Mr Shelley's mind was of 'too fiery a quality' to repose (for any continuance) on the probable or the true – it soared 'beyond the visible diurnal sphere', to the strange, the improbable and the impossible. He mistook the nature of the poet's calling, which should be guided by involuntary, not by voluntary impulses. He shook off, as an heroic and praiseworthy act, the trammels of sense, custom and sympathy, and became the creature of his own will. He was 'all air', disdaining the bars and ties of mortal mould. He ransacked his brain for incongruities, and believed in whatever was incredible. Almost all is effort, almost all is extravagant, almost all is quaint, incomprehensible and abortive, from aiming to be more than it is. Epithets are applied, because they do not fit: subjects are

chosen, because they are repulsive: the colours of his style, for
their gaudy, changeful, startling effect, resemble the display of
fire-works in the dark, and, like them, have neither durability,
nor keeping, nor discriminate form. Yet Mr Shelley, with all
his faults, was a man of genius; and we lament that uncontrollable violence of temperament which gave it a forced and false
direction. He has single thoughts of great depth and force, single
images of rare beauty, detached passages of extreme tenderness;
and, in his smaller pieces, where he has attempted little, he has
done most. If some casual and interesting idea touched his
feelings or struck his fancy, he expressed it in pleasing and un-
affected verse: but give him a larger subject, and time to reflect,
and he was sure to get entangled in a system. The fumes of
vanity rolled volumes of smoke, mixed with sparkles of fire,
from the cloudy tabernacle of his thought. The success of his
writings is therefore in general in the inverse ratio of the extent
of his undertakings; inasmuch as his desire to teach, his ambition
to excel, as soon as it was brought into play, encroached upon,
and outstripped his powers of execution. . . .

We pass on to some of Mr Shelley's smaller pieces and translations, which we think are in general excellent and highly
interesting. His *Hymn of Pan* we do not consider equal to Mr
Keats's sounding lines in the Endymion. His *Mont Blanc* is full
of beauties and of defects; but it is akin to its subject, and presents a wild and gloomy desolation. *Ginevra*, a fragment founded
on a story in the first volume of the *Florentine Observer*, is like a
troublous dream, disjointed, painful, oppressive, or like a leaden
cloud, from which the big tears fall, and the spirit of the poet
mutters deep-toned thunder. We are too much subject to these
voluntary inflictions, these 'moods of mind', these effusions of
'weakness and melancholy', in the perusal of modern poetry.
It has shuffled off, no doubt, its old pedantry and formality;
but has at the same time lost all shape or purpose, except that
of giving vent to some morbid feeling of the moment. The
writer thus discharges a fit of the spleen or a paradox, and
expects the world to admire and be satisfied. We are no longer

annoyed at seeing the luxuriant growth of nature and fancy clipped into arm-chairs and peacocks' tails; but there is danger of having its stately products choked with unchecked underwood, or weighed down with gloomy nightshade, or eaten up with personality, like ivy clinging round and eating into the sturdy oak! The *Dirge*, at the conclusion of this fragment, is an example of the manner in which this craving after novelty, this desire 'to elevate and surprise', leads us to 'overstep the modesty of nature', and the bounds of decorum.

> Ere the sun through heaven once more has roll'd,
> *The rats in her heart*
> *Will have made their nest,*
> And the worms be alive in her golden hair,
> While the spirit that guides the sun,
> Sits throned in his flaming chair,
>   She shall sleep.   [Reviewer's italics]

The 'worms' in this stanza are the old and traditional appendages of the grave; – the 'rats' are new and unwelcome intruders; but a modern artist would rather shock, and be disgusting and extravagant, than produce no effect at all, or be charged with a want of genius and originality. . . .

SOURCE: Extracts from unsigned review of *Posthumous Poems*, in *The Edinburgh Review* (July 1824).

John Stuart Mill (1833)

'SINGLE IMAGES . . . BUT NO PICTURE'

. . . Lyric poetry, as it was the earliest kind, is also . . . more eminently and peculiarly poetry than any other: it is the poetry most natural to a really poetic temperament, and least capable

of being successfully imitated by one not so endowed by nature.
All Wordsworth's attempts in that strain, if we may venture to
say so much of a man whom we so exceedingly admire, appear
to us cold and spiritless.

Shelley is the very reverse of all this. Where Wordsworth is
strong, he is weak; where Wordsworth is weak, he is strong.
Culture, that culture by which Wordsworth has reared from
his own inward nature the richest harvest ever brought forth
by a soil of so little depth, is precisely what was wanting to
Shelley: or let us rather say, he had not, at the period of his
deplorably early death, reached sufficiently far in that intellectual progression of which he was capable, and which, if it has
done so much for far inferior natures, might have made of him
the greatest of our poets. For him, intentional mental discipline
had done little; the vividness of his emotions and of his sensations had done all. He seldom follows up an idea; it starts into
life, summons from the fairyland of his inexhaustible fancy
some three or four bold images, then vanishes, and straight he
is off on the wings of some casual association into quite another
sphere. He had not yet acquired the consecutiveness of thought
necessary for a long poem; his more ambitious compositions
too often resemble the scattered fragments of a mirror; colors
brilliant as life, single images without end, but no picture. It is
only when under the overruling influence of some one state of
feeling, either actually experienced, or summoned up in almost
the vividness of reality by a fervid imagination, that he writes as
a great poet; unity of feeling being to him the harmonizing
principle which a central idea is to minds of another class, and
supplying the coherency and consistency which would else have
been wanting. Thus it is in many of his smaller, and especially
his lyrical poems. They are obviously written to exhale, perhaps
to relieve, a state of feeling, or of conception of feeling, almost
oppressive from its vividness. The thoughts and imagery are
suggested by the feeling, and are such as it finds unsought. The
state of feeling may be either of soul or of sense, or oftener
(might we not say invariably?) of both; for the poetic tempera-

ment is usually, perhaps always, accompanied by exquisite senses. The exciting cause may be either an object or an idea. But whatever of sensation enters into the feeling, must not be local, or consciously bodily; it is a state of the whole frame, not of a part only; like the state of sensation produced by a fine climate, or indeed like all strongly pleasurable or painful sensations in an impassioned nature, it pervades the entire nervous system. States of feeling, whether sensuous or spiritual, which thus possess the whole being, are the fountains of that poetry which we have called the poetry of poets; and which is little else than the utterance of the thoughts and images that pass across the mind while some permanent state of feeling is occupying it.

To the same original fineness of organization, Shelley was doubtless indebted for another of his rarest gifts, that exuberance of imagery, which when unrepressed, as in many of his poems it is, amounts even to a vice. The susceptibility of his nervous system, which made his emotions intense, made also the impressions of his external senses deep and clear: and agreeably to the law of association by which . . . the strongest impressions are those which associate themselves the most easily and strongly, these vivid sensations were readily recalled to mind by all objects or thoughts which had coexisted with them, by all feelings which in any degree resembled them. Never did a fancy so teem with sensuous imagery as Shelley's. Wordsworth economizes an image, and detains it until he has distilled all the poetry out of it, and it will not yield a drop more: Shelley lavishes his with a profusion which is unconscious because it is inexhaustible. The one, like a thrifty housewife, uses all his materials and wastes none: the other scatters them with a reckless prodigality of wealth of which there is perhaps no similar instance. . . .

Source: Extract from essay, 'Two Kinds of Poetry', in *The Monthly Repository* (November 1833); reprinted in *Mill's Essays on Literature and Society*, ed. J. B. Schneewind (1965)

Walter Bagehot (1856)

. . . The works of Shelley lie in a confused state, like the *disjecta membra* of the poet of our boyhood. They are in the strictest sense 'remains'. It is absurd to expect from a man who died at thirty a long work of perfected excellence. All which at so early an age can be expected are fine fragments, casual expressions of single inspirations. Of these Shelley has written some that are nearly, and one or two perhaps that are quite, perfect. But he has not done more. It would have been better if he had not attempted so much . . . .

His success, as we have said, is in fragments; and the best of those fragments are lyrical. The very same isolation and suddenness of impulse which rendered him unfit for the composition of great works, rendered him peculiarly fit to pour forth on a sudden the intense essence of peculiar feeling 'in profuse strains of unpremeditated art'. Lord Macaulay has said that the words 'bard' and 'inspiration', generally so meaningless when applied to modern poets, have a meaning when applied to Shelley. An idea, an emotion grew upon his brain, his breast heaved, his frame shook, his nerves quivered with the 'harmonious madness' of imaginative concentration. . . . In most poets unearthly beings are introduced to express peculiar removed essences of lyrical rapture; but they are generally failures. Lord Byron tried this kind of composition in *Manfred*, and the result is an evident failure. In Shelley, such singing solitary beings are almost uniformly successful; while writing, his mind really for the moment was in the state in which theirs is supposed always to be. He loved attenuated ideas and abstracted excitement. In expressing their nature he had but to set free his own.

Human nature is not, however, long equal to this sustained effort of remote excitement. The impulse fails, imagination fades, inspiration dies away. With the skylark it is well:

> With thy clear keen joyance
> Languor cannot be:
> Shadow of annoyance
> Never came near thee:
> Thou lovest; but ne'er knew love's sad satiety.

But in unsoaring human nature languor comes, fatigue palls, melancholy oppresses, melody dies away. The universe is not all blue sky; there is the thick fog and the heavy earth. 'The world', says Mr Emerson, 'is mundane.' A creeping sense of weight is part of the most aspiring nature. To the most thrilling rapture succeeds despondency, perhaps pain. To Shelley this was peculiarly natural. His dreams of reform, of a world which was to be, called up the imaginative ecstasy: his soul bounded forward into the future; but it is not possible even to the most abstracted and excited mind to place its happiness in the expected realisation of impossible schemes, and yet not occasionally be uncertain of those schemes. The rigid frame of society, the heavy heap of traditional institutions, the solid slowness of ordinary humanity, depress the aspiring fancy 'Since our fathers fell asleep, all things continue as they were from the beginning.' Occasionally we must think of our fathers. No man can always dream of ever altering all which is. It is characteristic of Shelley, that at the end of his most rapturous and sanguine lyrics there intrudes the cold consciousness of this world. So with his Grecian dreams [in *Hellas*]:

> A brighter Hellas rears its mountains
> From waves serener far;
> A new Peneus rolls its fountains
> Against the morning-star.
> Where fairer Tempes bloom, there sleep
> Young Cyclads on a sunnier deep.
>
> A loftier Argo cleaves the main,
> Fraught with a later prize;

> Another Orpheus sings again,
>   And loves, and weeps, and dies:
> A new Ulysses leaves once more
> Calypso for his native shore.

But he ends:

> O, cease! must hate and death return?
> Cease! must men kill and die?
> Cease! drain not to its dregs the urn
>   Of bitter prophecy.
> The world is weary of the past –
> Oh, might it die or rest at last!

In many of his poems the failing of the feeling is as beautiful as
its short moment of hope and buoyancy.

The excellence of Shelley does not, however, extend equally
over the whole domain of lyrical poetry. That species of art
may be divided – not perhaps with the accuracy of science, but
with enough for the rough purposes of popular criticism – into
the human and the abstract. The sphere of the former is of
course the actual life, passions and actions of real men, – such
are the war-songs of rude nations especially; in that early age
there is no subject for art but natural life and primitive passion.
At a later time, when from the deposit of the *débris* of a hundred
philosophies, a large number of half-personified abstractions are
part of the familiar thoughts and language of all mankind, there
are new objects to excite the feelings, – we might even say there
are new feelings to be excited; the rough substance of original
passion is sublimated and attenuated till we hardly recognise
its identity. Ordinarily and in most minds the emotion loses in
this process its intensity or much of it; but this is not universal.
In some peculiar minds it is possible to find an almost dizzy
intensity of excitement called forth by some fancied abstraction,
remote altogether from the eyes and senses of men. The love-
lyric in its simplest form is probably the most intense expression

of primitive passion: yet not in those lyrics where such intensity is the greatest – in those of Burns, for example – is the passion so dizzy, bewildering and bewildered, as in the *Epipsychidion* of Shelley, the passion of which never came into the real world at all, was only a fiction founded on fact, and was wholly – and even Shelley felt it – inconsistent with the inevitable conditions of ordinary existence. In this point of view, and especially also taking account of his peculiar religious opinions, it is remarkable that Shelley should have taken extreme delight in the Bible as a composition. He is the least biblical of poets. The whole, inevitable, essential conditions of real life – the whole of its plain, natural joys and sorrows – are described in the Jewish literature as they are described nowhere else. Very often they are assumed rather than delineated; and the brief assumption is more effective than the most elaborate description. There is none of the delicate sentiment and enhancing sympathy which a modern writer would think necessary; the inexorable facts are dwelt on with a stern humanity, which recognises human feeling though intent on something above it. Of all modern poets, Wordsworth shares the most in this peculiarity; perhaps he is the only recent one who has it at all. He knew the hills beneath whose shade 'the generations are prepared':

> Much did he see of men,
> Their passions and their feelings: chiefly those
> Essential and eternal in the heart,
> That mid the simple form of rural life
> Exist more simple in their elements,
> And speak a plainer language. [*Excursion*, Bk. 1]

Shelley has nothing of this. The essential feelings he hoped to change; the eternal facts he struggled to remove. Nothing in human life to him was inevitable or fixed; he fancied he could alter it all. His sphere is the 'unconditioned'; he floats away and an imaginary Elysium or an expected Utopia; beautiful into excellent, of course, but having nothing in common with the absolute laws of the present world. Even in the description of mere nature the difference may be noted. Wordsworth describes the earth as we know it, with all its peculiarities; where there are moors and hills, where the lichen grows, where the slate-rock juts out. Shelley describes the universe. He rushes away among the stars; this earth is an assortment of imagery, he uses it to deck some unknown planet. He scorns 'the smallest light that twinkles in the heavens'. His theme is the vast, the infinite, the immeasurable. He is not of our home, nor homely; he describes not our world, but that which is common to all worlds – the Platonic idea of a world. Where it can his genius soars from the concrete and real into the unknown, the indefinite and the void.

Shelley's success in the abstract lyric would prepare us for expecting that he would fail in attempts at eloquence. The mind which bursts forward of itself into the inane, is not likely to be eminent in the composed adjustments of measured persuasion. A voluntary self-control is necessary to the orator: even when he declaims, he must not only let himself go; a keen will must be ready, a wakeful attention at hand, to see that he does not say a word by which his audience will not be touched. The eloquence of *Queen Mab* is of that unpersuasive kind which is admired in the earliest youth, when things and life are unknown, when all that is intelligible is the sound of words.

Lord Macaulay, in a passage to which we have referred already, speaks of Shelley as having, more than any other poet, many of the qualities of the great old masters; two of these he has especially. In the first place, his imagination is classical rather than romantic. . . .

We need only to open Shelley to show how essentially classical in his highest efforts his art is. Indeed, although nothing can be farther removed from the staple topics of the classical writers than the abstract lyric, yet their treatment is nearly essential to it. We have said, its sphere is in what the Germans call the unconditioned – in the unknown, immeasurable and untrodden. It follows from this that we cannot know much about it. We cannot know detail in tracts we have never visited; the infinite has no form; the immeasurable no outline: that which is common to all worlds is simple. There is therefore no scope for the accessory fancy. With a single soaring effort imagination may reach her end; if she fail, no fancy can help her; if she succeed, there will be no petty accumulations of insensible circumstance in a region far above all things. Shelley's excellence in the abstract lyric is almost another phrase for the simplicity of his impulsive imagination. He shows it on other subjects also. We have spoken of his bare treatment of the ancient mythology. It is the same with his treatment of nature. In the description of the celestial regions quoted before – one of the most characteristic passages in his writings – the details are few, the air thin, the lights distinct. We are conscious of an essential difference if we compare the *Ode to the Nightingale*, in Keats, for instance . . . with the conclusion of the ode *To a Skylark*. . . . We can hear that the poetry of Keats is a rich, composite, voluptuous harmony; that of Shelley a clear single ring of penetrating melody.

Of course, however, this criticism requires limitation. There is an obvious sense in which Shelley is a fanciful, as contradistinguished from an imaginative poet. These words, being invented for the popular expression of differences which can be remarked without narrow inspection, are apt to mislead us when we apply them to the exact results of a near and critical analysis. Besides the use of the word 'fancy' to denote the power which adorns and amplifies the product of the primitive imagination, we also employ it to denote the weaker exercise of the faculty which itself creates those elementary products. We use the word 'imaginative' only for strong, vast, imposing, interesting conceptions: we use the word 'fanciful' when we have to speak of smaller and weaker creations, which amaze us less at the moment and affect us more slightly afterwards. Of course, metaphysically speaking, it is not likely that there will be found to be any distinction; the faculty which creates the most attractive ideas is doubtless the same as that which creates the less attractive. Common language marks the distinction, because common people are impressed by the contrast between what affects them much and what affects them little; but it is no evidence of the entire difference of the latent agencies. Speech, as usual, refers to sensations, and not to occult causes. Of fancies of this sort, Shelley is full: whole poems – as the *Witch of Atlas* – are composed of nothing else. Living a good deal in, and writing a great deal about, the abstract world, it was inevitable that he should often deal in fine subtleties, affecting very little the concrete hearts of real men. Many pages of his are, in consequence, nearly unintelligible, even to good critics of common poetry. The air is too rarefied for hardy and healthy lungs: these like, as Lord Bacon expressed it, 'to work upon stuff'. From his habitual choice of slight and airy subjects, Shelley may be called a fanciful, as opposed to an imaginative, poet; from his bare delineations of great objects, his keen expression of distinct impulses, he should be termed an imaginative rather than a fanciful one.

Some of this odd combination of qualities Shelley doubtless owed to the structure of his senses. By one of those singular results which constantly meet us in metaphysical inquiry, the imagination and fancy are singularly influenced by the bodily sensibility. One might have fancied that the faculty by which the soul roars into the infinite, and sees what it cannot see with the eye of the body, would have been peculiarly independent of that body. But the reverse is the case. Vividness of sensation seems required to awaken, delicacy to define, copiousness to enrich, the visionary faculty. A large experience proves that a being who is blind to this world will be blind to the other; that a coarse expectation of what is not seen will follow from a coarse perception of what is seen. Shelley's sensibility was vivid but peculiar. Hazlitt used to say, 'he had seen him; and did not like his looks'. He had the thin keen excitement of the fanatic student; not the broad, natural energy which Hazlitt expected from a poet. The diffused life of genial enjoyment which was common to Scott and to Shakespeare, was quite out of his way.

Like Mr Emerson, he would have wondered they could be content with a 'mean and jocular life'. In consequence, there is no varied imagery from human life in his poetry. He was an abstract student, anxious about deep philosophy; and he had not that settled, contemplative, allotted acquaintance with external nature which is so curious in Milton, the greatest of studious poets. The exact opposite, however, to Shelley, in the nature of his sensibility, is Keats. That great poet used to pepper his tongue, 'to enjoy in all its grandeur the cool flavour of delicious claret'. When you know it, you seem to read it in his poetry. There is the same luxurious sentiment; the same poise on fine sensation. Shelley was the reverse of this; he was a water-drinker; his verse runs quick and chill, like a pure crystal stream. The sensibility of Keats was attracted, too, by the spectacle of the universe; he could not keep his eyes from seeing, or his ears from hearing, the glories of it. All the beautiful objects of nature reappear by name in his poetry. On the other hand, the abstract idea of beauty is for ever celebrated in Shelley; it haunted his soul. But it was independent of special things; it was the general surface of beauty which lies upon all things. It was the smile of the universe and the expression of the world; it was not the vision of a land of corn and wine. The nerves of Shelley quivered at the idea of loveliness; but no coarse sensation obtruded particular objects upon him. He was left to himself with books and reflection.

So far, indeed, from Shelley having a peculiar tendency to dwell on and prolong the sensation of pleasure, he has a perverse tendency to draw out into lingering keenness the torture of agony. Of his common recurrence to the dizzy pain of mania we have formerly spoken; but this is not the only pain. The nightshade is commoner in his poems than the daisy. The nerve is ever laid bare; as often as it touches the open air of the real world, it quivers with subtle pain. The high intellectual impulses which animated him are too incorporeal for human nature; they begin in buoyant joy, they end in eager suffering.

In style, said Mr Wordsworth – in workmanship, we think

his expression was – Shelley is one of the best of us. This too, we think, was the second of the peculiarities to which Lord Macaulay referred when he said that Shelley had, more than any recent poet, some of the qualities of the great old masters. The peculiarity of his style is its intellectuality; and this strikes us the more from its contrast with his impulsiveness. He had something of this in life. Hurried away by sudden desires, as he was in his choice of ends, we are struck with a certain comparative measure and adjustment in his choice of means. So in his writings; over the most intense excitement, the grandest objects, the keenest agony, the most buoyant joy, he throws an air of subtle mind. His language is minutely and acutely searching; at the dizziest height of meaning the keenness of the words is greatest. As in mania, so in his descriptions of it, the acuteness of the mind seems to survive the mind itself. It was from Plato and Sophocles, doubtless, that he gained the last perfection in preserving the accuracy of the intellect when treating of the objects of the imagination; but in its essence it was a peculiarity of his own nature. As it was the instinct of Byron to give in glaring words the gross phenomena of evident objects, so it was that of Shelley to refine the most inscrutable with the curious nicety of an attenuating metaphysician. In the wildest of ecstasies his self-anatomising intellect is equal to itself.

There is much more which might be said, and which ought to be said, of Shelley; but our limits are reached. We have not attempted a complete criticism; we have only aimed at showing how some of the peculiarities of his works and life may be traced to the peculiarity of his nature.

SOURCE: Extracts from 'Percy Bysshe Shelley', *The National Review* (October 1856); reprinted in R. H. Hutton, ed., *Literary Studies by the Late Walter Bagehot*, 1 (1897).

Matthew Arnold (*1881*)

. . . Shelley, beautiful and ineffectual angel, beating in the void his luminous wings in vain.

SOURCE: Preface to *Poetry of Byron* (1881); reprinted as 'Byron', in *Essays in Criticism*, second series (Everyman edition, 1888).

T. S. Eliot (*1928, 1933*)

1. 'SOUND WITHOUT SENSE'

I have found that the more I studied the meaning of Crashaw's verse, and his peculiar use of image and conceit, the less resemblance the music of it seemed to have to Shelley's.[1] Take one of Crashaw's more extreme and grotesque figures, from *The Tear*:

> Faire Drop, why quak'st thou so?
> 'Cause thou streight must lay thy Head
> In the Dust? o no;
> The Dust shall never bee thy Bed:
> A pillow for thee will I bring,
> Stuft with Downe of Angels wing.

This imagery is almost the quintessence of an immense mass of devotional verse of the seventeenth century. But it has nothing to do with Shelley. Crashaw's images, even when entirely preposterous – for there is no warrant for bringing a pillow (and what a pillow!) for the 'head' of a 'tear' – give a kind of intellectual pleasure – it is a deliberate conscious perversity of language,

a perversity like that of the amazing and amazingly impressive
interior of St Peter's. There is brain work in it. But in *The
Skylark* there is no brain work. For the first time perhaps in
verse of such eminence, sound exists without sense. Crashaw
would never have written so shabby a line as 'That from heaven
or near it' merely to provide an imperfect rhyme for 'spirit'.

> Keen as are the arrows
> Of that silver sphere
> Whose intense lamp narrows
> In the white dawn clear,
> Until we hardly see, we feel that it is there.

I should be grateful for any explanation of this stanza; until
now I am ignorant to what 'sphere' Shelley refers, or why it
should have silver arrows, or what the devil he means by an
intense lamp narrowing in the white dawn; though I can
understand that we could hardly see the lamp of a 'silver'
sphere narrowing in 'white' dawn (why dawn? as he has just
referred to the pale purple even). There may be some clue for
persons more learned than I; but Shelley should have provided
notes. Crashaw does not need *such* notes.

And when Shelley has some definite statement to make, he
simply says it; keeps his images on one side and his meanings
on the other:

> We look before and after,
> And pine for what is not:
> Our sincerest laughter
> With some pain is fraught;
> Our sweetest songs are those that tell of saddest thought.

This is a sweeping assertion, and is rather commonplace in
expression; but it is intelligible. And it is not in the least like
Crashaw. . . .

SOURCE: Extract from 'A Note on Richard Crashaw', in *For
Lancelot Andrewes* (1928).

NOTE

1. Eliot is objecting to a comparison between Crashaw and Shelley made by L. C. Martin in his edition of *The Poems of Richard Crashaw.* [Ed.]

II. 'AN ABUSE OF POETRY'

The ideas of Shelley seem to me always to be ideas of adolescence – as there is every reason why they should be. And an enthusiasm for Shelley seems to me also to be an affair of adolescence: for most of us, Shelley has marked an intense period before maturity, but for how many does Shelley remain the companion of age? I confess that I never open the volume of his poems simply because I want to read his poetry, but only with some special reason for reference. I find his ideas repellent; and the difficulty of separating Shelley from his ideas and beliefs is still greater than with Wordsworth. And the biographical interest which Shelley has always excited makes it difficult to read the poetry without remembering the man: and the man was humourless, pedantic, self-centred and sometimes almost a blackguard. Except for an occasional flash of shrewd sense, when he is speaking of someone else and not concerned with his own affairs or with fine writing, his letters are insufferably dull. He makes an astonishing contrast with the attractive Keats. On the other hand, I admit that Wordsworth does not present a very pleasing personality either; yet I not only enjoy his poetry as I cannot enjoy Shelley's, but I enjoy it more than when I first read it. I can only fumble (abating my prejudices as best I can) for reasons why Shelley's abuse of poetry does me more violence than Wordsworth's.

Shelley seems to have had to a high degree the unusual faculty of passionate apprehension of abstract ideas. Whether he was not sometimes confused about his own feelings, as we may be tempted to believe when confounded by the philosophy

of *Epipsychidion*, is another matter. I do not mean that Shelley
had a metaphysical or philosophical mind; his mind was in
some ways a very confused one: he was able to be at once and
with the same enthusiasm an eighteenth-century rationalist and
a cloudy Platonist. But abstractions could excite in him strong
emotions. His views remained pretty fixed, though his poetic
gift matured. It is open to us to guess whether his mind would
have matured too; certainly, in his last, and to my mind greatest though unfinished poem, *The Triumph of Life*, there is evidence not only of better writing than in any previous long
poem, but of greater wisdom:

> Then what I thought was an old root that grew
> To strange distortion out of the hillside,
> Was indeed one of those [*sic*] deluded crew
> And that the grass, which methought hung so wide
> And white, was but his thin discoloured hair
> And that the holes he vainly sought to hide
> Were or had been eyes. . . .

There is a precision of image and an economy here that is new
to Shelley. But so far as we can judge, he never quite escaped
from the tutelage of Godwin, even when he saw through the
humbug as a man; and the weight of Mrs Shelley must have
been pretty heavy too. And, taking his work as it is, and without
vain conjectures about the future, we may ask: is it possible to
ignore the 'ideas' in Shelley's poems, so as to be able to enjoy
the poetry?

Mr I. A. Richards deserves the credit of having done the
pioneer work in the problem of belief in the enjoyment of
poetry; and any methodical pursuit of the problem I must leave
to him and to those who are qualified after him. But Shelley
raises the question in another form than that in which it presented itself to me in a note on the subject which I appended
to an essay on Dante. There, I was concerned with two hypothetical readers, one of whom accepts the philosophy of the
poet, and the other of whom rejects it; and so long as the poets

in question were such as Dante and Lucretius, this seemed to cover the matter. I am not a Buddhist, but some of the early Buddhist scriptures affect me as parts of the Old Testament do; I can still enjoy Fitzgerald's *Omar*, though I do not hold that rather smart and shallow view of life. But some of Shelley's views I positively dislike, and that hampers my enjoyment of the poems in which they occur; and others seem to me so puerile that I cannot enjoy the poems in which they occur. And I do not find it possible to skip these passages and satisfy myself with the poetry in which no proposition pushes itself forward to claim assent. What complicates the problem still further is that in poetry so fluent as Shelley's there is a good deal which is just bad jingling. The following, for instance:

> On a battle-trumpet's blast
> I fled hither, fast, fast, fast,
> Mid the darkness upward cast.
> From the dust of creeds outworn,
> From the tyrant's banner torn,
> Gathering round me, onward borne,
> There was mingled many a cry –
> Freedom! Hope! Death! Victory!

Walter Scott seldom fell as low as this, though Byron more often. But in such lines, harsh and untunable, one is all the more affronted by the ideas, the ideas which Shelley bolted whole and never assimilated, visible in the catchwords of creeds outworn, tyrants and priests, which Shelley employed with such reiteration. And the bad parts of a poem can contaminate the whole, so that when Shelley rises to the heights, at the end of the poem:

> To suffer woes which Hope thinks infinite;
> To forgive wrongs darker than death or night;
> To defy Power, which seems omnipotent;
> To love, and bear; to hope till Hope creates
> From its own wreck the thing it contemplates . . .

lines to the content of which belief is neither given nor denied, we are unable to enjoy them fully. One does not expect a poem to be equally sustained throughout; and in some of the most successful long poems there is a relation of the more tense to the more relaxed passages, which is itself part of the pattern of beauty. But good lines among bad can never give more than a regretful pleasure. In reading *Epipsychidion* I am thoroughly gravelled by lines like:

> True love in this differs from gold and clay,
> That to divide is not to take away . . .
> I never was attached to that great sect
> Whose doctrine is, that each one should select
> Out of the crowd, a mistress or a friend
> And all the rest, though fair and wise, commend
> To cold oblivion . . .

so that when I come, a few lines later, upon a lovely image like:

> A vision like incarnate April, warning
> With smiles and tears, Frost the anatomy
> Into his summer grave,

I am as much shocked at finding it in such indifferent company as pleased by finding it at all. And we must admit that Shelley's finest long poems, as well as some of his worst, are those in which he took his ideas very seriously.[1] It was these ideas that blew the 'fading coal' to life; no more than with Wordsworth, can we ignore them without getting something ˙ no more Shelley's poetry than a wax effigy would be Shelley. . . .

We may be permitted to infer, in so far as the distaste of a person like myself for Shelley's poetry is not attributable to irrelevant prejudices or to a simple blind spot, but is due to a peculiarity in the poetry and not in the reader, that it is not the presentation of beliefs which I do not hold, or – to put the case as extremely as possible – of beliefs that excite my abhorrence,

that makes the difficulty. Still less is it that Shelley is deliberately making use of his poetic gifts to propagate a doctrine; for
Dante and Lucretius did the same thing. I suggest that the
position is somewhat as follows. When the doctrine, theory,
belief, or 'view of life' presented in a poem is one which the
mind of the reader can accept as coherent, mature and founded
on the facts of experience, it interposes no obstacle to the
reader's enjoyment, whether it be one that he accept or deny,
approve or deprecate. When it is one which the reader rejects
as childish or feeble, it may, for a reader of well-developed
mind, set up an almost complete check. I observe in passing
that we may distinguish, but without precision, between poets
who employ their verbal, rhythmic and imaginative gift in the
service of ideas which they hold passionately, and poets who
employ the ideas which they hold with more or less settled
conviction as material for a poem; poets may vary indefinitely
between these two hypothetical extremes, and at what point
we place any particular poet must remain incapable of exact
calculation. And I am inclined to think that the reason why I
was intoxicated by Shelley's poetry at the age of fifteen, and
now find it almost unreadable, is not so much that at that age
I accepted his ideas, and have since come to reject them, as that
at that age 'the question of belief or disbelief', as Mr Richards
puts it, did not arise. It is not so much that thirty years ago I was
able to read Shelley under an illusion which experience has
dissipated, as that because the question of belief or disbelief
did not arise I was in a much better position to enjoy the poetry.
I can only regret that Shelley did not live to put his poetic gifts,
which were certainly of the first order, at the service of more
tenable beliefs – which need not have been, for my purposes,
beliefs more acceptable to me. . . .

SOURCE: Extract from 'Shelley and Keats', in *The Use of
Poetry and the Use of Criticism* (1933).

NOTE

1. He did not, for instance, appear to take his ideas very seriously in *The Witch of Atlas*, which, with all its charm, I think we may dismiss as a trifle.

Allen Tate (*1941*)

'AN INCOHERENT STRUCTURE OF IMAGES'

[Tate is discussing *When the lamp is shattered* and quotes the last stanza:]

> Its [Love's] passions will rock thee,
> As the storms rock the ravens on high:
> Bright reason will mock thee,
> Like the sun from a wintry sky.
> From thy nest every rafter
> Will rot, and thine eagle home
> Leave thee naked to laughter,
> When leaves fall and cold winds come.

The general 'argument' is that the passing of spiritual communion from lovers leaves them sad and, in this last stanza, the prey of lust and self-mockery, and even of the mockery of the world ('naked to laughter'). The first line sets the tone and the 'response' that the reader is to maintain to the end: we are told in advance what the following lines will mean: an abstraction that will relieve us of the trouble of examining the particular instances. Indeed, when these appear, the development of their imagery is confused and vague. The ravens in the second line are eagles in the sixth; but, after all, they are only generically birds; greater particularity in them would have compromised their poeticism as objects, or interfered with the response we are instructed to make to them. I pass over 'Bright reason', the self-mockery, for the mockery of the world. Are we to suppose that other birds come by and mock the raven (eagle), or are we to shift the field of imagery and see 'thee' as a woman? Now in the finest poetry we cannot have it both ways. We can have a multiple meaning through ambiguity, but we cannot have an incoherent structure of images. Shelley, in confusion, or carelessness, or haste, could not sustain the nest–bird metaphor and say all that he wished to say; so in order to say it, he changed the figure and ruined the poem. The more we track down the implications of his imagery, the greater the confusion; the more we track down the implications of the imagery in the best verse of Donne, Marvel, Raleigh, Milton, Hopkins, Yeats, Eliot, Ransom, Stevens, the richer the meaning of the poem. Shelley's poem is confused. Are we to conclude that therefore it offers an emotional experience?

SOURCE: Extract from 'Understanding Modern Poetry', in *Reason in Madness* (1941).

Donald Davie

SHELLEY'S URBANITY (1952)

I   THE SHELLEYAN SUBLIME

However we look at it, Shelley affects the sublime. We may not know what the sublime is, and yet know that, to be acceptable, it must include *The Triumph of Life* and *Prometheus Unbound*. Whatever we think of these poems (and the latter at any rate makes dull reading in my experience), there can be no doubt how high the poet aims in them, what large pretensions he makes. In short, whatever his performance, Shelley promises in these poems to move on a level where (for instance) 'urbanity' cannot count.

But this is what makes criticism of Shelley so difficult; he evades so many standards. In this he is peculiar even among the poets of the sublime. His sublimity is peculiarly indefinite and impalpable. From one point of view his poetry is certainly sensuous; but the sensuousness is not of a sort to bring into poetry the reek and grit of common experience. For Shelley goes as far as poetry can go, while it uses intelligible language, in cutting the hawsers which tie his fancies to the ground. His metaphors are tied so tenuously to any common ground in experience that it is peculiarly hard to arrive at their mooring in common logic or association. It was this, for instance, which gave Mr Eliot so much trouble with an image in *To a Skylark*:

> Keen as are the arrows
>   Of that silver sphere,
> Whose intense lamp narrows
>   In the white dawn clear
> Until we hardly see – we feel that it is there.

It is typical of Shelley's obscurity that as it happens I find no difficulty here, but only the accurate register of a sense-perception[1] – the fading of the morning-star. For Shelley evades as many standards as he can, and when he cannot evade them, makes their application as difficult as he can; or so it must seem to the harrassed critic. And as a result we can expect to find the critics even further than usual from agreement about the nature of his achievement. All one can say is that the period of un-critical adulation is past, and that we have learnt, since Dr Leavis's damaging scrutiny,[2] to be on our guard when Shelley is most sublime.

At any rate, if Shelley is great, in *Prometheus Unbound*, in *The Triumph of Life*, even in such shorter poems as *The Cloud*, he is so by virtue of *invention*, the characteristic virtue of the sublime. And the eighteenth-century critics would agree that in poems of this sort the poet has considerable licence. We can expect (and it is only right) that the diction of an epic or a hymn will be less chaste than the diction of a familiar epistle. And we can go so far as to say that in the case of such poems the question of diction should not be introduced at all. But this is not quite true. There are always limits. As Keats remarked, 'English must be kept up' – even in the epic. And Shelley as usual goes to the limit, or over it.

The Cloud is a good example:

> Sublime on the towers of my skiey bowers,
>   Lightning my pilot sits;
> In a cavern under is fettered the thunder,
>   It struggles and howls at fits;
> Over earth and ocean, with gentle motion,
>   This pilot is guiding me,
> Lured by the love of the genii that move
>   In the depths of the purple sea;
> Over the rills, and the crags, and the hills,
>   Over the lakes and the plains,
> Wherever he dream, under mountain or stream,

> The Spirit he loves remains;
> And I all the while bask in Heaven's blue smile,
> Whilst he is dissolving in rains.

The image is audacious to begin with. There is no reason in natural philosophy to give a basis in logic to the notion that a cloud is directed by electric charges. The image depends entirely on association, and the leap of association is something of a strain. However, it is made easier by the elaboration which makes the thunder a prisoner in the dungeons of the cloud. Natural philosophy lends its aid to the logical association of a cloud with the genii of the sea; and the lightning is supposed amorous of the sea – a link sanctioned by neither logic nor association (however 'free'), but carried as it were on the cloud's back. The real difficulty comes with the 'he', appearing three times in the last six lines. Is this 'he' the lightning, the actual cloud or the idea of the cloud which is always present even in a cloudless sky? We are given no indication that this 'he' is any other than 'the pilot', i.e. the lightning. And yet this is surely impossible in the last two lines:

> And I all the while bask in Heaven's blue smile,
> Whilst he is dissolving in rains.

Shelley means to say, I think, that the ideal cloud continues to bask while the actual cloud dissolves in rains; but in fact he says that the cloud, ideal or actual, rides high, while the lightning dissolves. And this is lunacy.

The fault here lies in the conduct and development of a metaphor, not, in the first place, in choice of language. And yet the two cannot be distinguished since the metaphor only comes to grief on the loose use of a personal pronoun. This looseness occurs time and again:

> The stars peep behind her and peer;
> And I laugh to see them whirl and flee,
> Like a swarm of golden bees,

> When I widen the rent in my wind-built tent,
>> Till the calm rivers, lakes, and seas,
> Like strips of the sky fallen through me on high,
>> Are each paved with the moon and these.

The grotesque 'and these' is an affront to all prosaic discipline.
So again:

> I am the daughter of Earth and Water,
>> And the nursling of the Sky;
> I pass through the pores of the ocean and shores;
>> I change but I cannot die . . .

– where 'ocean and shores' is unthinkable in speech or prose.
And finally:

> From cape to cape, with a bridge-like shape,
>> Over a torrent sea,
> Sunbeam-proof, I hang like a roof, –
>> The mountains its columns be.

Here the language is quite indiscriminate; the adjectival 'torrent' is a Latinate urbanity, 'sunbeam-proof' is an audacious coining, and 'The mountains . . . be' is a *naïveté*.

Obviously the conduct of the metaphor in the second stanza is a more serious flaw than any of these later examples. And obviously too, Shelley pitches his poem in a high key, to advise us not to expect nicety of discrimination and prosaic sense. The poem offers compensations. But all the same when the barbarities are so brutal and the carelessness so consistent, it may be doubted whether we can let them pass on any understanding. In poems of this sort, the weight to be given to diction and invention respectively is something that must be left to the taste of the reader. But this may serve as an example of how, even in sublime poems, the poet may take such liberties with his diction as to estrange his reader's sympathies. For one reader,

at any rate, *The Cloud* remains a poem splendid in conception
but ruined by licentious phrasing.

II SHELLEY AND THE FAMILIAR STYLE

This does not dispose of Shelley's pretensions to sublimity. They
confuse at almost every point the issue of his diction. In reading
Wordsworth it is comparatively easy to distinguish the 'sublime'
poems from the others, and to say that this poem begs the question of diction, this other does not. In the case of Shelley this is
not so easily done. And yet there are poems by Shelley which
plainly make no sublime pretensions. It was Ernest de Selin-
court, I think, who proposed Shelley as one of the masters of the
familiar style. The term, like all those which we find we need,
is out of fashion; but plainly it refers to a quality of tone, of
unflurried ease between poet and reader, in short to urbanity,
the distinctive virtue of a pure diction.

It is worth remarking how unlikely this was, in the period
when Shelley wrote. Plainly urbanity will come most easily to a
poet who is sure of his audience, sure that he and his reader
share a broad basis of conviction and assumption. The whole
pressure of Shelley's age was against anything of the kind.
Urbanity, except in the raffish version of Byron and Praed, was
out of fashion among critics and readers; but that was the least
of the difficulties. In the Elizabethan, the Caroline and the
Augustan ages, the poet moved in a society more or less stable
and more or less in agreement about social propriety. Most
poets moved in circles where manners were ceremonious. The
courteous usages were mostly hypocritical, but at least they
were consistent; and they furnished the poet with a model
urbanity which he could preserve in the tone of his writing.
This was as true of the ponderous decorum of Mrs Thrale's
drawing-room as of the elaborate frivolity of the court of
Charles II. Presumably, the violent dislocation of English society
at the end of the eighteenth century (the Industrial Revolution)
had destroyed the established codes of social behaviour. At any

rate, in the Godwin household, in the family of Leigh Hunt, in the extraordinary domestic arrangements of Lord Byron, personal suffering and passion broke through into conversation and social demeanour. These were people who lived on their nerves, whom an established code of behaviour no longer protected. Therefore we cannot expect to find in the poetry of 1820 the exquisite assurance, the confident communication between poet and reader, which dignifies the slightest pieces of Thomas Carew or Thomas Parnell. We cannot expect it; but we find it. It is only natural that Spenser and Dryden, Carew and Parnell, enjoy this assurance. It is anything but natural, it seems almost impossible, that Shelley should do so.

The familiar style in this sense derives from the mean style of the Elizabethans, distinguished by them from the high style, proper to the heroic poem and the hymn, and from the base style of satire and pastoral. It is related too, to what Coleridge, in *Biographia Literaria*, called the 'neutral' style. It is distinguished from the other styles, in the nineteenth century as in the sixteenth, by being comparatively prosaic. Now, according to Johnson, a diction was pure when it was sanctioned by speech-usage on the one hand, and by literary precedent (classic and neo-classic) on the other. The poet's needs tugged him now one way, now the other; to tread a middle course, in touch with both sorts of usage, was to write a pure diction. But as the literary models varied (Juvenal for satire, Virgil for epic), so did the spoken models. The speech of a cobbler was not the model for epic, nor the speech of bishops for satire. There survived, in fact, though mostly unacknowledged, Puttenham's rule that the model for the high style was the speech of courtiers and governors; for the mean style, the speech of merchants and yeomen; for the base style, the speech of peasants and menial trades. In theory Wordsworth ignored the other criterion, literary precedent, and, as Coleridge confusedly saw, came near to asserting that the only permissible style was the mean. In any of the styles, to maintain a pure diction was to preserve 'the tone of the centre' which Arnold was to esteem in Attic prose.

It is one way of explaining 'the sublime', to say that, as England
in the eighteenth century became a bourgeois state, the spoken
model for the high style disappeared, and in poetry which
'affected the sublime' (the Augustan version of the high style)
the question, whether the diction was pure, became meaningless. We are usually asked to acknowledge that Shelley's greatest
poetry was of this sort. But there are other poems which are in
the base and the mean styles; and it is among these that we
have to look for Shelley the master of the familiar style.

The clearest example of Shelley's base style is the *Letter to
Maria Gisborne*. If we continue to talk in terms of Elizabethan
decorum, this corresponds to *The Shepheard's Calender*, as *Julian
and Maddalo*, in the mean style, to *Colin Clout's Come Home Again*,
as *The Cloud*, in the high style, to *Fowre Hymnes*. Shelley himself
invites the Spenserian parallel:

> Near those a most inexplicable thing,
> With lead in the middle – I'm conjecturing
> How to make Henry understand; but no –
> I'll leave, as Spenser says, with many mo,
> This secret in the pregnant womb of time,
> Too vast a matter for so weak a rhyme.[3]

The archaism, like others ('I wist' . . . 'they swink') is used
partly as Spenser used it in *The Shepheard's Calender* or *Mother
Hubberd's Tale*, partly as Byron used it in *Don Juan*, to draw
attention to its ungainly self. But the *Letter to Maria Gisborne* is
neither Spenserian nor Byronic. It belongs to the tradition of
Donne and Browning, who use the base style to unusual ends.
There is no gainsaying that Shelley's verse resembles Browning's more than Donne's; it is an exercise in agility, not energy.
Still, it is heartening, not hearty; and affectionate without being
mawkish. It is too exuberant to be called urbane in the usual
sense. But it is so, in the sense that the poet is sure of his relationship with the person he addresses, that he knows what is due to
her and to himself, that he maintains a consistent tone towards
her. She is not a peg to hang a poem on, nor a bosom for him to

weep on, but a person who shares with him certain interests and certain friends and a certain sense of humour.

This poem is prosaic only in the relatively unimportant sense that it introduces things like hackney-coaches, Baron de Tott's Memoirs, 'self-impelling steam-wheels', and 'a queer broken glass With ink in it'. But like Donne's verse or Browning's, Shelley's is far more figurative than normal prose. For truly lean and bare prosaic language, we turn to *Julian and Maddalo*:

> I rode one evening with Count Maddalo
> Upon the bank of land which breaks the flow
> Of Adria towards Venice; a bare strand
> Of hillocks, heaped from ever-shifting sand,
> Matted with thistles and amphibious weeds,
> Such as from earth's embrace the salt ooze breeds
> Is this; an uninhabited sea-side,
> Which the lone fisher, when his nets are dried,
> Abandons; and no other object breaks
> The waste, but one dwarf tree and some few stakes
> Broken and unrepaired, and the tide makes
> A narrow space of level sand thereon,
> Where 'twas our wont to ride while day went down.

This of course represents a specifically Romantic purity – the adoption, from prose or careful conversation, of a vocabulary of natural description. At their best, the eighteenth-century poets had good reason for believing that features of natural appearance had to be dignified by figures, if they were to be pleasing and instructive; but more often their fussing with metaphors and personifications represented an impurity even by their own standards, for there can be little doubt that their practice in this particular was very far from any spoken usage. Shelley's assumption, that accuracy confers its own dignity, produced a much purer diction; and there are satisfying examples of this elsewhere in *Julian and Maddalo*, as elsewhere in his work.[4] But what the Romantics gained with one hand they lost from the other. For if Johnson, for example, was 'intolerably poetical' when he essayed natural description, he had an enviable prosaic assurance in his dealings with the abstractions of moral philosophy. And it is in this province that Shelley's diction is woefully impure. He expressed, in *The Defence of Poetry*, his concern for these large abstractions, and his Platonic intention to make them apprehensible and 'living' in themselves. In *The Witch of Atlas* he came near to effecting this; but more often, this programme only means that an abstraction such as Reason or Justice must always be tugged about in figurative language. The moment they appear in Shelley's verse (and they always come in droves) the tone becomes hectic, the syntax and punctuation disintegrate. In *Julian and Maddalo*, by inventing the figure and the predicament of the maniac, Shelley excuses this incoherency and presents it (plausibly enough) as a verbatim report of the lunatic's ravings: and in this way he preserves the decorum of the conversation piece (the poem is sub-titled 'A Conversation'). As a result, the whole of this passage, tiresome and unpoetic as it is, impairs but does not ruin the whole. The urbanity is resumed in the close:

> If I had been an unconnected man
> I, from this moment, should have formed some plan
> Never to leave sweet Venice, – for to me
> It was delight to ride by the lone sea;
> And then, the town is silent – one may write
> Or read in gondolas by day or night,
> Having the little brazen lamp alight,
> Unseen, uninterrupted; books are there,
> Pictures, and casts from all those statues fair
> Which were twin-born with poetry, and all
> We seek in towns, with little to recall
> Regrets for the green country. I might sit
> In Maddalo's great palace, and his wit
> And subtle talk would cheer the winter night
> And make me know myself, and the firelight
> Would flash upon our faces, till the day
> Might dawn and make me wonder at my stay.

The conversation we have attended to in the poem is just as civilized as the intercourse of Maddalo and Julian here described. It is in keeping that Julian should know little of Maddalo and not approve of all that he knows, but should be prepared to take him, with personal reservations, on his own terms. It is the habit of gentlemen; and the poet inculcates it in the reader, simply by taking it for granted in his manner of address. The poem civilizes the reader; that is its virtue and its value.

To Jane: the Invitation and *To Jane: the Recollection* were originally two halves of one poem, called 'The Pine Forest of the Cascine near Pisa'. In the second working over, *The Invitation* gained enormously, *The Recollection* hardly at all. The evolution of the latter poem illustrates very forcibly the process (analysed by Dr Leavis) by which the characteristically Shelleyan attitude emerges from a Wordsworthian base. The original version is strikingly Wordsworthian in metre and diction:

> A spirit interfused around,
>   A thinking, silent life;
> To momentary peace it bound
>   Our mortal nature's strife; –
>
> And still, it seemed, the centre of
>   The magic circle there,
> Was one whose being filled with love
>   The breathless atmosphere.

This becomes:

> A spirit interfused around,
>   A thrilling, silent life, –
> To momentary peace it bound
>   Our mortal nature's strife;
> And still I felt the centre of
>   The magic circle there
> Was one fair form that filled with love
>   The lifeless atmosphere.

As Dr Leavis notes, the changes ('thrilling' for 'thinking', 'being' to 'fair form', and 'lifeless' for 'breathless') are all in the direction of eroticism. It is more pertinent to the present enquiry to notice that they all remove the discourse further from prosaic sense. One could write, in sobʋr prose, of a 'breathless' atmosphere; one could never describe it as 'lifeless'. And by the same token a prose-writer can make us conceive how a person can seem to imbue a locality or a moment with a peculiar spiritual flavour; but that the emanation should be physical, an attribute of 'form' rather than 'being', is something far more difficult. It is, of course, part of the poetic function to persuade us of realities outside the range of prosaic sense. But this can hardly be done by the familiar tone; and certainly Shelley does not do it here. He does not persuade us of the novelty, he only tricks us into it. His verse neither appeals to an old experience, nor creates a new one. These passages are a serious flaw in such a short poem.

The other piece, *The Invitation*, is a nonpareil, and one of Shelley's greatest achievements. It maintains the familiar tone, though in highly figured language, and contrives to be urbane about feelings which are novel and remote. This poem presents the experience which *The Recollection* tries to define and rationalize; and the definition is there, already, in the expression. Jane's influence upon the scene where she moved is here entirely credible; what Shelley afterwards tries to express, first in Wordsworthian and then in erotic terms, here persuades us from the start with no fuss or embarrassment. It is the lack of fuss, the ease and assurance, which persuades us throughout. In other words, the poem is first and foremost a triumph of tone. We can accept Jane as 'Radiant Sister of the Day', largely because the lyrical feeling has already accommodated such seemingly unmanageable things as unpaid bills and unaccustomed visitors. It is an achievement of urbanity to move with such ease from financial and social entanglements to elated sympathy with a natural process; just as it is a mark of civilization to be able to hold these things together in one unflurried attitude.

III   *The Sensitive Plant* AND *The Witch of Atlas*

It is important that we should understand the reservations we
have to make about *The Recollection*. We dislike Shelley's eroticism, in the end, because it seems a vicious attitude, morally
reprehensible; but we dislike it in the first place only because it
produces a vicious diction, a jargon. In the end every true
literary judgment is a moral judgment. But many critics go
wrong, and many readers misunderstand them, because they
pass too rapidly into the role of moralist. Even so, those critics
are doing their duty better than others who think that moral
judgment is no part of their business. I think we should value
the significant ambiguity in such phrases as '*chaste* diction',
'*pure* diction', '*vicious* style', 'the *conduct* of a fable'. But I am
willing to let the ambiguity tell its own tale and to stop short,
in this argument, before the point at which literary criticism
moves over and becomes philosophical. It is best to think,
therefore, that we condemn Shelley's eroticism (as we do)
because it produces a jargon, and not because we dislike it 'in
itself'.

For the Elizabethan, the love-song (the 'praise' or the 'complaint') demanded the mean style, unless it used the pastoral
convention. And the best of Shelley's love-songs (not those,
like *Love's Philosophy*, which figure in the anthologies) are distinguished, like the best Caroline lyrics, by urbanity. As early
as 1814, the *Stanza, written at Bracknell* can control self-pity by
controlled and judicious phrasing:

> Thy dewy looks sink in my breast;
>   Thy gentle words stir poison there;
> Thou hast disturbed the only rest
>   That was the portion of despair!
> Subdued to Duty's hard control,
>   I could have borne my wayward lot:
> The chains that bind this ruined soul
>   Had cankered then – but crushed it not.

It is not serious, of course, only album-verse; as is some of Carew. It all depends on how good the album is; in other words, on the degree of civilization in the society which calls for such trifles. And of course there is no question of comparison with Carew. But the Caroline neatness in the third and fourth lines, and the Augustan echo in the fifth, represent an urbane control which Shelley later threw away. More urbane still are the stanzas, *To Harriet*, written in the same year:

> Thy look of love has power to calm
>   The stormiest passion of my soul;
> Thy gentle words are drops of balm
>   In life's too bitter bowl;
> No grief is mine, but that alone
> These choicest blessings I have known.
>
> Harriet! if all who long to live
>   In the warm sunshine of thine eye,
> That price beyond all pain must give, –
>   Beneath thy scorn to die;
> Then hear thy chosen own too late
> His heart most worthy of thy hate.
>
> Be thou, then, one among mankind
>   Whose heart is harder not for state,
> Thou only virtuous, gentle, kind,
>   Amid a world of hate;
> And by a slight endurance seal
> A fellow-being's lasting weal.
>
> For pale with anguish is his cheek.
>   His breath comes fast, his eyes are dim,
> Thy name is struggling ere he speak.
>   Weak is each trembling limb;
> In mercy let him not endure
> The misery of a fatal cure.

> Oh trust for once no erring guide!
> Bid the remorseless feeling flee;
> 'Tis malice, 'tis revenge, 'tis pride
> 'Tis anything but thee;
> Oh, deign a nobler pride to prove,
> And pity if thou canst not love.

Of course we cheapen the idea of urbanity by applying it to such polished nothings as these. But in their brittle elegance they represent a tradition which could have made Shelley's later love-verse a source of delight instead of embarrassment. The consciously elegant wording in places suggests another poet and even another period. Indeed there is more than a hint of pastiche; but that very period-flavour represents a discipline which Shelley threw away.

He can be seen doing so in the *Bridal Song* of 1821, which is admirable in its first version. In this first:

> O joy! O fear! what will be done
> In the absence of the sun!

– is as manly and wholesome as Suckling's *Ballad of a Wedding*. In the last version:

> O joy! O fear! there is not one
> Of us can guess what may be done
> In the absence of the sun . . .

– is just not true. And the familiar tone of 'Come along!' which securely anchors the first version, is merely silly in the others.

As Dr Leavis points out, it appears from parts of *Peter Bell the Third* that Shelley quite deliberately worked erotic elements into the Wordsworthian base of many of his poems. He seems to have mistaken for prudery the master's natural frigidity. No doubt, too, the erotic jargon was bound up with his dedicated flouting of all the sexual morality of his society. For whatever reason Shelley in his love-lyrics adopted a hectic and strident tone, and the urbanity of his early pieces never bore fruit. At the same time he threw into lyrical form more and more of his poetry. The lyric became confused with the hymn and so moved into the orbit of the sublime.

But the jargon came to be habitual with him, whatever sort of poem he wrote, until it taints them nearly all, sublime or not. One of the least tainted is *The Sensitive Plant*, which I find one of his greatest achievements, and of great interest from the point of view of diction. In this poem and *The Witch of Atlas* Shelley is as daring as ever in invention, making his fable as wayward and arbitrary as possible. In both poems the sensuousness is of his peculiar sort which makes the familiar remote. (He takes a common object such as a rose or a boat, and the more he describes it, the less we remember what it is.) In short, the vision in both these poems has all the difficulties of the Shelleyan sublime, impalpable and aetherial. What distinguishes these poems, however, from such a similar (and maddening) piece as *Alastor*, is the presence, at the end of each of them, of a tough hawser of sober sense which at once pulls the preceding poem into shape and (what amounts to the same thing) gives it as much prose meaning as it will bear.

The Sensitive Plant is in three parts, with a conclusion. The first part presents in ecstatic detail the garden in summer, and dwells with particular weight upon one plant in the garden, which appears endowed with almost human intelligence in so far as it seeks to express the love it feels and the beauty it aspires to. Devoid of bloom and scent, it is unable to do so. But this predicament is subordinate to the poet's more general purpose, which is, in Part I, to make the garden seem like a dream. He does so with persuasive ease, partly by metrical resourcefulness (the metres induce a dream, not a pre-Raphaelite swoon), partly by deliberate confusion between the five senses, and partly by exploiting the vaporous, atmospheric and luminous features in the scene which he describes. Part II is short and concerned with the presiding human deity of the garden, a woman who is a sort of human counterpart of the Sensitive Plant. Part III begins with the death of the lady and describes how the garden, through autumn and winter into the next spring, falls into un-weeded ruin.

In the scheme of this fable there is plainly room for an erotic element. The garden, for all its dream-like quality, pulses with germinating energy; and this 'love' is what the sensitive plant seeks to express:

> But none ever trembled and panted with bliss
> In the garden, the field, or the wilderness,
> Like a doe in the noontide with love's sweet want,
> As the companionless Sensitive Plant.

We know Shelley's eroticism is vicious only by the vicious diction it produces. Therefore we can have no complaints about the third line of this stanza, at the same time as we condemn the first. There the trembling and the panting and the bliss, coming thus together, are Shelleyan jargon, reach-me-down words which obviate the need for thinking and feeling precisely. The vice in question is not lasciviousness but more generally self-indulgence which betrays itself in lax phrasing as in lax conduct. Once we have read a certain amount of Shelley's verse, we recognize and dislike words from the private jargon, even when they are used with propriety:

> And the hyacinth purple, and white, and blue,
> Which flung from its bells a sweet peal anew
> Of music so delicate, soft, and intense,
> It was felt like an odour within the sense.

This is deliberate confusion between the senses, not used as later poets used it for definition of a compound sense-experi-ence, nor only for intensification, but to throw over waking experience the illusion of a dream. Unfortunately 'intense' is a word we learn to suspect in Shelley, and it irritates. So again:

> The plumed insects swift and free,
> Like golden boats on a sunny sea,
> Laden with light and odour, which pass
> Over the gleam of the living grass;
>
> The unseen clouds of the dew, which lie
> Like fire in the flowers ill the sun rides high,
> Then wander like spirits among the spheres,
> Each cloud faint with the fragrance it bears;
>
> The quivering vapours of dim noontide,
> Which like a sea o'er the warm earth glide,
> In which every sound, and odour, and beam,
> Move as reeds in a single stream.

Here the confusion between the senses is particularly persuasive, for it appeals to known facts about atmospheric conditions, or else to the evidence of the senses in such conditions. Unfortunately 'faint' and 'dim' are words from the jargon; and this perturbs the reader, even though both are plausible in this context.

Occasionally, too, there are flagrant violations of prosaic discipline:

> But the Sensitive Plant which could give small fruit
> Of the love which it felt from the leaf to the root,
> Received more than all, it loved more than ever,
> Where none wanted but it, could belong to the giver . . .

and:

> The snowdrop, and then the violet,
> Arose from the ground with warm rain wet,
> And their breath was mixed with fresh odour, sent
> From the turf like the voice and the instrument

– which is culpably ambiguous like Byron's lines which appalled Wordsworth:

I stood in Venice on the Bridge of Sighs
A palace and a prison on each hand.

And yet at the very crux of the argument lies the beautiful stanza:

And the beasts, and the birds, and the insects were drowned
In an ocean of dreams without a sound;
Whose waves never mark, though they ever impress
The light sand which paves it, consciousness.

This is memorably poetic, and yet, in the distinction between 'mark' and 'impress', and in the logical tautness of the whole image, it is 'strong' with the prosaic strength which Dr Johnson found in Denham.

The object of these many examples is not to pick holes in a masterpiece, still less to reduce judgment to some ridiculous balancing of good stanzas against bad. They are meant to illustrate what is after all the capital difficulty in reading Shelley – his unevenness. He has hardly left one perfect poem, however short. In reading him one takes the good with the bad, or one does without it altogether. The business of private judgment on his poems is not a weighing of pros and cons but a decision whether the laxity, which is always there, lies at the centre of the poem (as it often does) or in the margin. I have no doubt that the faults of *The Sensitive Plant* are marginal, and that at the centre it is sound and strong.

In any case, the second and third parts of the poem are an improvement on Part I. Part III, in particular, presents a rank and desolate scene as in *Julian and Maddalo* but in greater detail. It is done more poetically than by Crabbe, but no less honestly.

The six stanzas of the 'Conclusion' are of a quite different kind. They ask to be judged on the score of diction, and they triumphantly pass the test they ask for:

Whether the Sensitive Plant, or that
Which within its boughs like a Spirit sat,
Ere its outward form had known decay,
Now felt this change, I cannot say.

Whether that Lady's gentle mind,
No longer with the form combined
Which scattered love, as stars do light,
Found sadness, where it left delight,

I dare not guess; but in this life
Of error, ignorance, and strife,
Where nothing is, but all things seem,
And we the shadows of the dream,

It is a modest creed, and yet
Pleasant if one considers it,
To own that death itself must be,
Like all the rest, a mockery.

That garden sweet, that lady fair,
And all sweet shapes and odours there,
In truth have never passéd away:
'Tis we, 'tis ours are changed; not they.

For love, and beauty, and delight,
There is no death nor change: their might
Exceeds our organs, which endure
No light, being themselves obscure.

There is not a phrase here which would be out of place in un-
affected prose. If that is strange praise for a piece of poetry, it
is what one can rarely say of the poetry of Shelley's period. If
these stanzas stood by themselves, they might seem tame and
flat. In their place in the longer poem they are just what is
needed to vouch for the more florid language of what has gone
before.

The only comparable achievement, among Shelley's poems, is *The Witch of Atlas*. In most editions this poem is introduced by some loose-jointed jaunty stanzas in which Shelley replies to the objection that his poem is lacking in human interest. He compares it with *Peter Bell*:

> Wordsworth informs us he was nineteen years
>   Considering and re-touching Peter Bell;
> Watering his laurels with the killing tears
>   Of slow, dull care, so that their roots to Hell
> Might pierce, and their wide branches blot the spheres
>   Of Heaven, with dewy leaves and flowers; this well
> May be, for Heaven and Earth conspire to foil
> The over-busy gardener's blundering toil.

> My Witch indeed is not so sweet a creature
>   As Ruth or Lucy, whom his graceful praise
> Clothes for our grandsons – but she matches Peter,
>   Though he took nineteen years, and she three days
> In dressing. Light the vest of flowing metre
>   She wears; he, proud as dandy with his stays,
> Has hung upon his wiry limbs a dress
> Like King Lear's 'looped and windowed raggedness'.

> If you strip Peter, you will see a fellow
>   Scorched by Hell's hyperequatorial climate
> Into a kind of a sulphureous yellow:
>   A lean mark, hardly fit to fling a rhyme at;
> In shape a Scaramouch, in hue Othello.
>   If you unveil my Witch, no priest nor primate
> Can shrive you of that sin, – if sin there be
> In love, when it becomes idolatry.

The point of the comparison with *Peter Bell* is not very clear. The implication is that both poems are free fantasies, and that Wordsworth spoiled his by labouring it, whereas the essential virtue of such pieces is their spontaneity, and this Shelley claims to achieve. More interesting is the question how far such poems will bear scrutiny for meanings, how far such fantasies can be treated as allegorical. This I take to be the question of the last stanza above, and Shelley's answer is rather ambiguous. He begins by warning the reader not to rationalize at all, implying that Wordsworth came to grief by inviting such a reading; but then, in the teasing play with 'love' and 'idolatry', he seems to allow that to look for an allegory is perhaps the best tribute one can give. At any rate, it seems plain that *The Witch of Atlas*, like *Kubla Khan* no less than *Peter Bell*, is a flight of gratuitous fancy, a sort of iridescent bubble in which the reader looks for a 'message' only at his peril.

And of course the poem is all that Shelley says – a wayward fable, set in an unearthly landscape peopled by creatures neither human nor divine. Like *Alastor* and *The Sensitive Plant* it has no meaning except as a whole. It is one half of a vast metaphor with the human term left out; and this, its meaning for human life, emerges from the shape of the whole or else it is lost for ever. It was lost in *Alastor*, and to give the meaning in an Introduction (as Shelley did then) is not enough. The meaning may fit the myth, but it is not carried in the myth, and one always forgets what *Alastor* is about. *The Witch of Atlas*, which is just as wayward and inhuman, takes on meaning, as much meaning as it can bear without cracking the singing voice. Shelley takes care of the meaning:

> The priests would write an explanation full,
>   Translating hieroglyphics into Greek,
> How the God Apis really was a bull,
>   And nothing more; and bid the herald stick
> The same against the temple doors, and pull
>   The old cant down; they licensed all to speak
> Whate'er they thought of hawks, and cats, and geese,
>   By pastoral letters to each diocese.

It is absurd, of course. We cannot really believe that the ideal beauty of the vision means no more in moral terms than the regeneration of religious institutions, and their purification from superstition. But Shelley admits the absurdity, by his verse-form, at the same time as he implies that such a change must after all be *part* of any regenerated world. There is no danger of taking this too seriously, and thereby damaging the sheer creative *élan* of the poem. And by thus slipping back at the end of the poem, into the familiar, even slangy base style of the prefatory stanzas, Shelley guards this most visionary and fantastic poem from any rough handling. He casts his myth into a sort of rough-hewn cradle of coarse sense. The device is the same as that in *The Sensitive Plant*, except that here Shelley uses the base, where there he used the mean style. To complain that the poem is 'obscure' or 'lacking in human interest' is now out of the question. If one does so, one has missed the point, and made not a mistake only but a social blunder. To that extent Shelley's is an achievement, once again, of urbanity.

*

The poet I have considered here is a poet of poise and good breeding. Shelley was the only English Romantic poet with the birth and breeding of a gentleman, and that cannot be irrelevant. What is more surprising is the evidence that in other poems Shelley failed chiefly for want of the very tact which is here conspicuous. I am at a loss to explain how a poet so well aware of what he was doing should also have written *The Cenci*. But if urbanity depends on the relation between poet and public, then it may be that Shelley's failures in tact were connected with his being unread and neglected. In her notes on the poems of 1821, Mrs Shelley hinted as much:

Several of his slighter and unfinished poems were inspired by these scenes, and by the companions around us. It is the nature of that poetry, however, which overflows from the soul, oftener to express sorrow and regret than joy; for it is when oppressed by the weight of life, and away from those he loves, that the poet has recourse to the solace of expression in verse.

It is, alas, too true that many of Shelley's poems are the products of self-pity looking for 'solace' or compensation; and it is not strange that the 'slighter and unfinished poems', inspired by 'the companions around us', should be some of Shelley's best work. This is not the poetry 'which overflows from the soul', but the considered expression of an intelligent man.

SOURCE: *Purity of Diction in English Verse* (1952).

NOTES

1. Cf. from *Ode to Naples*:
          The isle-sustaining ocean-flood,
       A plane of light between two heavens of azure.
2. F. R. Leavis, *Revaluation*, pp. 203-40.
3. Or, as Sidney says (*Astrophel and Stella*),
          Too high a theme for my low style to show.
4. Notably in *Lines* (1815), *The Sunset* (1816), *Summer and Winter* (1820) and *Evening: Ponte al Mare, Pisa* (1821).

Ralph Houston

SHELLEY AND THE PRINCIPLE OF ASSOCIATION (1953)

'Shelley read incessantly; Hume's Essays produced a powerful impression on him . . .'

Matthew Arnold: *Essays in Criticism.*

The problem concerning Shelley to which I want to redirect attention, is posed for us by Dr F. R. Leavis in his essay on Shelley in *Revaluation*. Referring to the *Ode to the West Wind* Leavis says:

In the growth of those 'tangled boughs' out of the leaves, exemplifying as it does a general tendency of the images to forget the status of the metaphor or simile that introduced them and to assume an autonomy and a right to propagate, so that we lose in confused generations and perspectives the perception or thought that was the ostensible 'raison d'être' of imagery, we have a recognized essential trait of Shelley's: his weak grasp upon the actual (p. 206).

Leavis is rightly concerned with the vagueness (or, more often perhaps, the false appearance of precision) that can be found in Shelley's imagery. But is it entirely due to 'a weak grasp upon the actual'? It seems difficult to believe that the poet who wrote the following, for example, suffered from a weak grasp upon the actual:

> I have heard those more skilled in spirits say,
> The bubbles, which the enchantment of the sun
> Sucks from the pale faint water-flowers that pave

The oozy bottom of clear lakes and pools,
Are the pavilions where such dwell and float
Under the green and golden atmosphere
Which noontide kindles through the woven leaves;
And when these burst, and the thin fiery air,
The which they breathed within those lucent domes,
Ascends to flow like meteors through the night,
They ride on them, and rein their headlong speed,
And bow their burning crests, and glide in fire
Under the waters of the earth again.

                                    (*Prometheus Unbound*, II ii 70–82)

Yet the remarks that lead up to Leavis's final pronouncement
are not irrelevant here. Why, for example, 'pale' and 'faint'?
'Faint', clearly, has arrived because of its association with paleness; but fainting water-flowers seem to have little bearing on
the main theme of the passage; and if Shelley did not intend to
convey this meaning, then the word 'faint' is superfluous. This
may seem a small point, but it is symptomatic of the way a
chain of associations in Shelley's poetry tends to break down. A
clearer example of this tendency occurs a few lines earlier in the
same poem:

                    Those who saw
          Say from the breathing earth behind
          There steams a plume-uplifting wind
        Which drives them on their path.

The 'breathing earth' does steam in certain circumstances; but
'a plume-uplifting wind' does not. In effect, the chain of associations has broken in the middle; and examples of this kind of
breakdown are so numerous in Shelley's poetry that one is
forced, I think, to seek a cause other than, or in addition to, a
'weak grasp upon the actual'.

In his essay *A Defence of Poetry* Shelley says (my italics):

Man is an instrument over which a series of external and internal impressions are driven, like the alternations of an ever-changing wind over an Aeolian lyre, which move it by their motion to ever-changing melody. *But there is a principle within the human being . . .* which acts otherwise than in the lyre, and produces not melody alone, but harmony, by an internal adjustment of the sounds or motions thus excited to the impressions which excite them. It is as if the lyre could accommodate its chords to the motions of that which strikes them, in a determined proportion of sound; even as the musician can accommodate his voice to the sound of the lyre. A child at play by itself will express its delight by its voice and motions; and every inflection of tone and gesture will bear exact relation to a corresponding antitype in the pleasurable impressions which awakened it; it will be the reflected image of that impression; and as the lyre trembles and sounds after the wind has died away, so the child seeks, by prolonging in its voice and motions the duration of the effect, to prolong also the consciousness of the cause. In relation to the objects which delight a child, these expressions are what poetry is to higher objects.

Shelley is indebted to Hume for the phrase 'it will be the reflected image of that impression'; and Hume's presence in the rest of the passage is unmistakable. Compare, for example, Shelley's remarks on the child at play with the following from Book II, section ix, of Hume's *A Treatise of Human Nature*:

Each view of the imagination produces a peculiar passion, which decays away by degrees, and is followed by a sensible vibration after the stroke.

Compare, moreover, the following from the same section with Shelley's 'Man is an instrument . . .'

Now, if we consider the human mind, we shall find that, with regard to the passions, it is not of the nature of a wind-instrument . . . which, running over all the notes, immediately loses the sound after the breath ceases; but rather resembles a string-instrument, where, after each stroke, the vibrations still retain some sound, which gradually and insensibly decays. The imagination is extremely quick and agile; but the passions are slow and restive; for which reason, when an object is presented that affords a variety of views to the one, and emotions to the other, though the fancy may change its views with great celerity, each stroke will not produce a clear and distinct note of passion, but the one passion will always be mixed and confounded with the other.

The passion produced by the imagination 'decays away by degrees'; the vibrations of the human mind 'retain some sound, which gradually and insensibly decays'. Are not these remarks possibly the germs of Shelley's considered belief that 'the mind in creation is as a fading coal, which some invisible influence, like an inconstant wind, awakens to transitory brightness'? In view of this possibility an examination of Hume's epistemology may help us to name and clarify the principle that Shelley implicitly invokes in *A Defence of Poetry*; and this examination, I think, will lead us to the Principle of Association. This was, of course, an empiricist commonplace, and undoubtedly Shelley would have been acquainted with it through sources other than, and in addition to, Hume. But the Humian attitude and terminology, even the imagery, is so marked in *A Defence of Poetry* and in some of the poems (for example, 'Music, when soft voices die,/Vibrates in the memory') that to ignore it is to imperil our understanding of Shelley's work. . . .

Hume . . . begins his [*Treatise*] with an examination of the nature of Human Understanding. Man, he says, has no knowledge other than that obtained from experience. Experience is what is given us by perception, and he divides perception into (i) Impressions and (ii) Ideas. Impressions he defines as 'all sensations, passions and emotions as they make their first appearance in the soul': and Ideas are 'the faint images or copies of these impressions as used by us in thinking and reasoning'. These Ideas, generated by the Impressions, include the emotions of Pleasure and Pain and the passions of Desire and Aversion, which Hume calls 'impressions of reflection'. He insists that the Impression precedes the Idea, though the Idea may generate another Idea.

Hume next gives an account of Memory and Imagination:

Memory is any impression which reappears in the mind with a considerable degree of its original vivacity: Imagination, on the other hand, is recognized as such when the impression reappears in the mind without its original vivacity and strength. Memory, we are told, is 'tied down' to the original impression, whereas Imagination is free of it and does not retain the same form and order of the original impression. Memory, therefore, is reliable because of its exactness and strength; but Imagination, which is weak, inexact, even chaotic, is therefore suspect.

Here, however, Hume introduces the Principle of Association of Ideas, which, he says, prevents the activities of the Imagination from being completely unaccountable. This principle gives the Imagination some measure of uniformity with itself; and it brings to Ideas an order and uniformity by means of Resemblance, Contiguity of Time and Place, and Cause and Effect. It produces 'cohesion in our simple Ideas' in order to transform them into Complex Ideas such as Modes (e.g., Beauty) and Substances (e.g., Gold); and in the Imagination 'it supplies the place of that inseparable connection, by which they are united in the Memory'; and he describes it as 'a gentle force' or 'a kind of ATTRACTION, which in the mental world will be found to have as extraordinary effect as in the natural' (*Treatise of Human Nature*, Book I, part i, section 4).

Hume then proceeds to outline and agree with Berkeley's theory that all Abstract Ideas are nevertheless 'individual in themselves, even though they become general in representation'; and from this Hume deduces that in fact Abstract Ideas, as such, do not exist. The general or Abstract Idea merely signalizes the fact that we have associated certain simple ideas; it is a custom of the mind brought about by the automatic operation of the Principle of Association of Ideas.

Knowledge, then, is merely an aggregate of independent ideas which we build together to make a whole. But, Hume says, we cannot obtain our ideas of Time and Space in this way. How, then, do the ideas of Time and Space get into our minds? This, Hume replies, is quite inexplicable, and he rejects the three standard explanations so far put forward by philosophers: (i) that they arise from the object; (ii) that they are produced by the creative power of the mind; and (iii) that they are given by God. Hume therefore concludes that, since we cannot rationally demonstrate its existence, we cannot found our belief in an external order on Reason alone.

If, then, we cannot tell the difference between a 'true' and a 'false' idea of the external order of the world by means of Reason, is there any way in which we can? To this question Hume replies that we know a 'true' idea from a 'false' idea because it is superior in 'strength' and 'vivacity'. Thus a 'true' idea is only different from a 'false' idea in terms of *strength*, and by 'strength' Hume means strength of feeling – we 'feel' a 'true' idea more strongly than we do a 'false' idea; and this leads him to conclude that 'Belief is nothing but a strong and lively idea derived from a present impression related to it' (Book I, part iii, section 8). The foundation, then, of our knowledge of the world, according to Hume, is Sentiment (Feeling), rather than Reason. . . .

What did Hume mean by the 'strength' of an Idea or Impression? In chapters ix and x of his book *The Principles of Art*, R. G. Collingwood discusses this problem. The discussion is too lengthy to quote in full or paraphrase here, but . . . Collingwood concludes as follows (my italics):

The truth is that Hume does not distinguish the two meanings. An impression, for him, is distinguished from an idea only by its force or liveliness; but this force may be of two kinds. It may be the brute violence of crude sensation, as yet undominated by thought. Or it may be the solid strength of a sensum (by which Collingwood means 'that which we sense' by our five common senses) firmly placed in its context by the *interpretative work of thought*. Hume did not recognize the difference.

Collingwood's distinction is, I think, also valid if applied to the Principle of Association. Resemblance, which Hume makes one of the causes of Association, cannot be a cause until similarity has been *noticed*. We cannot associate certain ideas, except involuntarily and arbitrarily, until the mind has perceived some similarity between them. This implies *activity* of mind. Hume's theory depends upon the passive automatism of the mind, whereas in fact the mind is partly active and partly passive.

From much of Shelley's poetry and from his *A Defence of Poetry* one must deduce, I think, that Shelley thought his mind should, and indeed did, function in this passive way. At all events, it seems to me that this is how his mind was functioning when he wrote the following lines:

> Like rabid snakes, that sting some gentle child
>   Who brings them food, when winter false and fair
> Allures them forth with its cold smiles, so wild
>   They rage among the camp; . . .
>   (*The Revolt of Islam*, Canto v vii)

Here, I think, Shelley has attempted a Homeric simile; but there is no rational connection between the rabid snakes, the children taking food to them and the arbitrary setting in midwinter. The ideas have the solid strength of a sensum, but they are not firmly placed in their context by the interpretative work of thought.

The assumption that the human mind is merely a passive instrument leads Hume into another fallacy, this time in his Principle of the Association of Impressions. This principle provides an important link in the chain of reasoning that leads Hume to conclude that the Passions are the final arbiters of human action, for, Hume says, it is only when this Principle concurs with the Principle of Association of Ideas that *belief* results. Having reminded us of the Principle of Association of Ideas he continues (my italics):

The second property I shall observe in the human mind is the like association of impressions. All resembling impressions are connected together, and no sooner one arises than the rest immediately follow. Grief and disappointment give rise to anger, anger to envy, envy to

malice, and malice to grief again . . . it is difficult for the mind, when
actuated by any passion, to confine itself to that passion alone . . .
Human nature is too inconstant . . . Changeableness is essential to it.
And to what can it so naturally change as to affections and emotions,
which are suitable to the temper, *and agree with that set of passions which
then prevail*? (Book II, part i, section 4).

Thus, Hume concludes, when these two principles occur they
'bestow upon the mind a *double impulse*. The new passion, therefore, must arise with so much greater violence, and the transi-
tion to it must be rendered so much more easy and natural'.
The rapidly changing emotions, then, will inevitably flow into
the predominant emotion that happens to prevail in a particular
person at a particular moment. The *quantity of emotion*, then, is
what matters, not its *quality*. . . .

When this Principle of Association of Impressions (Emotions)
concurs with the Principle of Association of Ideas, Belief,
according to Hume, results. 'Imagination' was the faculty that
co-ordinated and associated ideas, but it was weak and power-
less to induce belief by itself and needed the help of the Principle
of Association of Impressions (Emotions). The latter, therefore,
becomes the more important of these two 'natural principles',
as Hume calls them. By 'Imagination', Shelley too, I suggest,
meant these two principles working together; and by inducing
belief in this way the poet, to Shelley, must be 'the unacknowledged legislator of the world'. . . . 'Imagination', in effect, has
become the power to sustain a permanent state of feeling; but,
as, according to Hume, one state of feeling cannot be held
constant in the mind for long, and must change rapidly into
another state of feeling, it follows that the mind in the act of
creation must be 'as a fading coal'.

[Houston then discusses John Stuart Mill's essay comparing
Wordsworth with Shelley, part of which is reproduced on
pages 57–9 above. – Ed.]

It would seem, then, that Hume, Shelley and Mill were
committed, intentionally or unintentionally, to the idea that
the human mind is fundamentally a passive instrument func-

tioning automatically by means of the Principles of Association
of Ideas and Impressions (Emotions). We must now consider
the logical consequences of this as far as poetry is concerned.
As I see it, then, there will be, firstly, a failure to *select* among the
reflected images of impressions presented to the mind, so that
the associative links become a matter of mere chance; secondly,
a failure to relate these images to a central and controlling
theme; and thirdly, a tendency towards greater compression,
since the associative links are not presented to the reader who
has to supply them for himself. The first two consequences can
be disastrous and are causes of much bad modern poetry; the
third, however, can be productive of good poetry, provided
that the first two faults are not committed, that is, given the
active selection of independent impressions so that the reader
can relate them or contrast them and in turn connect them to a
central theme.

Thus I would suggest that Leavis's sense of dissatisfaction
with *Ode to the West Wind* is partly due to Shelley's lapses into
involuntary and arbitrary associative thinking, when, as Mill
puts it, 'all the thoughts which those feelings suggest are floated
promiscuously along the stream'. In those 'tangled boughs of
Heaven and Ocean' Shelley's mind, under pressure and moving
at speed, has telescoped the shattered autumn landscape with
a stormy Heaven and Ocean and produced, while conveying a
vague meaning, a muddle which I for one find impossible to
straighten out. And there are other examples of this telescoping
of associations in the Ode. The West Wind buries the 'winged
seed' until her azure sister of the spring shall blow

> Her clarion o'er the dreaming earth, and fill
> *(Driving sweet buds like flocks to feed in air)*
> With living hues and odours plain and hill

Here Shelley has telescoped the idea of the spring wind
driving the flocks out to feed and the idea of new buds opening
in the spring air. Both ideas are associated with spring and can
be associated with each other, but not in the way Shelley does.

In the following extract, again, the plethora of associations, introduced while the simile is allowed to extend itself, leaves the reader bewildered by the time he reaches 'So came a chariot':

> When on the sunlit limits of the night
> Her white shell trembles amid the crimson air,
> And whilst the sleeping tempest gathers might –
>
> Doth, as the herald of its coming, bear
> The ghost of its dead mother, whose dim form
> Bends in dark aether from her infant's chair, –
>
> So came a chariot on the silent storm . . .
>
> (*The Triumph of Life*, 80–6)

I suggest that this habit of involuntary associative thinking leads Shelley into a form of 'Impressionism', the basis of which is compression, and therefore inimical to the Homeric simile; and I would suggest that there is a conflict in much of Shelley's poetry between a desire to pursue fulsome, detailed and particularized descriptions in the manner of Milton, and this tendency towards 'Impressionism'. It is this basic conflict, I think, that causes what for me is the unsuccessful Homeric simile in Canto v, vii, of *The Revolt of Islam*. That Shelley was, in fact, somewhere between Milton on the one hand, and the extreme compression of, say, T. S. Eliot on the other, is shown I think by the following examples:

> (*a*)   Southward through Eden went a river large,
>   Nor changed his course, but through the shaggy hill
>   Pass'd underneath ingulf'd; for God had thrown
>   That mountain as his garden mould, high raised
>   Upon the rapid current, which *through veins*
>   *Of porous earth with kindly thirst updrawn,*
>   *Rose a fresh fountain,* and with many a rill
>   Water'd the garden; . . .
>
>   (*Paradise Lost*, IV 223–30)

(*b*)   The Earth.   I am the Earth,
        Thy Mother; *she within whose stony veins,*
        To the last fibre of the loftiest tree
        Whose thin leaves trembled in the frozen air,
        Joy ran, as blood within a living frame,
        When thou didst from her bosom, like a cloud
        Of glory, arise, a spirit of keen joy!
                            (*Prometheus Unbound*, I 153–8)

  (*c*)   The goat coughs at night in the field overhead;
        Rocks, moss, stonecrop, iron, merds.
                            (*Gerontion*)

Milton's 'through veins/Of porous earth with kindly thirst
updrawn' is straightforward; and we can accept Shelley's 'stony
veins' of earth; but when Shelley suddenly compresses, transferring, by implication, the 'stony veins' to the tree, one cannot,
I think, assent. Mr Eliot, on the other hand, relies entirely on
presenting a series of distinct impressions to the reader, all carefully linked to a central and controlling theme, that of Gerontion,
'an old man in a dry month . . . waiting for rain'. It would seem
that there can be no compromise between Mr Eliot's method
and Milton's, though it was this compromise, I suggest, that
Shelley was subconsciously attempting.

I do not wish to suggest, however, that Shelley, either in his
poetry or his criticism, was consciously writing in accordance
with Hume's philosophy (which was fundamentally an attempt
to outline a psychology). No true poet creates in that way. Yet
he seems to have echoed Hume in much the same way that he
echoed Shakespeare in *The Cenci*. Perhaps he was predisposed,
as a child of that particular period of time, to be influenced by
Hume's writings in the sense that he found himself happy to
agree with them. At least Hume seems to have presented
Shelley with a psychological 'schema' such as Freud and Jung
have given modern poetry. I would urge, then, that it is to
Hume, rather than to Plato, that we should now turn for a

better understanding of Shelley's poetry and criticism, and, in
so doing, of Shelley's descendants today.

SOURCE: Extracts from 'Shelley and the Principle of Association', in *Essays in Criticism* (January 1953).

William Milgate, David V. Erdman and Valerie Pitt

READING SHELLEY (1954)

I. WILLIAM MILGATE

Mr Ralph Houston's useful study of the relation of Shelley's work to Hume's [see foregoing essay – Ed.] corrects in some degree Dr Leavis's opinion that Shelley's 'weak grasp upon the actual' is 'a recognized essential trait'. Like Dr Leavis, however, Mr Houston seems to approach Shelley's grasp upon the actual only through his use of visual imagery. He objects to 'from the breathing earth behind/There steams a plume-uplifting wind (*Prometheus Unbound*, II ii 52–3) because, while the 'breathing earth' does steam in certain circumstances, a 'plume-uplifting wind' does not. It is true that Shelley writes that 'those who *saw* /Say from the breathing earth . . .' etc.; 'saw' suggests a visual connection (as 'seeing' is understood of the world of spirits). Nevertheless it is not true that 'the chain of associations has broken down in the middle'; for the association of 'steams' and 'wind' is, as so often in Shelley's imagery, one of impulsive *force* ('plume-uplifting'). Shelley has picked up a new association, from an aspect of 'steams' other than the visual one. Opinions may differ as to his success in suggesting the world of spiritual forces by this swift breaking down of distinctions between one sense and another; but it seems unfair to assume at the outset that the only possible method is the use of cohesive *visual* imagery, and then to attribute Shelley's failure to the admitted lack of this particular sort of cohesion. (Other critics show that it becomes even more difficult to assess Shelley if one excludes from one's notion of 'the actual' that spiritual world whose quality and landscape he at any rate thought real enough to describe; a certain imaginative acceptance at least will give the reader a clearer idea of what Shelley is doing.)

Another of Mr Houston's examples from *Prometheus Unbound* illustrates a misreading of a different kind. Earth describes herself (1 i 153–8) as

> she within whose stony veins,
> To the last fibre of the loftiest tree
> Whose thin leaves trembled in the frozen air,
> Joy ran, as blood within a living frame,
> When thou didst from her bosom, like a cloud
> Of glory, arise, a spirit of keen joy!

Here, says Mr Houston, we can accept the 'stony veins' of earth; 'but when Shelley suddenly compresses, transferring, by implication, the "stony veins" to the tree, one cannot, I think, assent'. But surely no one would readily assume that Shelley is 'compressing' to the extent of ascribing 'stony veins' to a tree? What has happened is obviously a syntactical phenomenon, a compression not of imagery but of construction; joy ran *within* earth's stony veins and *from* them to the tips of the leaves. The 'loose' syntax might be regarded as another poetic method of suggesting an idea which it is difficult to realize in poetry while observing the usual distinctions, not only in sense-imagery, but in syntax also. (There is a certain reluctance nowadays to allow Shelley the freedom in these matters which is ungrudgingly allowed to others.) The weakness in *imagery* here seems to me to rest in the word 'living' – in the comparison by simile of things already more powerfully identified in metaphor: an elaboration which is weak, not *because* it is an elaboration, but because its effect is *weakening*. We can readily enough 'assent' to the imagery in the earlier lines (153–5); there the doubtful point is the degree of success achieved in relation to the extent of disturbance in the syntax. (Are the distortions in syntax both necessary to and justified by the poetic effect achieved?) Here Shelley's method is not 'somewhere between' Milton's and

Eliot's; it is Milton's, modified by a syntactical compression through which Shelley conveys a sense of the *unity* of earth and tree – a sense which normal syntax (as my expansion of the idea shows) would weaken or altogether destroy.

In addition to confining the associative process to visual imagery, and to overlooking kinds of 'compression' which have nothing to do with imagery, Mr Houston's way of reading Shelley suggests a prejudice in favour of one certain type of poetry (a prejudice which he shares with Dr Leavis). Quoting from *The Revolt of Islam* (v vii 1774–7):

> Like rabid snakes, that sting some gentle child
> Who brings them food, when winter false and fair
> Allures them forth with its cold smiles, so wild
> They rage among the camp;

Mr Houston remarks that here 'Shelley has attempted a Homeric simile; but there is no rational connection between the rabid snakes, the children taking food to them and the arbitrary setting in mid-winter'. Adapting Collingwood's phrases used in a discussion of Hume, he adds: 'The ideas have the solid strength of a sensum, but they are not firmly placed in their context by the interpretative . . . thought.' The emphasis on the *rational* comes out also in Mr Houston's remark that 'there is a conflict in much of Shelley's poetry between a desire to pursue fulsome, detailed and particularized descriptions in the manner of Milton, and this tendency towards "Impressionism" '. Even if one does not admit 'impressionism' as a legitimate way of writing poetry and one insists on a clearly statable rational progression throughout the poem, Mr Houston's example seems an unfortunate one. Snakes hibernating are deluded by a warm winter day ('false' because it is 'fair') into coming out to seek food, and bite the hand that feeds them. (In Australia, I know, people who carelessly associate hibernation with torpor are sometimes bitten by snakes in midwinter; and, even though the validity of the image does not depend on this, the same would be true in the locale of Shelley's poem.)

The image is fully 'rational' in its context; the 'grasp upon the actual' is firm; the ideas *have* 'the solid strength of a sensum'. (For another instance of misreading by a critic intent upon demonstrating the lack of 'rational connection' in Shelley, see Professor F. A. Pottle's examination of a criticism by Mr Allen Tate [in Part One above – Ed.].) The weakness of Shelley's imagery here lies in the slightly sentimental imaging of the 'good' people in the context by 'gentle child' in the fairly trite level of imagination, and in the local use of 'snake' in opposition to the symbolism of the 'serpent' with which the poem begins. I am not suggesting that here Shelley is writing great poetry; but it is better poetry than Mr Houston's reading makes of it. (Critics, perhaps not including Mr Houston, who look only for 'rational connections', usually favour poetry built on principles of paradox, irony, tension of attitudes and so on; to them Shelley's 'cold smiles' would have a paradoxical quality probably too weak to be noticed.)

As a further instance of Shelley's 'involuntary and arbitrary associative thinking' to be added to those already gathered by Dr Leavis from the *Ode to the West Wind*, Mr Houston mentions the telescoping of images in

> Thine azure sister of the Spring shall blow
> Her clarion o'er the dreaming earth, and fill
> (Driving sweet buds like flocks to feed in air)
> With living hues and odours plain and hill.

The ideas of the spring wind driving flocks out to feed and of new buds opening in the spring air, he says, 'are associated with spring and can be associated with each other, but not in the way Shelley does'. But *why* not in this way? Does the reader find this a 'muddle', as Mr Houston finds those 'tangled boughs of Heaven and Ocean' a muddle? Does the organization of the lines suggest that they arose from a creative process both involuntary and arbitrary? It seems to me that here we have an elaboration which does not weaken, but which reinforces, the poetic effect. Blue skies and warm spring breezes call forth irresistibly ('driving') both buds and flocks, two harmonious symbols of new life and increase ('living', 'fill'). Nothing is more striking in the passage than the intellectual grip with which Shelley fuses distinct things into an organized and compressed harmony; and by the fusion he conveys a rich sense of an underlying unity. (Hunters of the 'ambiguity' would note an effective one in the word 'blow', but might feel that 'driving' has had placed upon it a heavy, and risky, burden.) Mr Houston, indeed, seems to condemn elaboration as such (Shelley's detail is not 'full' but 'fulsome'). In a passage which he quotes from *Prometheus Unbound* (ii ii 70–82), he objects to 'pale' and 'faint' in

> The bubbles, which the enchantment of the sun
> Sucks from the pale faint water-flowers that pave
> The oozy bottom of clear lakes and pools . . .

'Faint' has clearly arrived, says Mr Houston, 'because of its association with paleness; but fainting water-flowers seem to have little bearing on the main theme of the passage; and if Shelley did not intend to convey this meaning, then the word "faint" is superfluous' – another example, in Mr Houston's opinion, of 'the way a chain of associations in Shelley's poetry tends to break down'. The sense of 'faint' does not seem to be obviously, or even possibly, 'fainting'; the flowers *are* 'pale', and they *look* 'faint' below the water. There does not seem to be any tendency at all for the chain of associations to 'break down'. Indeed this very accuracy of vizualizing ought to have appealed to Mr Houston, who rightly finds it difficult to believe that the poet who wrote the passage 'suffered from a weak grasp upon the actual'. In a *firmly* conceived passage, surely, the more elaboration there is the more 'grasp upon the actual' there is *likely* to be. We have already seen one example, however, in which the elaboration unnecessarily weakens a firm conception. Nevertheless much more of the elaboration in Shelley's poems that Mr Houston's reading would suggest plays a part in an intellectually controlled scheme. One such scheme is usefully

proposed by Mr Bateson in connection with the very Ode to
which Mr Houston, following Dr Leavis, objects: the use of
associations to *enrich* the symbol (*English Poetry*, pp. 213–14n.).

I do not wish to underestimate the value of Mr Houston's
main study – the relation of Shelley's theory and practice to the
psychology of Hume. Mr Houston is alive to the danger of
reading poetry in the light of the poet's psychology or of his
theory of psychology (Shelley was not 'consciously writing in
accordance with Hume's philosophy. No true poet creates in
that way'). The danger is shown clearly enough by Lowes's
account of *Kubla Khan*, as Mr House has . . . demonstrated
(*Coleridge*, pp. 114ff). Nevertheless the whole tenour of Mr
Houston's article suggests that he has been reading (or misreading) Shelley to prove that Shelley's (or Hume's) conception of psychology accounts for and, indeed, determines his
practice (e.g. 'From much of Shelley's poetry . . . one must
deduce, I think, that Shelley thought his mind should, and
indeed did, function in this passive way'). After suggesting that
Shelley agreed with Hume's theory of the inducing of belief,
Mr Houston adds that this 'helps to explain why the confused
image quoted from Canto v, vii, of *The Revolt of Islam* is primarily
emotive rather than rational'. Hence to Mr Houston, every
fusion in Shelley tends to be confusion. The 'rational' use of
'primarily emotive' images, which he seems to praise in Mr Eliot,
he does not allow for in the reading of Shelley. He also assumes
too easily that Mill's comments on Shelley accurately describe
his poetry. 'Why should not the feelings excited by thoughts',
asks Mr Houston, 'be as strong as the feelings excited by anything else?' There is no reason, of course; and the feeling in
much of Shelley's poetry *is* thus excited. 'The logical consequences' of the psychology of Hume . . . and Shelley will be
poetry exhibiting a failure to select, so that the associative links
'become a matter of mere chance'. This happens in Shelley's
poetry far less often than Mr Houston's way of reading it
suggests. Another result will be 'a failure to relate these images
to a central and controlling theme'; Mr Houston's reading

exaggerates (or creates) this failure because he has limited too much the ways in which images can be so 'related'. The third result will be 'a tendency towards greater compression', and this tendency has possibilities for good as well as for evil.

That so often Mr Houston makes them evil in Shelley's work may be due to the influence of the current fashion for using Shelley as the scapegoat of certain kinds of poetry that modern taste disdains. The eighteenth century is sometimes disparaged because of the critical dogmatism which recognized rules and methods and tones appropriate to poetic 'Kinds'. At least there was a general recognition in readers then that they had a duty to hoist themselves on to the plane upon which the poetry took its stand; and at least the older dogmatism is preferable to the modern one that restricts acceptable ways of creating a poem to one or two. Mr Houston may have succumbed a little, and temporarily (for him, at any rate, Shelley is a 'true poet'), to a fashion of disparagement, in which the more violent the disparagement the less ability is shown in *reading* the poem. Can it be, too, that because Mr Houston does not find Shelley's procedure 'rational' he wishes to divert our attention from such ideas as Shelley's poetry *does* contain to interests of another kind – 'I would urge, then, that it is to Hume, rather than to Plato, that we should now turn for a better understanding of Shelley's poetry and criticism, and, in so doing, of Shelley's descendants today'? Mr Houston's reading of Shelley does not altogether encourage us to do so.

2. DAVID V. ERDMAN

It is really too bad that the very issue headed by Mr Bateson's welcome manifesto against irresponsibility in criticism (*Essays in Criticism*, January 1953, 1–27) should contain one of the most extravagantly irresponsible pieces of criticism one has seen in many years. I refer to Mr Ralph Houston's 'Shelley and the Principle of Association', in which quotation after quotation from Shelley is either simply misread or is declared to be so bewildering as to produce in the reader's mind 'a muddle which I for one find impossible to straighten out'.

I leave on one side Mr Houston's thesis about Shelley's predisposition 'subconsciously' to follow Humian passivity or 'passive automatism' in the creative process – except to note that in the passage that Mr Houston quotes from *A Defence of Poetry*, Shelley is *not* declaring for the passivity of the Aeolian lyre; rather he is saying that the human mind adds an active principle not found in the lyre and that in doing so the mind produces a harmony beyond the simple melody of passive reflection. Mr Houston, reading for the words 'impressions' and 'reflected image', so ignores all the rest that when he comes up with the wisdom allegedly unavailable to Shelley – that 'in fact the mind is partly active and partly passive' – he is evidently not 'conscious' that he is but restating Shelley's idea. But the chief irresponsibility lies in his refusal to find any sense in Shelley's poetry.

Three instances may be cited, of several, and there is not room here to pursue the aesthetic implications. Quoting an allusion in *Prometheus Unbound* (II ii 51–4) to a 'plume-uplifting wind' which 'steams' 'from the breathing earth', Mr Houston exclaims: 'The "breathing earth" does steam in certain circumstances; but "a plume-uplifting wind" does not.' The 'chain of associations has broken in the middle' – yes, but the chain in *his* mind, not that in Shelley's. For the plume *is* the breath of steam, as we soon learn if we read on to Shelley's next page. There we discover (II iii 1–10) that the uplifted plume is composed of 'oracular vapour . . . hurled up' from a Delphic chasm in the earth. Apparently Mr Houston had in mind some irrelevant image of a feather in a gale.

Further on, dipping into *The Revolt of Islam* (v vii) and mistaking luxuriance for irrationality, he supposes that Shelley's mind was functioning passively when he wrote of 'rabid snakes, that sting some gentle child/Who brings them food, when winter false and fair/Allures them forth with its cold smiles'. There 'is no rational connection between the rabid snakes, the children taking food to them and the arbitrary setting in mid-winter', we are told. 'The ideas have the solid strength of a sensum, but they are not firmly placed in their context by the interpretative work of thought.' With a little interpretative work on his own part, the reader should be able to discover the rational connections – certainly a reader who can manage the connections of 'Rocks, moss, stonecrop, iron, merds'. Snakes lured out of hibernation by the 'cold smiles' of a winter day that seems like spring ('false and fair') are brought food by a child, who gets stung for his pains. Far from being arbitrary, a mid-winter setting is of the essence of hibernation. As for the place of these ideas 'in their context' – for here, we are told, 'Shelley has attempted a Homeric simile' – the simile fails for Mr Houston quite evidently because he is unwilling to examine the lines preceding and following his excerpt. But where else would one look for the point of a Homeric simile? Shelley's rational meaning is there, for anyone who reads the poem consecutively and is not engaged merely in culling illustrations of 'involuntary and arbitrary associative thinking'.

Finally, of *Prometheus Unbound*, I 153–8, Mr Houston declares: 'we can accept Shelley's "stony veins" of earth; but when Shelley suddenly compresses, transferring, by implication, the "stony veins" to the tree, one cannot, I think, assent.' Here one has assented too quickly if one 'can accept' Earth's stony veins as *stones*. Ice is stony but it is not stone; Earth's veins, a reader of all her lines in the poem would see, are the sapbearing veins of the world's vegetation; they have been made stony by the 'frozen air' of the dark night of oppression; she now is simply saying that the rise of Prometheus caused the sap of joy to run within her 'stony veins, to the last fibre of the loftiest tree'. What Mr Houston had had to 'accept' in order to reject Shelley is apparently some absurd image of 'veins' of ore running with blood. But Shelley, at least, is not a punster comparing rock strata and blood vessels because both happen to be called 'veins'. In the passage in question he is making two easy comparisons: of frozen vegetation to stone and of sap running in vegetable 'fibre' to blood running 'within a living frame'.

The whole line of approach, deriving from Dr F. R. Leavis's notion of Shelley's 'weak grasp upon the actual' . . . cannot be examined here but may at least be questioned when it leads to such misreadings. Dr Leavis's own example, of 'the growth of those "tangled boughs" out of the leaves', is itself a doubtful illustration of Shelley's weak grasp. A curious image it is, 'the tangled boughs of Heaven and Ocean', but the responsibly curious critics can find out what Shelley meant and need not assume that his 'perception or thought' was lost 'in confused generations and perspectives'. When the kind of storm Shelley is describing in the *West Wind* was driven across the bay of Leghorn, the rain clouds and the ocean sometimes intertangled: 'sometimes the dark lurid clouds', explains Mary Shelley, 'dipped towards the waves, and became water spouts, that churned up the waters beneath, as they were chased onward, and scattered by the tempest' (Preface to *The Cenci*). This was a curious phenomenon which Shelley had never seen before. I have not yet seen it, but I can credit the poet with having had a firm grasp upon both perception and metaphor when he wrought the phrase that describes it.

3. VALERIE PITT

Mr Houston makes, and then confuses together, two distinct assertions about the study of Shelley. One, that Shelley's imagery can be profitably examined in the light of Hume's theory of association, is justified by Mr Houston's interesting if arguable analyses. But it must be said that the theory is his tool, and not Shelley's. The other assertion, that Shelley consciously or unconsciously adapted his practice to Hume, cannot be maintained without more evidence than Mr Houston gives, and by making it he himself passes from the study of the poet's technique to that of his philosophy. It is legitimate, therefore, to point out that Mr Houston has ignored a good deal of what Shelley himself says about the mind and its workings in the essay *On Mind,* and elsewhere, and has misread both in itself and in its context, the passage he quotes from the *Defence of Poetry.* This passage follows a definition of the powers of reason and imagination acting on the sense impressions received, and proceeds to an assertion that the mind responds to stimulus not by an echo of, but in harmony with the impression received. Mr Houston has also missed this passage:

> Thought
> Alone, and its quick elements, Will, Passion,
> Reason, Imagination, cannot die;
> They are, what that which they regard appears,
> The stuff whence mutability can weave
> All that it hath dominion o'er, worlds, worms,
> Empires, and superstitions.

This is Berkleian, not Humian, and it implies, at the very least, an interaction between the forces of consciousness and the forces of change in the external world.

The words 'active' and 'passive' are however misleading. There is not space here to describe, without distortion, what Shelley thought about the mind. His theory arises from the sort of experience described in the essay *On Life* in which the mind can realize no distinction between itself and the outer world. From this Shelley evolves a modified idealism, expressed in images of the human mind as the image of the Eternal Mind, or as a mirror in which man watches the reflected world,

> One mind, the type of all, the moveless wave
> Whose calm reflects all moving things that are.

Or again it is expressed in the images of the Universal mind as a wind, or a stream, passing through and taking colour from the human mind. Mr Houston may object that this philosophizing does not help us with the understanding of Shelley's technique, but it does, I think, indicate what that technique is. Shelley's medium is that of the mental symbol; his fantasies are

significant because they symbolize the operations of the outer
world, for example, in political action; his descriptions of the
outer world, as in the journeys of Alastor, symbolize the life of
the Mind. This is in accordance with this theory, and the theory,
together with the experience from which it arises, throws light
on Shelley's idiom, his fantasies, his abstractions, his curious
intellectualization of sense data. His descriptive passages have
often enough the brightness of mirror images,

> Quivering within the wave's intenser day,

where the image is sharply defined, but is, in spite of this,
curiously unreal.

This seems, perhaps, to frustrate Mr Houston's rescue, and
deliver Shelley to the strictures of Dr Leavis. But Dr Leavis's
condemnation is only valid where we accept his conception of
'the actual', and accede to his demands. Shelley's method is
contrary to that of Keats: it proceeds, not to the intensification
of sense experience, but away from it, to the point at which
sense experience is formalized into a mental representation with
the function of a symbol:

> Through the gray, void abysm,
> > Down, down!
> Where the air is no prism,
> And the moon and stars are not,
> And the cavern-crags wear not
> The radiance of Heaven,
> Nor the gloom of Earth given,
> Where there is One pervading, One alone,
> > Down, down!

This is not 'actual', and is not meant to be 'actual'. Even the
words themselves are given an abstract quality; the attention is
directed away from single images to the song as whole, and as
a representation of a pattern of meaning.

To return to Mr Houston's arguments: the method I have described involves, in practice, not over-passivity, but an over-activity of the poet's reasoning power.

> The tongueless Caverns of the craggy hills
> Cried 'Misery!' then; then hollow Heaven replied,
> 'Misery!' And the Ocean's purple waves,
> Climbing the land, howled to the lashing winds,
> And the pale nations heard it, 'Misery!'.

This illustrates what seems to me Shelley's major fault – that of over-elaboration. There is again the presentation not of an experience, but of a mental pattern of horror, and the pattern is only too obvious. The poet is consciously aware of his arrangement of land, sea and heaven, and of the verbal patterning of 'Caverns-craggy-cried', 'Hills-Heaven-hollow' which accompany it – so conscious that he overlays, and nearly destroys, the intended effect of reverberating echo. His intelligence is too active and the machinery creaks. The passage also shows the fault which Dr Leavis points out, and Mr Houston tries to explain – that of the break between mental pattern and sense experience. Formalized sense experience is one thing, the substitution of convention for real experience is another – the 'pale nations' and 'purple waves', belong to a literary and un-realized mental pattern – they are mere counters, and it is at the moments when the mere counters of Shelley's beliefs (Mr Houston's snakes are an example) the sneering kings, the charnel houses, the white and quivering brows, thrust their way into the verse that his images fall apart. These, however, illustrate my main point, for they show the symbol faded to a mere formula.

That was by way of digression. The method at work in the speech of the Earth – the poet's exploitation or creation of a mental link – succeeds in other passages:

> It is the unpastured sea hungering for calm.

This image, for instance, depends, not on association, but concealed analogy. Or there is this passage:

> Each one
> Of that great crowd sent forth incessantly
> These shadows, numerous as the dead leaves blown
>
> In autumn evening from a poplar tree.
> Each like himself and like each other were
> At first, but some distorted seemed to be
>
> Obscure clouds, moulded by the casual air;
> And of this stuff the car's creative ray
> Wrought all the busy phantoms that were there,
>
> As the sun shapes the clouds.

This is pure but significant fantasy. It is built on the pattern of a literary reminiscence from Lucretius, and in the similes there is again the method of analogy, an analogy incidently with Shelley's recollections of science behind it. It will be seen that these similes have an apparent and a real function; the shadows are *numerous* as dead leaves, but the impression of number is less important than the image of the poplar tree in movement, which carries to the mind the associations of flimsiness, lightness, in its movements and fuses them with its impression of 'these shadows'. Mr Houston might claim this as an example of association; yet it does not show the poet as passive, but as actively exploiting not only his own associations but the reader's. In its fusion of elements the whole passage illustrated the synthesizing power of the imagination of which Shelley speaks in the *Defence of Poetry*; here the mind is indeed acting on its materials, but acting under the direction of the artist's will.

SOURCE: Extracts from discussion article, 'Reading Shelley', *Essays in Criticism* (January 1954).

G. M. Matthews

SHELLEY'S GRASP UPON THE ACTUAL (1954)

Mr Houston's much-mistaken commentary [reproduced above] on the working of Shelley's mind and his rearguard action against 'bad syntax' point the truth of the old warning that the criticism of Shelley's verse in isolated fragments is 'a fruitless task: we have not the language'. It is not a bit of good extracting the nucleus of a highly-organized system of associations in *Prometheus* and then calling it a broken chain of imagery, or rejecting one of Aesop's fables in *Islam* on the ground that it is an unsuccessful Homeric simile.

As Dr Erdman hinted in his admirable reply, the whole line of approach implied in the charge of a 'weak grasp upon the actual' is so very wrong that little can be achieved by tinkering with details. I wish only to revert to the 'plume-uplifting wind' extract from *Prometheus Unbound* II, ii, since this belongs to a crucial episode in the poem and invites a different kind of analysis.

Shelley himself tells us what he does with the actual after grasping it, in a passage more often admired than explained. A poet, he says,

> . . . will watch from dawn to gloom
> The lake-reflected sun illume
> The yellow bees in the ivy-bloom,
> Nor heed nor see, what things they be;
> But from these create he can
> Forms more real than living man. . . .
>
> (*Prometheus Unbound* I 734–8)

Shelley sets out, that is, from a scientifically-observed piece of
reality (the insects and flowers are identified; the source and
angle of the lighting defined), but he is not interested in physical
details as details (like Clare), nor in bees as bees (like Keats):
what he perceives in the natural world gives only a physical
basis for what concerns him as a poet – the essence of the
human situation reflected in art ('Forms more real than living
man'). The bees are on a mission of renewal amid forms of life
that spring irrepressibly, like the 'tyrant-quelling myrtle', over
the ruins of Roman greatness and oppression.

Shelley's major images all have a similar origin. Their
peculiar quality doesn't arise from visionary's palsy, but from
the cocoon of symbolism which is drawn purposefully round
some central physical fact and hides its metamorphosis. The
'plume-uplifting wind' is such an image. It contains no scientific
or syntactical errors. Mr Houston can make a plume-uplifting
wind steam merrily any time he likes by putting on his kettle,
or by simply quoting *Gerontion* in his bedroom in January. The
physical basis of the image is an exhalation of vapour from a
volcanic crack, which condenses to a plume of steam in the
cold air ('A Pinnacle of Rock among Mountains'). By borrowing the 'subterranean wind' of Pelorus and *thundring Aetna* from
Paradise Lost (i 230–3), Shelley converts the vapour into an
agent of revolutionary change; but he himself was one of 'those
who saw' similar phenomena, first in the hot springs at Bath
(he refers to the legend of the founding of Bath by Bladud in
Prometheus Unbound iv 388–93 – another non-Homeric simile, by
the way), and later at the Grotta del Cane, near one of the
places that suggested the realm of Demogorgon.

Threads of association are attached to this concept from all
parts of the poem. Shelley's science, of course, makes no distinction between radioactive and volcanic processes, and the form
of the exhalation is meant to suggest both a medicinal steam
(capable of healing the pains of mankind) and a suppressed
revolutionary force. The volcano is an obvious symbol of social
revolution, as in the contemporary lines on Peterloo:

> And that slaughter to the Nation
> Shall steam up like inspiration,
> Eloquent, oracular;
> A volcano heard afar.
>
> (*Mask of Anarchy*, LXXXIX)

Demogorgon inhabits a quiescent volcano, as the Titan Typhon lay beneath Etna in Aeschylus, and the 'oracular vapour' hurled up from his realm is oracular in several senses: it bodes no good to Jupiter, and it makes those who breathe it eager to grasp the future (Oracles in ancient time had used such vapours to induce a prophetic trance). Those affected are inspired and compelled to 'follow'; they thus become agents of the power that converted them; and the whole complex of symbols expresses a relation between historical necessity and human action which is fundamental both to the poem and to Shelley's views on the writer's role in society. (Some exhalations, incidentally, are poisonous, and any who breathe these are liable to become agents of imperialism. *Prometheus Unbound* III iii 124–30.)

It is obviously wrong to deny to Shelley the supporting 'ambiguities' that would be credited to other poets as a matter of course. The steaming wind uplifts its own plume, but it is also 'plume-uplifting': it ruffles the complacent feathers of those who feel it, and it makes them cocky and militant. The whole passage is not only thoroughly sound in itself, but radiates imagery which keeps all parts of the poem in touch with this particular theme. Objections to it based on syntax or association-breakdown are not so much wrong as meaningless and frivolous, like some of the Augustan objections to Elizabethan metaphor. . . .

SOURCE: 'Shelley's Grasp upon the Actual', *Essays in Criticism* (July 1954).

John Holloway

SHELLEY'S ACHIEVEMENT IN PERSPECTIVE (1960)

. . . Literary history is full of confusions which have been bred from the confusions which preceded them. Shelley's present reputation in many circles is an example of this: just as Milton's is another. Milton was once admired for the 'organ-note' of his poetry. When it came, very properly, to be thought that poetry was not made good merely by such notes as that, the diagnosis was left essentially unchanged, the verdict founded on it was reversed. (Yeats's line comes again to mind.) Shelley was once admired for the ethereal beauty, the intangible quintessential music, the haunting unreality of his verse (and personality). These qualities have come to seem trivial in themselves, and to have regard to them has come to seem the hallmark of an exasperating *belle-lettrisme*. The exasperation is indulged, Shelley is condemned, and the fact that, through the critics' hastiness, we have been, in Dryden's phrase, 'cozened by a jelly', and now cozened not once but twice over, remains unnoticed.

There is so much to say of a positive kind about the nature and development of Shelley's poetry, and it would be a pity to use up space rebutting errors and confusions about it which are easily removed by a truly attentive and open-minded reading of his poetry itself. Yet certain preliminary points are worth making. The tabloid version of English poetic history which we owe to T. S. Eliot's early essays ('. . . a dissociation of sensibility set in, from which we have never recovered . . .') seems now to be losing the hold on readers' minds which it once had. In its time it encouraged the idea that in Shelley's poetry the intellect naturally did either no work at all, or only the inappropriate work of supplying a mass of poetically indigestible philosophical or political doctrines. This is a plain error of fact, one which is made plain not so much by noticing the considered and multiple corrections and changes in the manuscripts of Shelley's poems, as from such poems as *An Exhortation* or *Rarely, rarely, comest thou*, or *To Jane*, or, finally, the *Ode to Heaven*. There is no need to look further than these poems, which save for the last are all comparatively simple, to recognize how Shelley's intelligence could operate not as that of a philosopher in his verse, but essentially as that of a poet, thinking and working through the detailed fabric of the verse, controlling and modulating the tone, and creating a train of thought, intricate and exact yet unforced and unostentatious, of which the metre, the rhyming, the stanza, come to form the necessary vehicle.

I point to these poems . . . because they bring decisively to notice a Shelley who has been overlooked. Yet the capacity to conduct an argument in poetry is a modest talent, even though it is one which a poet should not be without: and the first two poems mentioned above are modest achievements in that they go little beyond this. Once we have learnt, however, to look in Shelley for qualities of mind which the tabloid account of English poetic history encouraged us to assume were absent, a genuinely poetic mental life, controlling and manoeuvring material much more varied than the steps of any argument, and doing so with an intricacy and dexterity which few English poets have equalled, begins to be apparent in much of his work. To many readers this will sound surprising and unplausible; I can only add that it is something which I have had to teach myself, against the current of a now widespread opinion about Shelley, slowly and with difficulty and incredulity. . . . Dr Leavis has severely censured the [*Ode to the West Wind*] for (in part) the absence of just such qualities of exact and intelligent organization as I am now attributing to it: but his discussion gives one every reason to suppose that he has simply not recognized, save in a vague and inaccurate way, the realities with which Shelley was dealing. This is a decisive defect, but hardly an unnatural

one: part of the difficulty of Shelley's work (the point will be
considered again later) is that his facts are often distinctive and,
to many modern readers, recondite. When the *Ode* is understood at every point, it is still not a perfect poem, but that it is
an extraordinary achievement of the whole mind of a true poet
comprehensively at work to unify a great variety of poetic
material in its linguistic embodiment, seems to me simple truth.
The fact is, that Shelley's poetry is far from easy; often enough
it is too difficult for his detractors and his champions both. . . .

Probably most readers are less troubled by the supposed defects
in Shelley's poetic intelligence than by those in his emotions.
As is the case (though in very different ways) with Wordsworth,
Shelley has roots deep in the eighteenth century; or rather, in
some of the less pedestrian and also less sound sides of that
period. We can see this in the resonance and sometimes even
stilted formality of his prose; in his early addiction to the 'gothic'
novel, an addiction which had its effect not only in his two early
(and worthless) prose romances, but also here and there in his
later work; and again, in a kind of emotionalism which is
reminiscent of the cult of sensibility, the self-conscious tears of
Sterne and the rest, and the verse of his early correspondent
Felicia Hemans. It is no part of my purpose to defend this
strain in Shelley; though, if we are concerned for the moment
with what it reveals of the man, we must recall such facts as
that he never published many of the poems to which objection
may be made along these lines, and that *Stanzas written in
Dejection near Naples*, with *Lines written among the Euganean Hills*,
followed closely upon the death of his daughter Clara, while the
Ode to the West Wind stands in a not dissimilar relation to the
death of his son William. Besides this, it is clear that Shelley's
literary isolation, lack of readers in England, and receipt of little
hut sustained calumny from many English reviewers, oppressed
bim deeply throughout his last years. For all that, this part of
his poetry remains what it is.

Yet if this train of thought is taken further, it will bring the reader to certain vital facts which must be borne in mind before much of the poetry of this period (not Shelley's alone, but often enough, that of his contemporaries as well) can be accurately assessed. The modern reader, over and over again, is likely to form the impression that Shelley must have had his thoughts and feelings, and hence of necessity his language, only half under control. Felicities and ineptitudes appear to alternate in his work with bewildering abruptness. This is something which his admirers have scarcely faced: often enough they have been those who barely see the problem. But to the reader who is not satisfied until he can sense the poem growing like a living thing from individual word to word,

> Let the tyrants pour around
> With a quick and *startling* sound
> Like the loosening of a sea,
> Troops of armed emblazonry.
> > (*The Mask of Anarchy*, 303–4)

seems like a sudden lapse into lameness.

> Thou young Dawn,
> Turn all thy dew to *splendour*
> > (*Adonais,* 362–3)

seems a typical piece of strained Shelleyan vagueness. When, in the *Hymn to Intellectual Beauty*, Shelley writes,

> Sudden, thy shadow fell on me;
> *I shrieked, and clasped my hands in ecstasy!*

his poem seems to become disastrously embarrassing. When, in *The Sensitive Plant*, we read of

> A *Lady*, the wonder of her kind,
> Whose form was upborne by a *lovely mind*.

it is much easier to think that we are confronting the language,
and the emotional response, of Wardour Street than of a major
poet.

Yet that is an attitude which it is impossible to sustain, even
for two lines further:

> a lovely mind
> Which, *dilating, had moulded her mien and motion*
> *Like a sea-flower unfolded beneath the ocean.*

Here after all, if only we could ignore those sudden false notes,
like a wolf on a violin, is a genuinely imaginative perception of
how the mind of a human being can exalt everything about the
body; a perception confirmed in a true poet's metaphor, apt
yet remote, and also one intrinsically beautiful. Wardour Street
is a world away. What, then, is going on? And do the lines from
the *Hymn to Intellectual Beauty* take on another appearance, when
they are set beside the closing lines of Keats's *Hyperion*, to which
they bear an intriguing resemblance?

> During the pain Mnemosyne upheld
> Her arms as one who prophesied. – At length
> *Apollo shriek'd*; – and lo! from all his limbs
> Celestial Glory dawn'd; he was a god.[1]

The fact is, that the poetry of this period confronts the modern
reader with a difficulty which has scarcely been remarked on,
although it is pervasive and acute. It may be seen as a matter of
emotions, responses and attitudes, or of the vocabulary in which
these are expressed. Ideally it should be seen as both of these
together. Leading attitudes and feelings of earlier times, often
also pervasive in the poetry of those times, have in many cases
entirely disappeared from the modern mind. When this happens, the words which gave them expression either become
obsolete, or entirely lose the particular sense of associations
which they were lent by the obsolete attitude or feeling. Both
attitude and meaning are overlooked by the general reader,
and are carefully recovered and restored by the scholarly one.

This would be the case, for example, with the idea of universal hierarchy which (as who does not now know?) was so influential in Shakespeare's time, and with a word like 'relation' which, through this idea, then meant something a good deal richer emotionally than it does today.

The special problem with a poet like Shelley is that many of the attitudes, situations and ideas in his work are such as a modern reader can neither remain unaware of nor recover in a mint state. The isolation of the artist, 'ideal beauty', idealized love between men and women, skylarks singing, the sensations of incipient syncope which appear to be a frequent concomitant, even among the flyest, of extreme physical desire, and the notion of a great social and spiritual regeneration of mankind, are things in quite a different class from cosmic correspondence or universal hierarchy. Nothing is harder than to take them strictly at their face value in a poem. This is so because (whatever critics may have come to prefer) it is the ideas and attitudes and emotions which the Romantic Movement minted that have now penetrated down into every corner of modern life and modern awareness; that have been cheapened everywhere around us; that have descended to ubiquitous banality through a thousand channels. Legitimate burlesque then completes what vulgarization began. It is not a matter of Shelley alone, though he suffers more than the others. Echoes of Wordsworth's *Immortality Ode* may turn up in a Children's Home appeal, of Keats on the Nightingale or Coleridge on the artist across the sleeve of a long-playing record, of Shelley's 'glorious Phantom' [in *Sonnet: England in 1819* – Ed.] from a Marble Arch stump-orator. There is no need to prolong the dreary catalogue, painful in itself, and doubly so for what it has done to our literature.

As with the feelings and ideas, so of necessity with the language. 'Lovely mind' could once mean something exact and significant. In contemporary English it can only justify a shudder. The newspaper has deprived 'startling' of its original connexion with awakening from sleep, and 'splendour' (useful for coronations and reviews of the Fleet) of its connexion with sparkle and

radiance. These are the meanings which transform what
Shelley wrote from vague or banal to precise and appropriate:
from the occurrence of these words elsewhere in Shelley than
the passages quoted above, and also in his contemporaries, it is
clear that these are the meanings which they legitimately had
for him. Something similar applies very often to the language
of the Romantics. Lamb obligingly records perhaps the first
stage by which 'awful' became the sort of word which now
seems only embarrassing in serious poetry ('she is indeed, *as the
Americans express it,* something awful'; 1834, *O.E.D.*). Business
correspondence has presumably transformed the tone of 'the
same', an idiom not infrequent in Shelley, Keats and Browning
(I believe that it occurs at least once in Wordsworth) and
rendered it poetically preposterous. Words and phrases like
'madness' (poetic rapture), 'green wilderness', and 'maniac'
(*Prometheus Unbound,* IV 470, where it means 'mantic'), also
require a certain mental adjustment if they are not to seem to
strike false notes. 'Lady' (compare Coleridge's *Dejection Ode*),
'sweet', and 'thrilling' are examples too obvious to need
comment. . . .

Shelley's work is intimately of its time in more ways than these.
Professor Grabo and others have indicated how the science of
the period, or at least (as is reasonable) the more or less popular
science, enters into his work. Shelley was widely and variously
informed about, for example, astronomy and meteorology; and
sometimes, a detail picked on by a modern critic for censure on
the ground of arbitrariness or confusion has a genuine basis in
the scientific opinion of the time. Dr Davie, for example, con-
demns Shelley's *Cloud* for saying:

> Sublime on the towers of my skiey bowers
> The lightning my pilot sits.

'There is no reason in natural philosophy to give a basis in
logic to the notion that a cloud is directed by electric charges'

is his comment.[2] In making it, Dr Davie was presumably ignorant that this (no doubt erroneous) theory is exactly what Shelley had learnt from his teacher of science, Dr Adam Walker, who was reputable enough to be employed as a visiting lecturer at Eton, and in whose *Analysis of a Course of Lectures on Experimental Philosophy* we can find other ideas, besides this, like those of Shelley's poem. Not that Shelley's knowledge of science adds much directly to his stature as a poet. Here *Queen Mab* is instructive. Just as this poem draws on Rousseau, Hume, Godwin, Baron d'Holbach and Condorcet for its political and religious ideas, and makes of them (as might be expected) something strained and rhetorical, so it draws widely on eighteenth-century cosmic poetry for a kind of buoyant and grandiose cosmic emotion, and its usually didactic, declamatory tone has clear affinities with Akenside's *Pleasures of the Imagination* or Brooke's *Universal Beauty*. To a large extent, it is an eighteenth-century work of a conventional kind.

But one major key to Shelley's development as a poet is, that what begins as mere knowledge of theory becomes in the course of time more intimately a part of his personal experience and response; and the indirect impact of his interest in science on his poetry was great, if it is this which led to the quite special area of experience where (despite legends to the contrary) Shelley as a descriptive poet has a firm and intimate grasp of reality. To an extent, this is true about the reality of ordinary conversation and everyday surroundings. The *Letter to Maria Gisborne* and *The Boat on the Serchio* bring this out clearly. . . . Shelley's free rendering of the Homeric *Hymn to Mercury*, which is one of his most enjoyable pieces, . . . shows peculiarly well how wit, liveliness and everyday realism could fuse with the more imaginative side of his mind. In the end, though, it is this more imaginative side of Shelley which is most remarkable, which is unique; and the point here is that it has a realism of its own.

Shelley, more perhaps than any other poet, possesses an imaginative insight into nature as a world of events and processes,

especially those which occur through a great volume of space.
His imagination comes to life before the movements of the sun
and planets as tangible realities, the transmission of light or
sound through the air, the development of things as they grow,
the great cycles of interaction between sea, land and air which are
the determinants of climate. It is a gift such as might start with
the insight of science, but it has become the insight of a poet
or an artist. In the universal cataclysms of the geological past

> the blue globe
> Wrapped deluge round it like a cloak.
>
> (*Prometheus Unbound*, IV 314–15)

Spring comes

> Driving sweet buds like flocks to feed on air
>
> (*Ode to the West Wind*, 11)

an image of which I at least never saw the point, until I watched
great flocks of sheep, spreading across a whole landscape, being
slowly driven up to their summer mountain pastures. When
Shelley makes *The Cloud* say

> I pass through the *pores* of the ocean and shores
>
> (*The Cloud*, 75)

there seems again, behind the emphatic concrete word, a real
sense of the passage of river into the sea and sea into vapour.
And here is Shelley's account of how the nightingale sings (it
is from *Rosalind and Helen*, written in 1817):

> Daylight on its last purple cloud
> Was lingering grey, and soon her strain
> The nightingale began; now loud,
> Climbing in circles the windless sky,
> Now dying music; suddenly
> 'Tis scattered in a thousand notes,
> And now to the hushed ear it floats
> Like field smells known in infancy,
> Then failing, soothes the air again.

The same concrete awareness is plain: air is a volume, sound spreads in it and through it like a moving thing or a perfume. (Those who wish to dwell on the fact that smells do not float to the ear are free to do so.) It would be easy, of course, to attack this passage from a position one jump behind the writer: 'Climbing in circles' will seem a fantastic phrase, to those who cannot recall the gradual pealing *crescendo* of the nightingale's song which it so unexpectedly and then so exactly conveys. Something of this kind, perhaps, is widely relevant to criticizing poetry on points of factual detail. The poet is likely – what is often forgotten – to be always right as against the critic. A man who refers in a poem to the nightingale, thereby strongly suggests that he has interested himself in nightingales as well as poems. There is an antecedent likelihood that he will know something of what he writes about. But the critic is in a different position. He in no way criticizes a poem that refers to a nightingale because of any interest in that bird; and the likelihood that he will be even as well informed as the poet, on not one but a variety of subjects which the latter exclusively has chosen, is virtually nil. Nor, very often, can he easily remedy his ignorance, even if he is honest enough to recognize it. All this seems obvious enough; but failure to think these issues out must be behind the arrogance and ineptitude of much that critics have written to correct poets on matters of detail. It is merely a question of who, under the circumstances, may expect to learn from whom. This is very relevant to one of Mr Eliot's disparagements of Shelley. With regard to the lines:

> The world's great age begins anew
> The golden years return,
> The earth doth like a snake renew
> Her winter weeds outworn:

he writes 'It is not . . . easy to see the propriety of an image which divests a snake of "winter weeds" '. That this critic should be so ignorant of snakes as to think that 'weeds' in this passage means 'plants', is difficult to believe: but I can find no

less feeble explanation for his bewildering objection. At such a
level, only too often, has been the dismissal of Shelley.

In the situation which exists today, when Shelley is likely to be
relied on by every budding critic as a safe quarry from which
to chip specimens of almost any kind of poetic ineptitude, this
discussion has concentrated on disposing of some of the hostile
errors about Shelley, and on bringing out the coherence and
reality of his work. Since a true perspective, however, is by no
means of necessity created through erasing the caricatures of
others, something remains to be said or at least to be underlined.
In the first place, although his achievement as a poet is altogether outstanding, although there is a sense in which his work
is more clearly irreplaceable than the work of greater poets, I
think it must be recognized that in another sense his achievement is a clearly limited or perhaps one should say delimited
one. This is not to point out that much of his early work is prosy
declamation. That is obvious enough. But even in his later
work, the kinds of thing that he can do, the notes that he can
strike, the aspects or areas of human life which he can exploit
or illuminate at least directly, do not spread very wide. The
recurrent quality of his images, his situations, has often been
noticed. Again, *The Mask of Anarchy* is more like *Prometheus
Unbound* than perhaps it should be, in view of its utterly different intention and *genre*. Johnson's phrase 'the want of human
interest is always felt' is one which comes to mind. As it stands,
it does not fit the case; as I have argued already. Yet a want
of human interest created directly, created simply, coming not
from a great effort but, let us say, from those corners of the poem
which the writer seems to have completed with least effort of all
– this kind of human interest, and the relaxing reassurance that
it brings, is indeed to some extent wanting. It is certainly not
always wanting. . . . But by comparison with many other poets
of equal genius, it is not really conspicuous in Shelley. That his
dramatic work (*Prometheus Unbound* is in a quite special class) is

not among his best has its relevance here. There are some poets whose minds, and whose work, have spread so wide, that as we read them and become immersed in them, they begin to create an impression that what they have produced is something approaching not merely a *speculum vitae*, but a *speculum artis* as well. It is an exaggeration, yet the sensation grows in us that if all other poetry were lost, men could at least make this corpus of work, by this one man, lead outwards to most or all that poetry can do. Chaucer, Milton and Yeats (there is no need to invoke Shakespeare) seem all to be more or less of this kind: beauty, learning, good and evil in life, humour, satire, indignation, an understanding and sometimes a love of individual people and their meanest doings, a grasp of the affairs of states and of men, and many other things beside, seem all to enter their work with mastered ease. Shelley is not among them. His work is as remarkable as theirs, but decisively less capacious. He is not, to use his own words once again, among

> . . . the great bards of elder time, who quelled
> The passions that they sung, as by their strain
> May well be known.
>
>   (*The Triumph of Life*, 274–6)

There is something else, too, which that quotation points to clearly: in one respect, the limitation of range on what Shelley could achieve peculiarly increases the difficulty and reduces the pleasure of reading him. Shelley himself has diagnosed the matter far better than those who rely upon the word 'immature', which is no diagnosis at all, but merely a form of self-insurance. 'I cannot but be conscious, in much of what I write, of an absence of *that tranquillity which is the attribute and accompaniment of power*' (letter to Godwin; my italics). This is a very penetrating remark, both in particular and in general. The fact is, Shelley is hard to read not only because his language and indeed his punctuation are not quite our own, not only because what he intends to convey is sometimes condensed and esoteric, not only because his intelligence is dexterous enough, and in evidence enough, often to make what he writes more intricate than the work of others. It is difficult because there is, with trying regularity, a tension and an eagerness about it that leads the reader hardly to expect the control which he very often finds. One might almost put this point by saying that Shelley's sensibility was too emphatically unified to be altogether tolerable. No one ought to feel so passionately, so intensely as this, and yet move in thought with such virtuosity. Or perhaps it is better put as an excessive demand which Shelley makes on his readers; but it is not an excess merely in the sense of being above the powers of ordinary able men, it is an excess in which there is a hint of eccentricity, or rather of hypertrophy. If these powers are to be as great as these, others must suffer – a price is to be paid. Often enough in Shelley, and on a final judgement, I think, over his work seen as a whole, the price is a fatiguing intensity of intellectual and emotional response, within a range which is fatiguing in its narrowness. Only in *The Triumph of Life*, at the very end of his career, does one hear, sustained throughout a long and wholly serious work, that note of composure and calm, and indeed of dry shrewdness, which offers the reader of this very difficult poem a kind of reassurance new in Shelley. For this reason, he will never be universally admired; and his readers will be those prepared to experience a certain strain or discomfort for the things where he was a master. . . .

SOURCE: Extracts from the Introduction to *Selected Poems of Percy Bysshe Shelley* (1960).

NOTES

1. The last line is completed here from the Woodhouse MS.
2. D. Davie, *Purity of Diction in English Verse* (1952) p. 135 [see p. 79 above – Ed.].

PART THREE

Studies of Individual Poems 1941–73

Edward B. Hungerford

ADONAIS (1941)

Shelley's *Adonais* is the most complex poem based on a mythological theme produced by any poet of the Romantic generation. So complex, indeed, is the mythological understructure of the poem that its true character has been scarcely observed.

Adonais is based upon the legend of Aphrodite and Adonis, a legend which is adapted throughout the entire length of the poem. The reason why that fact is not more apparent is that Shelley so generalized the myth in order to make it fit his purposes, and availed himself of such a loose and diversified application, that the presence of the myth in the structure of the poem has been nearly obscured.

Adonais is a poem in which a mythological theme is made to be the vehicle of certain related purposes. As in poems fashionable in the Renaissance, the poem follows the general outlines of a myth, with different levels of application. Thus in *Adonais* there is a mythological level of the poem which rests upon the story of Aphrodite and Adonis. There is a literal level in which that legend is made to apply to the death of John Keats. There is what may be described as a polemical level, in which the myth becomes the vehicle for an attack upon the element of conservative society to which Shelley and his friends were hostile. And there is a philosophical level. In this the myth supports Shelley's statement that the only escape from the evil of the world is for the soul to free itself by death from the limitations of the world and, like Keats, to achieve participation in the Divine Love. Thus the poem proceeds at four parallel but disparate levels of thought, all developed simultaneously. In the dexterity with which Shelley sustains and integrates these levels of meaning, one may see why Shelley described *Adonais* as a 'highly wrought piece of art'. In the recognition of the difficulties which the poet encountered and the manner in which he met them, a proper criticism of the poem may commence.

The recognition of the fable, the story of Aphrodite and Adonis, is the key to the understanding of *Adonais*. It is the linking theme; in its implications all the meanings are folded. Yet Shelley deliberately veiled the most obvious clues by which we should recognize the fable. The name Adonis has been lengthened to Adonais. Aphrodite appears under the title Urania, an epithet meaning 'heavenly', which properly belongs to her but which is not ordinarily associated with the fable. The boar of the legend has been generalized to a symbol of evil, the 'unpastured dragon' of the poem. These alterations may appear at first thought so striking as to cause the reader to doubt that Shelley had the fable of Aphrodite and Adonis in mind at all. But the details of the fable are followed too closely to sustain that doubt. The alterations were deliberately introduced in order to generalize and to apply the theme.

There is no single treatment of the Adonis myth in Greek or Latin literature which tells the full story. The outlines of the whole legend must be put together from a number of sources. Relevant portions of the story are as follows. Adonis was a beautiful young shepherd who was very fond of hunting. Aphrodite, the goddess of love and beauty, fell in love with him and persuaded him to become her lover. Fearful that he might be killed in the hunt, she tried to dissuade him from the pursuit of savage beasts. But one day, when Aphrodite was absent, presiding over ceremonies in her honor, Adonis returned to the hunt, and was mortally injured by a wild boar. Some say that Ares, jealous of Aphrodite's love for the shepherd boy, instigated this disaster. Informed of the injury to her lover, Aphrodite returned to his side, lamenting his fate and grieving that she could not die with him. Her companions mourned with her. At her caresses Adonis revived slightly, and she implored him for a last kiss. According to some, Aphrodite turned his dead body into an anemone. According to others, she followed him to the lower world, where Persephone fell in love with him and refused to give him up. Aphrodite pleaded with Zeus for his return, and at last, with the consent of Hades, Adonis was allowed to return to earth for six months of each year, during the spring and summer. This time he spent with Aphrodite. The return of Adonis was celebrated in an Adonis festival. Annually a song was sung embodying the lament of Aphrodite, and a day of mourning was followed by a day of rejoicing at his revival.

In Shelley's poem no such simple narrative as this is told, but all of its elements may be detected, even though the poet's wing merely brushes them with light allusiveness. Adonais is a beautiful young shepherd whose flocks are, figuratively, Keats's poetic thoughts. The Aphrodite who is in love with him is Urania, the celestial goddess of love and beauty, the Aphrodite Ourania of the Greeks. She appears as an actual goddess, with a distinct and visible from, but in the latter part of the poem she becomes progressively less individual until, at the end, she is not a goddess with the conventional attributes and companions of Aphrodite, but Divine Love, abstractly conceived. Aphrodite's warning to the young shepherd is transposed to her lament, after the injury, that Adonais had not been dissuaded from his boldness in hunting. As in the myth, the injury to Adonais takes place while Urania is absent, presiding over ceremonies in her honor. In this poem she is listening, in her secret paradise, to a young poet read aloud the poems which he had composed under the inspiration of love and beauty. The allusion is probably to Kirke White, whose fate had been somewhat similar to that of Keats. Adonais has, in the meanwhile, been mortally wounded by a beast in the hunt, but has not yet died. When Urania is informed of the injury, she returns to his side, lamenting his fate and grieving that she cannot die with him. The various personifications which mourn for the wounded Adonais are, under English names, the conventional companions of Aphrodite. Adonais revives slightly. She implores him for a last kiss, after which he dies. The legend that Adonais was turned into an anemone is alluded to obscurely, in a fashion which I shall describe later, as are also the descent into the lower world and the refusal of Persephone to give him up.

In the earlier portion of the poem the following of the Adonis myth is fairly clear. In the latter portion the connection is not so readily observed but it is nevertheless sustained. Shelley links the return of Adonis with the survival of the poet's influence after death. The fable is thus continued, as the return of Adonais to the world is imagined and his union with Urania, or Aphrodite, takes place. But since Keats does not return annually for a six-month residence on earth, the fable takes on a symbolic character, developing the theme that the poet's thoughts survive in the world as a quickening influence. For this purpose Shelley had recourse to interpretations of the myth, both ancient and modern.

Ancient writers had recognized in the fable of Adonis a nature myth symbolizing the reawakening of life in the spring-time. Macrobius, for instance, had interpreted Adonis as the sun, the boar as the killing winter, Aphrodite as the earth abandoned by the warmth of the sun in the wintertime, and the revival of Adonis as the return of the sun to the earth in the spring and summer. The union of Adonis and Aphrodite thus symbolized the uniting of earth and sunlight to bring forth life. The little baskets of spring flowers, comparable to our May Day baskets, which women carried in the ancient Adonis festival, were in honour of Adonis as the symbol of quick-growing vegetation.

Mythologists of Shelley's time had developed this interpreta-tion of the myth somewhat extravagantly. Hancarville and Knight had read the fable as merely one version of a myth which frequently recurs in the mythology of all countries. Enumerat-ing various pairs of mythical lovers, Hancarville had declared that they were all twofold representations of the generative god, the active and the passive elements of the generative act, or the male and female aspects of the single act of generation. Richard Payne Knight had developed Hancarville's thesis extensively.

The allegorical tales of the loves and misfortunes of Isis and Osiris
. . . are an exact counterpart of those of Venus and Adonis (Astarte
and Baal); which signify the alternate exertion of the generative and
destructive attributes. Adonis, or Adonai, was an Oriental (Phoeni-
cian and Hebrew) title of the Sun, signifying Lord; and the boar,
supposed to have killed him, was the emblem of Winter; during
which the productive powers of nature being suspended, Venus was
said to lament the loss of Adonis until he was again restored to life.

The boar, which Knight explained as a symbol of 'the
destroying or anti-generative atttibute', he linked to the monster
Typhon, whose dismemberment of Osiris had the same meaning
as the boar's slaying of Adonis. The Aphrodite who represents
the passive generative power is the Mother-Goddess, the Venus –
Urania, personified as goddess of love or desire.

The myth of Aphrodite and Adonis was then, according to
Knight, a myth in which Aphrodite, the Venus Urania, represented the passive principle of generation. Adonis represented
the active principle, and the boar was the destructive principle.
Knight believed that the ancients conceived of 'female or
passive powers of production supposed to be inherent in
matter'. When the passive power which pervaded earth was
joined to the active principle, the united force produced
vegetation.

By seizing hold of the idea that Adonis was a symbol of fertility, Shelley was able to make that aspect of the myth serve his
celebration of the poet's continued influence after death.
Without departing from the story, he attempted, as the poem
progressively unfolded, to continue the application of the myth
to Keats. The return of Adonis, or Adonais, and his union with
Aphrodite, Shelley imagined in language appropriate to the
resurgence of life in the springtime, when the warm sunlight
operates upon the earth to produce vegetation. But since the
object of the poem was to celebrate not the annual return of
springtime, but the perpetually vitalizing influence of Keats's
poetry, the imagery was broadened to sustain the additional
burden. As Adonis, Adonais represents the fructifying power

without which nature is inanimate, but as Keats, Adonais represents the fructifying power of poetry in the world, surviving the death of the poet.

Shelley does not desert the legend even when he has finished his statement of the immortal influence of the poet's thought. The understructure of the myth is sustained to the end of the poem. As Adonais has, by his death, achieved union with Aphrodite, so the spirit of like-minded persons (such as Shelley himself) may, through the death of the body, unite with that high love of which the Uranian Aphrodite is an emblem. 'No more let Life divide what Death can join together', is the final message of the poem, but it is still stated in terms of the fable. Urania, divested now of her nature symbolism and her individuality, becomes an allegorized personification of that divine love in which the soul desires to participate. As Shelley, in the prophetic image of the shipwreck, looks forward to the final divestiture of the spirit from its mortal body, the soul of Adonais, which has already attained its union with the divine love, is the guiding beacon.

We may perceive, then, that what I have described as the mythological level of the poem is maintained in one form or another from beginning to end.

On the literal level, the application of the fable to Keats is readily apparent. The shepherd youth, slain in the hunt by the wild boar, is Keats, mortally wounded, as Shelley supposed him to have been, by the savage criticism of *Endymion*. The hostile critic is the savage beast of the legend. The interval elapsing between the criticism of *Endymion* and the death of Keats in Rome is the interval between the wounding of Adonis and the return of Aphrodite to his side to witness his death. The promise of immortality for Keats's name and poetry are figured, as I have already said, under the fiction of the resurgence of Adonais.

It is a familiar fact that Keats and Shelley were not close friends – that, indeed, Shelley had not greatly admired Keats's poetry before reading *Hyperion*. His admiration for Keats was

carefully qualified in his prose statements, and even after he had
written *Adonais* he admitted to Byron that he felt that he had
overpraised Keats in the poem. To Shelley, Keats was a symbol
of the just man persecuted by the unjust. The theme of justice
is nearly as significant in the poem as the theme of immortality.
Shelley believed, and rightly, that Keats suffered at the hands
of the reviewers more because of association with Leigh Hunt
than because of his poetry. 'The offence of this poor victim,' he
wrote, 'seems to have consisted solely in his intimacy with Leigh
Hunt, Mr Hazlitt, and some other enemies of despotism and
superstition.' When Keats died, Shelley indignantly seized
upon the fact of his death – and its supposed cause in the harsh-
ness of the *Quarterly Review* – as an occasion for some pointed
observations. The reviews of the time were politically controlled, and Shelley had spent a lifetime in revolt against the
Tory state of mind, if not the actual Tory party which controlled them. He had himself suffered intensely from the injustice of the representatives of the established powers. Personal
abuse of Shelley, calumny, willful distortion and vilification
were flung across the pages of *Blackwood's*, and this vilification
had been constantly on the increase.

Shelley probably would have refrained from taking issue with
his enemies had not his friends and principles been at stake, and
had not the whole affair culminated in the death of Keats. It
should be remembered that Shelley himself had been linked in
Blackwood's Magazine with the 'Cockney School', of which
school Keats and Hunt were the most condemned, and it is
doubly significant that *Blackwood's* had pointed out that Keats
belonged to 'the Cockney School of Politics as well as to the
Cockney School of Poetry'. Keats had committed himself to this
school with his sonnet *Written on the Day That Mr. Leigh Hunt
Left Prison*, in which he had charged that Hunt was shut in
prison 'for showing truth to flatter'd state'. In reality Shelley
belonged to no school, but he admired Hunt and was indebted
to him for that appreciation of his own ideas and poems which
Hunt had long publicly shown in the *Examiner*. Shelley was

otherwise involved with the reformers of his day. His adventures in Irish reform in his youth, his *Declaration of Rights*, his Marlow pamphlets, his connection with Godwin, his acquaintance with the minor reformers Richard Carlile, Francis Place, the Irish radicals Peter Finnerty, Daniel Isaac Eaton, Robert Owen, and his connection with General Sir Ronald Cranford Ferguson, had not left him in an isolated position. While his interest in reform was mainly philosophical, it was not wholly so.

The curious tactics of *Blackwood's* had put him in a position in which it was difficult to act. *Blackwood's* had all along insisted that Shelley was a gentleman, a scholar and a poet of great ability. Under cover of these compliments, his character, poetry and convictions had nevertheless been assailed even more savagely than those of Keats. This difficult situation in respect to *Blackwood's* was probably the reason why he selected the review of Keats in the *Quarterly*, rather than the more savage one in *Blackwood's*, for his special attack, although he had ample personal reason for feeling that both the *Quarterly* and *Blackwood's* deserved rebuke.

It appears to have been Shelley's original intention to stress the polemical purpose of his poem. But cancelled passages of the preface and cancelled stanzas reveal that he toned down this aspect of his work. He deleted from the preface important passages relating to himself. He cut out such passages as the following:

Persecution, contumely, and calumny, have been heaped upon me in profuse measure; and domestic conspiracy and legal oppression have violated in my person the most sacred rights of nature and humanity.

From the poem itself he struck out a revolutionary passage in which he speaks of those who keep

> A record of the wrong which, though they sleep,
> Die not, but dream of retribution.

But much of the polemical remains. *Blackwood's* had warned Shelley to seek better companions than Leigh Hunt and 'Johnny Keats'. In *Adonais* Shelley not only declares an admiration for Keats but says that he will follow Keats's soul as a beacon. *Blackwood's* had, in a nasty passage, compared Shelley to Hunt in contemptuous fashion:

But of Mr. Shelley much may be said with truth, which we not long since said of his friend and leader Mr. Hunt: he has not, indeed, all that is odious and contemptible in the character of that person; so far as we have seen he has never exhibited the bustling vulgarity, the ludicrous affectation, the factious flippancy, or the selfish heartlessness, which it is hard for our feelings to treat with the mere contempt they merit.

In *Adonais* Shelley avows his admiration for Hunt:

> What softer voice is hushed over the dead?
> Athwart what brow is that dark mantle thrown?
> What form leans sadly o'er the white death-bed,
> In mockery of monumental stone, –
> The heavy heart heaving without a moan?
> If it be He, who, gentlest of the wise,
> Taught, soothed, loved, honoured the departed one,
> Let me not vex, with inharmonious sighs
> The silence of that heart's accepted sacrifice.

It is idle to say, as some critics have said, that this praise might better have been applied to Joseph Severn. *Adonais* without reference to Leigh Hunt would not have fulfilled Shelley's intention. It is similarly pointless to say that Shelley makes poets mourn for Keats who did not actually mourn for him. Shelley's mourning poets are not so much friends of Keats as common allies in the cause of justice. Thus the Pilgrim of Eternity mourns at the tomb of Keats, not as a personal friend, but as one who, like Keats, had been attacked as the champion of liberal causes, and who had, like Keats, been followed by

> the mingled howl
> Of Northern Wolves, that still in darkness prowl;
> A coward Brood, which mangles as they prey,
> By hellish instinct, all that cross their way.

Nor was it friendship for Keats that led the Tom Moore of the poem to mourn at the tomb of Keats, but the fact that he was 'the sweetest lyrist' of Ireland's 'saddest wrong'.

Of the dead poets who welcomed Keats in the Unapparent, Chatterton was selected not alone because Keats had admired him, but because he was, as Keats had believed, the victim of 'base detraction' in an 'ingrate world'. Sidney is pictured as welcoming Keats because Sidney was the defender of poetry from the attacks of the Puritan *School of Abuse*. Lucan, 'by his death approved', who had conspired to kill the tyrant Nero when Nero had oppressed the poets by refusing them the right of free speech, likewise appears as a champion of liberty. Thus each of these men was not only a poet who, like Keats, had died young, but each was a man who, like Keats, had dared 'the unpastured dragon in his den'. *Blackwood's* had warned Shelley that if he did not turn from his present practices he would 'sink like lead to the bottom' and be forgotten. Shelley replied that those who have 'waged contention with their time's decay' are among 'the kings of thought . . . and of the past are all that cannot pass away'. To *Blackwood's* condemnation of his 'proud spirit' he defiantly replied with a description of himself as 'A pardlike Spirit beautiful and swift'.

The polemical character of the poem, then, cannot be ignored. The preface, even without the cancelled passages, is a flaming and angry invective. The poem begins with an appeal to Justice to declare the wrong which has been done and to make of Keats's sad fate an echo and a light unto eternity. Milton is at once introduced as a man who, despite the enmity of his contemporaries, had in the justice of time come to rule over the thoughts of men because he had dared to oppose the tyrannies of his day and champion the cause of human liberty.

Keats is pictured as one who was destroyed because he dared the unpastured dragon in his den. Those living poets who are the champions of noble causes mourn his fate, and Shelley in particular weeps his own fate in that of Keats. Defiantly Shelley praises that in Keats's poetry which has been condemned by the critics. He boldly associated himself with those who had been outcast by society, scorning the advice of the critics. Although he privately detested the poetry of Hunt, he singles out Hunt for special praise in defiance of the prevailing hatred of him. He makes the dead champions of great causes welcome Keats in the Unapparent. And he points out that ultimately the influence of those who have fought for the right prevails. So much for the polemical level of the poem.

On the philosophical level, the poem passes beyond any mere celebration of the greatness of Keats and of the ultimate triumph of his influence in the world. Nor does it rest with the idea that those who have waged contention with their time's decay will survive those who have opposed reform. Neither the beauty of the world nor the thought of the ultimate triumph of causes which Shelley held dear could finally compensate for the inadequacy and impermanence of earthly things. Shelley had ample cause in his own life to be weary of the world, and in the contemplation of the pure Being of which all earthly things are but an imperfect shadow, he yearned to be rid of the body which kept his soul from participation in unchanging essence. In imagining the soul of Keats freed at last from the limitations of its earthly dwelling, Shelley offered one more pertinent reflection as his final message. If death is all that keeps us from what we seek, why linger when by dying we may attain it? Shelley was not the first nor the last to reach that great conviction, but his expression of it is one of the noblest utterances of English poetry. He did not have long to wait before his desire for death was fulfilled. He did not take his own life, but it is strange to remember how very closely the circumstances of his death resemble the imagined scene of the closing lines of *Adonais*.

It would perhaps not be fanciful to compare the fourfold

structure of *Adonais* with that of a musical composition for four instruments, in which the theme is now sustained by one, now by another, or by two or more in harmony, and in which variations of the theme may be explored without loss of unity. Shelley is often dexterous in making the imagery fit the various themes. He does not, indeed, attempt to force a fourfold allusiveness upon each line, but rarely is any passage limited to a single meaning. An instance in which the imagery brilliantly coincides with three of the themes occurs at the beginning of the poem. Shelley, announcing his lament for *Adonais*, addresses himself to one of the Hours, with the 'h' capitalized:

> And thou, sad Hour, selected from all years
> To mourn our loss, rouse thy obscure compeers,
> And teach them thine own sorrow.

Here in a literal sense the sad Hour is the hour in which Keats had died, and the obscure compeers the hours which had not been distinguished by such an event as the death of Keats. But the Hours are mythological personages, Dike, Eunomia and Eirene, who, as the companions of Aphrodite, always accompany her in her lament for Adonis, and it is appropriate that Shelley should call upon them on this occasion. A polemical significance may be equally discerned. We may suppose the 'sad Hour' to have been Dike (Justice), whose function it was to inform the gods when an injustice had been done. Her 'obscure compeers' would be Eunomia and Eirene (Harmony and Peace), whose obscurity in the world Shelley deplored. It was their duty to superintend the moral world of human life. Shelley calls upon them to make 'an echo and a light unto eternity' out of the injustice done to Keats by his politically inspired enemies.

In other instances the myth and the facts are not so congruent. Keats died in February, while the lamentation for Adonis took place later in the springtime, a convention which Shelley followed in the poem. Rossetti notes that:

This introduction of Spring may be taken as implying that Shelley supposed Keats to have died in the Spring: but in fact he died in the Winter – February 23.

It is more likely that Shelley merely could not adjust the fable to the fact at this point. A more striking instance of the stubbornness of the material is shown in the incident of the final kiss. It is difficult to imagine that this portion of the story could be applied to Keats, but Shelley attempted to make use of it. By imagining that the interval between the wounding of Adonis and the return of Aphrodite for the final kiss could be compared to the interval between Keats's wounding by the critic of *Endymion* and his death in Rome, Shelley attempted to fit the disparate themes together. But since he had already begun, in conventional elegiac fashion, to lament the death of Adonais, he was forced rather awkwardly to imagine Adonais merely as lying under the vault of the blue Italian sky, as though in sleep, while death and corruption dared not deface him. The analogy between Keats dying of tuberculosis in Rome and Adonais awaiting the shadow of 'white Death', is plausible but faint. Then, upon Urania's return, demanding the final kiss, Shelley declares:

> In the death-chamber for a moment Death
> Shamed by the presence of that living Might,
> Blushed to annihilation, and the breath
> Revisited those lips, and life's pale light
> Flashed through those limbs, so late her dear delight.

There was no analogous incident at the death of Keats.

In other ways Shelley encountered difficulties in applying the details of the fable to the poet. In order to make later use of the symbolism of the return of Adonis, it was necessary at least to allude to the descent of Adonis into the underworld, where Persephone became enamored of him and refused to give him up. Since the application of that portion of the fable to Keats was pointless, Shelley was forced to say vaguely:

> For he is gone, where all things wise and fair
> Descend; – oh, dream not that the amorous Deep
> Will yet restore him to the vital air;
> Death feeds on his mute voice, and laughs at our despair.

Adonis in the fable was a shepherd. In order to use this detail, Shelley availed himself of the conceit that the poetic thoughts of Keats were his flocks.

> The quick Dreams,
> The passion-wingèd Ministers of thought,
> Who were his flocks, whom near the living streams
> Of his young spirit he fed, and whom he taught
> The love which was its music, wander not, –
> Wander no more, from kindling brain to brain,
> But droop there, whence they sprung; and mourn their lot
> Round the cold heart, where, after their sweet pain,
> They ne'er will gather strength, or find a home again.

To preserve the convention that the companions of Aphrodite mourned over Adonais, Shelley struck upon the device of selecting the conventional companions of Aphrodite whose names, translated into English, might be taken as descriptive of Keats's poetic inventions. Thus Aphrodite in Greek myth is conventionally attended by the Desires and Loves: Eros and Anteros, Himeros and Potheros. These become the Desires and Adorations which mourn for the dead poet. Her companions Aglaia (Splendor) and Peitho (Persuasion) become the Splendours and the Persuasions of the poem. The activities of these mourners are developed elaborately from the seventh stanza of Bion's *Lament for Adonis*. The device is ingenious but not wholly satisfactory as a description of the poetic qualities of Keats.

The incident of the conversion of the dead body of Adonis into an anemone, mentioned by Bion, suggested the lines:

> The leprous corpse touched by this spirit tender
> Exhales itself in flowers of gentle breath;
> Like incarnations of the stars, when splendour
> Is changed to fragrance, they illumine death
> And mock the merry worm that wakes beneath.

The 'flowers of gentle breath' are from the Greek *anemone* (windflower), from *anemos* (wind or breath). The star shape of the anemone, or Adonis flower as it is still called, suggested the 'incarnations of the stars'. But the delicate allusiveness of the passage is not readily detected, since the incident is not narrated. It is merely touched upon in this almost hidden fashion.

A recent critic has objected, reasonably enough, to the comparison of Keats to so many fragile things. Keats was made of sterner stuff than the 'pale flower', the 'bloom, whose petals nipped before they blew', or the 'broken lily'. Shelley was recalling the association of Adonis with the delicate springtime vegetation, such as was carried in the Adonis baskets in the ancient festival, but the idea was not a felicitous one if we consider it in terms of Keats's character. Much of the language of the poem is appropriate not to Shelley or Keats but to Aphrodite, 'most musical of mourners'. The amorous character of the language in which Shelley mourned for Keats led a psychoanalytically minded critic to interpret the passages as an indication that Shelley was homosexual. Pointing to the fact that in *Adonais* Shelley was 'portraying and glorifying a *Man*' (the italics are his), he asks:

Yet how are the love-expressions in it to be taken? Are they to be put aside as amiable but rather meaningless enthusiasms, or are they to be interpreted directly and candidly, as *meaning what they say*?

The critic was doubtless thinking of such a line as that echoed from Bion's *Lament*: 'Kiss me, so long but as a kiss may live.' He did not realize that Shelley was speaking in terms appropriate to Aphrodite mourning for her lover. He had missed the mythological element of the poem altogether, or had mistaken it as those critics do who interpret Urania as the Muse of Astronomy. But his comment points to conspicuous flaws in the poem: the awkwardness in which the elaborate device involved Shelley, and the inappropriateness of parts of the poem to Keats.

When one considers also that Keats was not killed by the wound of the critic, as Shelley supposed, the application of the legend to Keats loses its chief justification. Shelley learned the true facts about the death of Keats after *Adonais* had been written, but obviously he could not correct his error without destroying the whole scheme of the poem.

On what I have described as the literal level of the poem, the application of the myth to John Keats, the device proved, then, not very successful. In order to make it work at all, Shelley had to be so vague that the details of the fable were all but lost, and the picture of Keats which it was intended to give was faulty at the time and still more obviously faulty once the character of Keats and the facts of his life and death were better known. The best passages dealing with Keats are those which were not tied down to the fable: allusions to his poetry; the magnificent lines,

> To that high Capital, where kingly Death
> Keeps his pale court in beauty and decay,
> He came; and bought with price of purest breath
> A grave among the eternal. . . .

the beautiful description of his grave in the Protestant cemetery at Rome near the pyramid of Cestius; and the very fine stanzas that Shelley developed from Keats's own sonnet *To Chatterton.*

The polemical element of the poem was adjusted to the basic myth with less distortion than was necessary in the narrative of the death of Keats. The chief difficulty which the modern reader finds in this whole aspect of the poem lies, however, in the fact that we do not regard Keats as Shelley regarded him. Keats was not slain by the critic; Shelley exaggerated Keats's role as the daring champion of liberal causes; and the immortality of his poetry had practically nothing to do with his having waged contention against his time's decay – in any political sense, at least. Moreover, much that the critics had said of Keats's poetry was true, as Keats himself recognized.

It was in exploring the symbolism of the Adonis myth and in attempting to adapt it to the philosophical affirmations at the end of the poem that Shelley employed himself most subtly. One cannot avoid the feeling, however, that the poem becomes too subtle, and it is certainly in the latter part of the elegy that one most easily loses the meaning. Shelley's problem was to find and sustain an analogy between the annual return of Adonis and the survival of Keats's poetry. By exploiting the fable as a nature myth – taking Adonis as the sunlight and Aphrodite as the 'abandoned earth', he imagined the return of Adonis as bringing the resurgence of springtime. This conception was made applicable to Keats by identifying the voice of Keats – that is, his poetry – with the music of reanimated nature. By drawing upon the symbolic interpretation of Hancarville and Knight, Shelley made Adonis, or Adonais, represent the active aspect of the creative spirit, an idea which was, of course, applicable to the influence of the creative spirit of Keats in the world after his physical death. In the imagery which sustains this motif, Aphrodite becomes the passive element of the creative spirit, on which the active spirit operates. The union of Adonais and Urania thus produces the 'one Spirit', that is, the twofold principle of fertility. Hence the intricate imagery in which Adonais becomes the 'plastic stress' of the 'one Spirit'. The weakness of the poetic idea is that in attempting to amalgamate the nature myth and Keats, Shelley made nothing very clear of either one. Keats does not revive annually in the springtime, as Adonis did. Nor does his poetry produce vegetation. Adonis is neither wholly Adonis nor wholly Keats. The symbolic character attached to him does not perfectly fit either the idea of sunlight bringing the vegetation to life or the creative spirit of a poet vitalizing the world of thought after his death. Furthermore, it is difficult to follow the manner in which Adonais and

Urania lose their individuality, fading from distinct and visible personages into nature myths.

This difficulty is the more marked as Shelley advances to the concept of Urania not merely as a personage of a fable nor merely as a principle in a nature myth, but as a philosophical abstraction. Urania becomes the Divine Love, the Platonic One; she is the permanent and unchanging essence, participation in which constitutes the final refuge of the soul. We are thus faced with an extraordinary number of guises in which Urania appears in the poem. In the first place it is a little difficult to recognize Urania as the Aphrodite of the myth at all, for Shelley does not confine her to a single mythological form. She is the goddess who is in love with Adonis; she is also what that goddess stands for – love and beauty as the object of the poet's desire. But Shelley shifts her into other aspects of Aphrodite. For instance, in virtue of her role in myth as Venus Genetrix, the mother of all forms, Shelley makes her 'the mighty Mother', and Adonais is temporarily her son, instead of her lover. Shelley speaks of her as in her widowhood, which would seem to be an allegory based on the idea that love and beauty are widowed in the modern world. She becomes the earth abandoned by the sunlight in the wintertime. She becomes a principle of fertility. And she becomes the unchanging essence of which all earthy things are an imperfect image. It is hard to keep one's grasp upon her as she passes through these Protean changes, and one may well wonder whether her intricacies are worth the trouble.

Because *Adonais* contains many echoes of the language of the classical elegies and because Shelley has borrowed from the elegies many of their conventional devices, the elegies of Bion and Moschus, together with some of the pastoral verses of Theocritus, are commonly spoken of as Shelley's models or sources. No more mistaken notion could be expressed in a criticism of the poem. *Adonais* is highly original, both in form and conception. The imitation of the language and conventions of the classical elegies was a deliberate device intended to impart a traditional character to the poem. But to describe the classical

elegies as models for *Adonais* does Shelley's poem no service.
Shelley must have supposed the capacity to perceive these
borrowings as the elementary equipment necessary to read the
poem at all. The very originality of *Adonais* consists of the fact
that intentionally recognizable elegiac conventions have been
made to subserve a novel and subtle purpose. It is quite likely
that as Shelley devised, 'in the accents of an unknown land', a
new lament for the 'most musical of mourners', he had studied
the whole literature of Adonis laments, including the many
Italian versions of the theme. In many instances Shelley's
language, even when he is closest to the fable, more nearly resembles the ornate style of the Italians than the simpler one of
the Greeks. The 'secret Paradise' of Urania is reminiscent of the
garden of love in which the goddess resides in Girolamo Para-
bosco's *Favole d'Adone*. In at least one case a borrowing from the
Italian may be clearly detected. In Marino's *L'Adone*, just before Venus is aroused to return to her dying Adonis, the poet
writes:

> L'Aurora intanto che dal suo balcona
> Gli humidi lumi abbassa a la campagna
> Vede anelante e moribondo Adone.

Shelley's lines are:

> Morning sought
> Her eastern watch-tower, and her hair unbound,
> Wet with the tears which should adorn the ground,
> Dimmed the aërial eyes that kindle day.

Here the phrase 'eastern watch-tower' is a literal translation of
the word *balcona*, which is derived from the Arabic *bala*, 'look-
out place', and was used in early Italian for the 'sky', or the
'East', or as 'window of Heaven'. Considering the common
theme of the two poems and the similar position of the incident
in the parallel fables, Shelley's use of the phrase must indicate
that he had his eye upon the famous Italian poem. In a letter
dated November 9, 1815, Shelley had ordered from Lackington,

Allen and Co., 'an Italian poem by Marino called L'Adone' –
a fact which would seem to indicate an early interest in the
Adonis fable. But we should regard the Italian poems no more
than the Greek as Shelley's models. The epithet 'most musical
of mourners' which Shelley applies to Urania shows that he is
aware of the many poets who have composed laments for
Aphrodite on the death of Adonis. We are to understand that
Shelley's poem is operating upon a long mythological and
literary tradition, and our consciousness of the fact is requisite
to a perception of the composite character of the poem.

Adonais is brilliant but not always clear. Despite the fact that
Shelley's finest powers were employed in it, and that it contains
some of his noblest verse, one feels that he has not overcome the
immense difficulties which he laid in his own way. For Shelley's
attempt to carry a complicated device throughout the poem, a
dexterity and superficial brilliance were needed, alien to a great
poetic conception. The myth which constituted the enfolding
theme of the poem had to be generalized until it was obscured
and in the manifold applications weakened until it meant no
single thing. The figure Adonais became so diaphanous that it
did not emerge wholly either as Keats or as Adonis. Shelley so
involved himself in the intricacies of his medium that, despite
an ingenuity of which no other poet of his generation was capable, he did not effect a clear-cut poetic conception.

SOURCE: 'Shelley's *Adonais*', in *Shores of Darkness* (New York,
    1941); reprinted in paperback (1963).

I. J. Kapstein

THE MEANING OF *MONT BLANC* (1947)

Shelley composed *Mont Blanc*[1] upon the occasion of his first visit to the Swiss Alps. 'The immensity of these aerial summits', he tells us, 'excited when they suddenly burst upon the sight, a sentiment of extatic [*sic*] wonder, not unallied to madness.'[2] Of *Mont Blanc*, which resulted from this experience, he says that 'it was composed under the immediate impression of the deep and powerful feelings excited by the objects which it attempts to describe',[3] and then evidently aware of the poem's difficulty, describes it as 'an undisciplined overflowing of the soul'.[4]

Had Shelley composed the poem in tranquility, he might not have permitted the tensions that disrupt its logic and obscure its meaning. But in the poem as it stands, there is a hidden conflict: Shelley struggles to assert the freedom of his mind against his conviction that nothing in the universe is free. It is this conflict that is responsible for the ambiguities and equivocations in phrasing that make *Mont Blanc* such difficult reading, ambiguities so powerful as to force the poem into anti-climax. The real difficulty in reading *Mont Blanc* is not that its subject matter is ontology, but Shelley's conflicting attitudes towards the subject matter – his simultaneous acceptance and rejection of the conclusion to which his ontological speculations led him.

The particular subject matters of *Mont Blanc* are the nature of mind, the nature of knowledge, the nature of reality and the relation of the human mind to the universe. These matters the poem tries to integrate in the doctrine of Necessity, long a central element in Shelley's thought as *Queen Mab* (1813) and

the *Refutation of Deism* (1814) indicate. Up to the last three lines
of the poem Shelley's attitude is awe and worship of the remote,
amoral power of Necessity ruling eternally the mutable universe
of matter and the human mind. Of this power the towering
peak of Mont Blanc is the central symbol of the poem. Shelley's
submission to the rule of Necessity is sustained up to the last
three lines of the poem, but in the course of his exposition of the
doctrine he balks in a number of crucial places at accepting it.
The reluctance implicit in the confused and ambiguous phrasing
finally becomes explicit in the last three lines; here with a shift
of attitude from worship to defiance of the power of Necessity,
Shelley's logic also shifts, so that in contradiction of what he
has been saying for a hundred and forty-one lines he brings the
poem to an anti-climax.

   The poet's ambiguous attitude towards his subject at once
makes difficulty in reading the first eleven lines, comprising, in
Shelley's division, the first section of the poem. Here he makes
a statement about the content of mind and the mind's activity
in knowledge of 'the everlasting universe of things':

> The everlasting universe of things
> Flows through the mind, and rolls its rapid waves,
> Now dark – now glittering – now reflecting gloom –
> Now lending splendour, where from secret springs
> The source of human thought its tribute brings
> Of waters, – with a sound but half its own,
> Such as a feeble brook will oft assume
> In the wild woods, among the mountains lone,
> Where waterfalls around it leap for ever,
> Where woods and winds contend, and a vast river
> Over its rocks ceaselessly bursts and raves.

At first glance it appears that Shelley is asserting by 'the everlasting universe of things' the substantial existence of the universe independent of mind. He repeats the phrase 'universe of
things' in l. 40 and speaks of the 'Strength of things' in l. 139.

If by 'things' he means material objects, then he is echoing John Locke whose *Essay Concerning Human Understanding* he had read as early as 1810,[5] and had read again, according to Mary Shelley,[6] in 1815, the year before he composed *Mont Blanc*. Read in accordance with Locke's theory of knowledge, the passage means that a 'vast river' of sensory impressions of material objects flows into the mind where it unites with the mind's own 'feeble brook' of ideas to make up the total content of the mind.

Locke's theory of knowledge distinguishes between the primary and the secondary qualities of matter, the primary – solidity, extension, figure and mobility – being inherent in matter, and the secondary – colour, taste, smell, sound, etc. – being produced in the mind by the operation of the primary qualities upon it. That Shelley may have been thinking of this distinction seems borne out by his statement that the darkness and the glitter of the stream of things, its gloom and its splendour, these being secondary qualities, have their source in mind. Yet in saying that the source of thought has 'secret springs', Shelley holds back from complete acceptance of Locke's theory of knowledge, for he appears to be saying by 'secret' that however feeble may be the stream of ideas that the mind holds in contrast to the vast flood it takes in from the external world, it still is mysteriously free and creates to some degree the objects of its knowledge.

While the phrase 'secret springs/The source of human thought' suggests a withdrawal from acceptance of Locke's sensationalism, the syntax and the punctuation of the passage permit a strong alternative reading of the passage, dependent upon a wholly different theory of knowledge. It is clear enough that 'its' in l. 5 refers to 'source of human thought', but the 'its' of l. 6 has ambiguous reference. At first glance it seems also to refer to 'source of human thought', so that in reading ll. 5 and 6 one takes them to say: 'The source of human thought with a sound but half its own brings its tribute of waters.' But the comma and dash which come after 'waters' in l. 6 make an emphatic separation of 'with a sound but half its own' from 'the source of human thought its tribute brings of waters', so that the 'its' of l. 6 may be taken to refer, as does the 'its' of l. 2, to 'the everlasting universe of things'. If this is the reference Shelley intended, then the passage demands a reading of the 'universe of things' as the 'feeble brook' of l. 7 while the waters from the 'secret springs of human thought' become the 'vast river' of l. 10.

Read in this reversal of the roles of 'vast river' and 'brook' the passage says that the 'everlasting universe of things', the river flowing through the mind, is the creation of mind from which the feeble brook of sense borrows – the 'lending' of l. 4 should be noted in connection with this reading – its reality. . . .

What freedom Shelley's ambiguity in the passage reserves for the mind foreshadows his less equivocal assertion of the mind's complete freedom in the last three lines of the poem. But up to the very point of this assertion Shelley keeps stating the complete passivity of the mind in knowledge and the submission of both the material universe and the human mind to the power of Necessity. The idea of this power is introduced in the next section of the poem in ll. 16–17; it constitutes the major theme of the poem, but Shelley holds off its development until l. 75.

In the meantime, the second section of the poem, ll. 12–48, begins by comparing the flow of thought through the mind with the flow of the river Arve through its Ravine. Shelley describes the Arve as the medium through which the power of Necessity reveals itself:

> . . . Power in likeness of the Arve comes down
> From the ice-gulfs that gird his secret throne (ll. 16–17)

which is to say that Necessity reveals its power in the 'universe of things' of which the river Arve is the symbol.

Shelley now turns to some sixteen lines of literal description of the sights and sounds of the Ravine and then picks up again the theme with which he began the poem – the relation between the universe and the human mind, this time his own mind, whose symbol is the Ravine:

> Dizzy Ravine! and when I gaze on thee
> I seem as in a trance sublime and strange
> To muse on my own separate fantasy,
> My own, my human mind. . . .   (ll. 34–7)

By 'fantasy' Shelley means the illusion that his mind is an entity
separate from and independent of the 'universe of things',
anticipating here a conclusion he came to in the essay *On Life*
where he says,

. . . The existence of distinct individual minds, similar to that which
is employed in now questioning its own nature, is likewise found to
be a delusion.[7]

Actually, says Shelley in the next few lines of *Mont Blanc*, the
mind is only what the mind contains; its knowledge is created
by the mingling of sensory impressions of the external world
with the mind's own ideas. But again he does not make it clear
whether these ideas are produced in the mind by the operations
of the sensory impressions upon it, or whether they exist independently and are imposed upon or added to the sensory impressions:

> My own, my human mind, which passively
> Now renders and receives fast influencings,
> Holding an unremitting interchange
> With the clear universe of things around   (ll. 37–40)

The word 'passively' makes the ambiguity in these lines. If
it is taken to qualify 'now' only, then Shelley means that his
mind is passive at this particular moment, though free at others
– passive now because it is momentarily overwhelmed by the
scene he has just finished describing. But if 'passively' is taken
as qualifying 'now renders and receives', Shelley means that his
mind is always passive whether it is rendering (i.e., contributing
its own ideas to the total content of mind), or whether it is
receiving impressions from the external world. Its 'unremitting

interchange' is wholly involuntary; what the mind adds to knowledge is determined by what the external world produces in its operation upon mind. By this reading, therefore, Shelley is saying that the mind has no freedom in the creation of its knowledge. . . .

At this point, then, in *Mont Blanc* he seems to have put aside the reservation of some freedom for mind in the creation of knowledge, the reservation ambiguously implied in the opening lines of the poem, and to have accepted the complete passivity of mind. But this submission does not sit well with the poet, and his uneasiness creates the tangled ambiguities of the lines immediately following where Shelley, still addressing the Ravine, describes the 'influencings' both rendered and received, the content of his mind as

> One legion of wild thoughts, whose wandering wings
> Now float above thy darkness, and now rest
> Where that or thou art no unbidden guest,
> In the still cave of the witch Poesy,
> Seeking among the shadows that pass by –
> Ghosts of all things that are – some shade of thee,
> Some phantom, some faint image; till the breast
> From which they fled recalls them, thou art there! (ll. 41–8)

The plain sense of the first four lines of this passage is that the poet's mind, i.e., the 'legion of wild thoughts', wandering over the landscape of the Ravine finally settles down to recreation of the scene in poetry. By 'that' in l. 43 Shelley means his mind, the 'legion of wild thoughts', and by 'thou' he means the Ravine. That both are not unbidden guests in the cave of Poesy is Shelley's way of saying that both poetic activity and the object it makes poetry about are welcome to his mind.

What occupies Shelley for the next three lines of the passage is the real nature of the object he is making poetry about, and again he hesitates between two theories. First, he may be saying that his mind in the act of creating poetry seeks out among all

its impressions of the external world the particular impression
of the Ravine, an impression variously described as shade,
phantom, image because the mind does not create the reality
of the object, but merely receives an impression of it. Or, if
'ghosts of all things that are' be taken to stand for words, Shelley
means that he is seeking in his mind for words descriptive of the
Ravine, but that these also being remote from the material
reality of the Ravine are therefore merely its shades, phantoms,
images. By both these readings, consonant with the theory of
knowledge set out at the beginning of the passage, Shelley
takes the 'universe of things' to have substantial existence.

But another reading must also be considered. Shelley's reference to the 'cave of the witch Poesy' and the 'shadows that pass
by' are reminiscent of Plato's myth of the Cave and seem to
come from the same area of Shelley's thought which produced
the Platonic elements in the *Hymn to Intellectual Beauty*, written
in the same year as *Mont Blanc*. Shelley may mean, then, that
his mind in the creative act seeks out among all the phenomena
of the world of sense – which are merely shadows of their real
Forms in the realm of the Ideas – the Ravine, in itself merely a
shadow of reality, as its subject matter. But if the ideas as well
as the imagery of the lines be taken as Platonic, then Shelley by
denying real existence to the object known by his senses is
contradicting the alternative readings of the lines as well as
those previous passages in the poem (ll. 1–11; 38–40) where he
seems to acknowledge the substantial existence of the material
universe.

The last sentence in the passage, 'till the breast/From which
they fled recalls them, thou art there', sustains the ambiguity
of the whole. Shelley is still addressing the Ravine ('thou') and
saying that it is in the cave of Poesy ('there'). If 'breast' is meto-
nymical for the poet's mind, Shelley means that until his mind,
free to do as it likes, withdraws its impressions from the cave of
Poesy, he will continue to make poetry about the Ravine. On
the other hand, if 'breast' stands for the universe, Shelley may
mean that until the universe recalls all of its impressions, 'ghosts

of all things that are', that it stamps upon his passive mind, he must retain his impressions of the Ravine and make poetry about it. It seems plain here that Shelley is troubled again about the nature of the poetic process; he is not certain whether it is determined by the operation of the external world upon the mind, or whether the mind is free in the creation of poetry, i.e., knowledge. . . .

II

Towards the conclusion of the thirty-five lines that make up the third section of the poem Shelley comes at length to exposition of the central theme of *Mont Blanc* – the rule of the universe by Necessity. First, in stunned awe at the sight, he describes the great peak, the symbol of Necessity, towering serenely above the wild desolation of the torn and jagged slopes and lesser peaks. In the last eight lines of the section he makes a statement about the relation of the savage wilderness to mankind, a statement foreshadowed by the reference to Power in l. 16 and now elaborated throughout the rest of the poem.

> The wilderness has a mysterious tongue
> Which teaches awful doubt, or faith so mild,
> So solemn, so serene, that man may be
> But for such faith, with nature reconciled;
> Thou hast a voice, great Mountain, to repeal
> Large codes of fraud and woe; not understood
> By all, but which the wise, and great, and good
> Interpret, or make felt, or deeply feel.   (ll. 76–83)

The difficulty of this passage lies in its first four lines. The paradox of a tongue which can teach either doubt or faith can be explained, however, by Shelley's earlier intellectual history. The overwhelming spectacle of Mont Blanc towering serenely above the awful desolation of the wilderness below re-evoked in Shelley those ideas about nature and its rule by Necessity which had once dominated his thought. These ideas he had found set out generally by Godwin[8] and in detail in D'Holbach,[9] and he himself had presented them in *Queen Mab* and its notes. . . .

The 'universe of things', described in the first lines of the poem as a mountain stream, is now revealed under the rule of Necessity to be 'a flood of ruin/ . . . that from the boundaries of the sky/Rolls its perpetual stream' (ll. 107–9). The torrents of this stream plunging through the 'vast caves' (l. 120) below the mountain well up from their 'secret chasms' (l. 122) and become 'one majestic River' (l. 123) that 'for ever/Rolls' (ll. 124–5). These caves and chasms, like the Ravine of the Arve earlier in the poem, are symbolic of the human mind through which flows 'the everlasting universe of things' (l. 1). . . .

Embedded, however, in his account of the mutable flux of life is Shelley's description of Necessity, the power remote from the turbulence it creates –

> Power dwells apart in its tranquillity,
> Remote, serene, and inaccessible   (ll. 96–7)

– and to this power Shelley devotes the fifth and final section of *Mont Blanc*. Against the devastation of its slopes and the turbulence of its torrents, Shelley once more sets the detached calm of the towering peak. 'The power is there' (l. 127), he says, and then, coming to the climax of the poem, asserts the power of Necessity not only over the material universe, but – and this time without ambiguity – its power over mind as well.

> The secret Strength of things
> Which governs thought, and to the infinite dome
> Of Heaven is as a law, inhabits thee!   (ll. 139–41)

On the surface this is the assertion towards which the entire poem moves. Mont Blanc becomes for Shelley a symbol of natural law ruling the passive universe and the passive mind of man. The peak is a symbol of the polarity that creates the dramatic situation in many of his poems, a symbol of the One against the Many, Eternity against Time, Necessity against Mutability.

But the climax of *Mont Blanc* is not its conclusion. Its conclusion is its anti-climax where Shelley, still addressing the mountain, says,

> And what were thou, and earth, and stars, and sea,
> If to the human mind's imaginings
> Silence and solitude were vacancy?   (ll. 142–4)

In these last lines of the poem its earlier evasions, equivocations and ambiguities reach their own climax. Shelley's reluctance to accept his own conclusions, the thread of denial that tangles and knots his crucial statements, now comes boldly to the surface to reveal the disruptive tension of the poem. Both the tone and the sense of the lines explain why Shelley never fully commits himself to the ontology he expounds when he discusses the relation between the 'universe of things' and the mind of man. For the anti-climax of the poem contradicts the climax by saying that it is not external Necessity, but the mind of man that creates our knowledge and makes the reality of the universe.

This is not to say that the pressure of doubt is so strong as to make the denial clear and explicit. On the contrary, the three lines are capable of at least three different readings in relation to what has been said before them. Whatever the reading, one sees, nevertheless, more clearly than at any other point in the poem that Shelley cannot submit to the conclusion towards which the epistemology of materialism presses him. The essay *On Life* reveals with what relief Shelley was to seize upon the epistemology of idealism as his escape from the materialistic power of Necessity.

Materialism is a seducing system to young and superficial minds. . . . But I was discontented with such a view of things as it afforded; man is a being of high aspirations. . . . Whatever may be his true and final destination, there is a spirit within him at enmity with nothingness and dissolution. . . . Such contemplations as these, materialism and the popular philosophy of mind and matter alike forbid; they are only consistent with the intellectual system.[10]

But in *Mont Blanc* Shelley had not yet rejected materialism. The tension created by his desire to be free in conflict with his conviction that nothing in the universe is free forces such ambiguity into the last three lines of the poem as to permit at least three interpretations of their meaning:

a) The 'universe of things', the material universe, has no substantial existence; it exists only as it is perceived by mind.

This reading of the lines would make them contradict the assertion that the 'secret Strength of things/ . . . governs thought' (ll. 139–40) and also contradicts the poem's previous statements of the mind's passivity.

b) The mind is passive and governed like everything else in the universe by Necessity; it is, however, part of the operation of Necessity that it excite the mind to discovery of the presence and power of Necessity in the universe. If the 'human mind's imaginings' did not discover the One and the Many, Necessity and Mutability, as the polar opposites of reality, then the 'silence and solitude' of nature would be 'vacancy', i.e., vacant of meaning.

By this reading, Shelley's idea of reality would follow Locke's theory that the primary qualities of matter have the power to produce in the mind the secondary qualities which the mind assigns to matter. This reading is consonant with the alternative reading of the opening lines of the poem which say that the glitter and gloom of the Arve are supplied by thought. In this sense the anti-climax represents Shelley's attempt to reserve some freedom for the mind. While mind can have no knowledge except what is given or produced by sensory experience of the universe of matter, the universe of our knowledge is not complete unless the mind assigns certain qualities to it. Reality, therefore, though dictated by matter, is, nevertheless, not wholly material; it is a confluence of the vast river of matter and the feeble brook of mind.

c) The material universe exists independently of mind, but the mind, too, is independent since it 'renders' as well as 'receives fast influencings,/Holding an unremitting interchange/ With the clear universe of things around' (ll. 38–40).

Thus the universe of matter can have reality only as the mind by reflection upon the data of sense comes to the assignment of meaning and so creates knowledge. Mind as the value-seeking, judgment-making process of the universe is superior to the processes of nature no matter what their spectacular force and grandeur.

This reading of the lines gets some support from the tone of mingled defiance and condescension with which they begin: 'And what were thou . . .?' as if Shelley were saying, 'What would you amount to if it were not for me?' Indeed the tone of the lines gives the only consistency to their ambiguity. For in whatever sense they are read Shelley seems to be asserting the ironic attitude of a slave towards his master. The slave, admitting his master's power over him, yet resentful that he is a slave, consoles himself by saying that if it were not for his existence as a slave his master's power would have no significance. Or again, the slave in self-consolation says that his master's power rises from the labor of the slave which converts the raw materials supplied by the master into objects of value. . . .

SOURCE: Extracts from 'The Meaning of Shelley's *Mont Blanc*', *PMLA*, LXII (1947).

NOTES

[Notes retained or revised from the original text are here renumbered]

1. First published by Mary Shelley in *History of a Six Weeks' Tour through a Part of France, Switzerland, Germany, and Holland* (1817). Subsequent references to this and to other works by Shelley are from Roger Ingpen and Walter E. Peck, *The Complete Works of Percy Bysshe Shelley*, Julian Edition, 10 vols (London, 1926–30), hereinafter noted as Julian, *Works*.

2. Julian, *Works*, VI 137.

3. *Ibid.*, VI 88.

4. *Ibid.*

5. Thomas Jefferson Hogg, *The Life of Percy Bysshe Shelley*, ed. Edward Dowden (London, 1906) p. 70.

6. 'Mary Shelley's Reading Lists', in Newman Ivey White, *Shelley*, 2 vols (New York, 1940) II 541.

7. Julian, *Works*, VI 196. The date of this essay and of the essay *Speculations on Metaphysics* has been much discussed, but it appears from the relationship of their ideas to those in *Mont Blanc* that both essays were written after 1816 rather than in 1815 as has been conjectured.

8. William Godwin, *An Enquiry Concerning Political Justice*, 2 vols (London, 1793) I 283–317.

9. Baron D'Holbach [under pen-name 'M. Mirabaud'], *Le Système de la Nature*, 2 vols (Londres [sc. Leyden], 1770) I 1–70.

10. Julian, *Works*, VI 194.

G. M. Matthews

THE LYRICS (1969)

It is easy to slip into the assumption that 'self-expression' was among the objectives of the early English Romantics. T. S. Eliot may unwittingly have made it easier, by combining a distaste for Romanticism with his principle that 'Poetry is not a turning loose of emotion, but an escape from emotion; it is not the expression of personality, but an escape from personality'; if so, this would be ironical, for it is from the Romantics that his principle derives. When Eliot says: 'the more perfect the artist, the more completely separate in him will be the man who suffers and the mind which creates', he is developing Shelley's view that 'The poet and the man are two different natures';[1] when he affirms, of the poet, that 'emotions which he has never experienced will serve his turn as well as those familiar to him', he is generalizing from Shelley's endeavour in *The Cenci* 'to produce a delineation of passions which I had never participated in'.[2] The word 'self-expression' dates from the nineties, and the idea that an artist wants to express his own 'individuality' in art is alien to the early Romantic poets, all of whom would have repudiated, or did explicitly rule out, any such notion. Shelley would have had difficulty in even making sense of it. Every great poet, he agreed, left the imprint of an individual mind on all his works, but that imprint was the brand of his limitation as much as of his greatness; it was a by-product of his real aims. For an artist to seek, or a critic to praise, 'self-expression' would have seemed absolutely meaningless to him.

This has never deterred critics from assuming not only that the lyrical heart-cry is Shelley's typical utterance, but that he is liable to utter this cry at virtually any moment. Charles Kingsley and F. R. Leavis have recognized even the Catholic murderess Beatrice Cenci as Percy B. Shelley. Turn but a petticoat and start a luminous wing. David Masson decided in 1875 that Shelley's poetry was 'nothing else than an effluence from his personality',[3] and in 1965 the medical psychologist Dr Eustace Chesser declared that Shelley 'does not even *notice* the existence of the hard, external world which pays no attention to his wishes. His gaze is directed all the time on his own emotional states'.[4] The present essay tries to remove a major obstacle in the way of a more intelligent discussion; and it is first necessary to see in plain figures what Shelley's contribution as a lyrical poet really was.

From *Original Poetry* (1810) to *Hellas* (1822) Shelley published twelve volumes of verse. Seven of these contain no separate lyrics. *Original Poetry* had four 'personal' lyrics,[5] all bearing on Shelley's attachment to Harriet Grove. *Posthumous Fragments of Margaret Nicholson* was artfully-packaged propaganda, and its concluding poem is the only personal one it contains. *Alastor* has ten shorter poems: three addressed to Coleridge, Wordsworth and Napoleon respectively; two translations; and again one 'personal' lyric, the *Stanzas – April 1814*, which concern the Boinville-Turner entanglement. *Rosalind and Helen* (1819) has three shorter poems, *Lines written in the Euganean Hills, Hymn to Intellectual Beauty* and *Ozymandias*, the second of which contains a striking autobiographical passage. The *Euganean Hills* I believe to have even less reference to Shelley himself than Donald Reiman has already ably argued.[6] *Prometheus Unbound* contains nine shorter poems, including the allegorical *Sensitive Plant*,[7] once again, the only lyric with unequivocal personal application is the *Ode to the West Wind*. A total of seven or eight 'personal' lyrics in twelve volumes of verse, only half of these in the last eleven volumes – a modest ration, one might think, for a monotonously self-regarding narcissist whose genius was essentially lyrical. This is not quite the full story, of course. Two volumes had 'personal' dedications; Shelley himself called *Epipsychidion* 'an idealized history of my life and feelings'[8] (though nobody can explain the history it records, and it is not a lyric). Two other proposed volumes would have affected the statistics: the early 'Esdaile' collection (at least 57 poems, of which about 23 have direct personal significance), and *Julian and Maddalo*, intended to contain, Shelley said, 'all my saddest verses raked up into one heap'.[9] But these were not published, and after a few unanswered inquiries Shelley seems to have lost interest. *Epipsychidion*, in an anonymous edition of 100 copies, was suppressed by its author within twelve months.[10] Shelley also cancelled a passage intended for the *Adonais* preface 'relating to my private wrongs'.[11] Medwin's story that the poet's self-portrait in *Adonais* was also 'afterwards expunged from it'[12] may be a muddle, but it is a fact that Shelley had enjoined his publisher to make an 'omission' in the second edition,[13] while the draft proves that the 'frail Form' who comes to mourn Adonais in stanza 31 was almost certainly not, in conception, Shelley himself but some idealized figure born not later than Buonaparte and contrasted with him – perhaps Rousseau.[14]

From *Alastor* onwards, then, Shelley actually published in book form (excluding dedications) four personal or semi-personal poems: *Stanzas – April 1814*, *The Euganean Hills*, *Intellectual Beauty* and the *West Wind*. His ten poems in periodicals were all offered anonymously; of these only *On a Faded Violet* and possibly *The Question* might be called 'personal' (*Sunset* and *Grief* appeared with all the personal parts omitted). *Epipsychidion* was repudiated and suppressed. Four of *Adonais*'s 55 stanzas are personal, but allegorized. Some of *Rosalind and Helen* was suggested by a family friendship. This is all. It now seems necessary to ask: how is it that so reticent a poet has gained a reputation for emotional exhibitionism? Shelley's evolution into a lyricist was accidental. Like most poets, he bestowed, over the years, a few[15] complimentary or occasional verses on his intimates, less in the manner of a celebrity dispensing autographs than of an uncle covertly fishing out tips. They were private gifts, and Shelley often kept no copy. 'For Jane & Williams alone to see', he directed on the manuscript of *The*

Magnetic Lady, and 'Do not say it is mine to any one', on that of *Remembrance*; 'The enclosed must on no account be published' (*Letter to Maria Gisborne*); '– if you will tell no one *whose* they are' (*Lines on a Dead Violet*). Later, his widow tried to retrieve everything possible from his worksheets and acquaintances, and was able to publish about 110 short poems and fragments by 1840, when her second edition of the *Poetical Works* appeared. Many of Shelley's best-known lyrics now first emerged: the *Stanzas in Dejection, O world! O life! O time!, I fear thy kisses, When the lamp is shattered, Music when soft voices die, With a Guitar, to Jane*. Mary Shelley was right to print all she could find, but it meant salvaging the equivalents of doodles on the telephone-pad, such as *O Mary dear, that you were here*, as well as drafts whose illegibility made them half-incomprehensible, such as *Rough wind, that moanest loud*. This has not worried the critics much, who have rarely questioned a poem's origins or purpose, being content merely to find it exquisite or shoddy; some, indeed, outdoing Coleridge, profess to be given most pleasure by Shelley when he is not perfectly understandable. Swinburne hailed one half-completed line as 'a thing to thrill the veins and draw tears to the eyes of all men whose ears were not closed against all harmony',[16] and Donald Davie has found another nonsensical fragment manly and wholesome.[17] So Mary Shelley's conscience is partly responsible for the dogma that besides being trivial and self-obsessed, Shelley was negligent of grammar, syntax and logical structure, with an incapacity to punctuate verging on feeblemindedness.[18]

Yet although Shelley's negligence is axiomatic, it would not be easy to illustrate by anyone prepared to look into the transmission of his examples. As for self-obsession, Shelley withheld his lyrics from publication for the same reason that Samuel Johnson wrote his private poems in Latin: to keep them private. To treat these intimate verses ('you may read them to Jane, but to no one else, – and yet on second thoughts I had rather you would not') as if they were manifestoes is rather like breaking into a man's bathroom in order to censure his habit of indecent exposure. Still, the reminder that certain poems were printed without Shelley's consent is no defence of their quality. It did not help poor Midas that the secret of his ears was only whispered into a hole in the ground. What that reminder should do is inhibit any pronouncement on a given poem's qualities until the *nature* and *function* of the poem have been inquired into. A straightforward example, not a 'personal' one, is the *Bridal Song* or *Epithalamium* of 1821.[19]

Here the reader must first decide which of three 'versions' constitutes the poem. Close consideration will show that neither of the first two versions makes sense; however, as the poet is Shelley, it is perhaps begging the question to suggest that this throws doubt on their integrity. The 'third version' (Hutchinson tells us) derives from Shelley's holograph, and its use as a gloss makes the conjecture a pretty safe one that Versions One and Two represent the foul papers and a Bad Quarto respectively of the authentic Version Three. Nevertheless, one critic has thought it

admirable in its first version. In this first:

> O joy! O fear! what will be done
> In the absence of the sun!

– is as manly and wholesome as Suckling's *Ballad of a Wedding*. In the last version:

> O joy! O fear! there is not one
> Of us can guess what may be done
> In the absence of the sun . . .

– is just not true. And the familiar tone of 'Come along!' which securely anchors the first version, is merely silly in the others.[20]

The First Version begins by calling down sleep on the lovers in the middle of begetting a child, and goes on to advocate, among other things, what Lionel Trilling once memorably criticized in the Sexual Behaviour of the American Male ('Haste, swift Hour, and thy flight Oft renew'). Professor Davie's stricture on the Third Version bears hardly on Catullus, whose Epithalamium (62) was Shelley's model. Here is the text of the Third Version:

Boys Sing.   Night! with all thine eyes look down!
        Darkness! weep thy holiest dew!
    Never smiled the inconstant moon
        On a pair so true.
    Haste, coy hour! and quench all light,
    Lest eyes see their own delight!
    Haste, swift hour! and thy loved flight
        Oft renew!

Girls Sing.   Fairies, sprites, and angels, keep her!
        Holy stars! permit no wrong!
    And return, to wake the sleeper,
        Dawn, ere it be long!
    O joy! O fear! there is not one
    Of us can guess what may be done
    In the absence of the sun: –
        Come along!

Boys.   Oh! linger long, thou envious eastern lamp
        In the damp
            Caves of the deep!

Girls.   Nay, return, Vesper! urge thy lazy car!
        Swift unbar
            The gates of Sleep!

Chorus.   The golden gates of Sleep unbar,
        When Strength and Beauty, met together,
    Kindle their image, like a star
        In a sea of glassy weather.
    May the purple mist of love

> Round them rise, and with them move,
> Nourishing each tender gem
> Which, like flowers, will burst from them.
> As the fruit is to the tree
> May their children ever be.[21]

In a conventional Epithalamium, the desire and misgiving which both partners feel are polarized on to a reluctant bride, with her mock-modest virgin attendants, and an avid groom, incited by his troop of wanton boys. Catullus's girls ask, 'Hespere, qui caelo fertur crudelior ignis?', to which the boys retort, 'Hespere, qui caelo lucet jucundior ignis?' and later (still addressing Hesperus) comment:

> at libet innuptis ficto te carpere questu.
> quid tum si carpunt tacita quem mente requirunt? (36–7)

which Peter Whigham has rendered:

> for maidens' acts belie their mock complaints,
>   affecting aversion
>   for what they most desire[22]

Mock-trepidation, 'tender-whimpring-maids',[23] were essential to the ceremony. But the girls' feigned ignorance of what the lovers will do in bed is stressed here for an important reason. This was commissioned work, written for the climactic scene of a play, a wedding-banquet in a 'magnificent apartment' where wealth literally rivals nobility. To compare it with Suckling's mock-turnip *Ballad of a Wedding* is like comparing a State funeral with Finnegan's wake. The plot is that of Novel ix from the tenth day of the *Decameron*, and concerns a Pavian wife's promise to wait a year, a month and a day after her husband's departure to the Crusade before remarrying. The time having expired, she unwillingly consents to marry a former suitor; but after the ceremony her consort reappears, the new bridegroom renounces this claim, and the play ends in amity. The girls' declaration, therefore, that not one of them can guess what may be done in the absence of the sun just *is* true: contrary to every expectation, *nothing* will be done – not, at any rate, by those newly licensed to do it. How the 'tone' of a poem can be so confidently criticized without the slightest interest in that poem's provenance or purpose is a mystery darker than Hymen's.

The first line presents in one immediate image the antiphonal unity which structures the poem: the sociable stars are invited to watch the lovers with the *voyeur* relish of the males who are singing, but also with the bashful, downcast gaze of the bride. The lovers are to be seen and unseen at once, hidden in darkness under the eyes of stars, moon, and one another; for this is a supremely social and an intensely private occasion. The weeping of 'holiest dew' suggests both the modest sanctity of the encounter and its fruitful sensuality,[24] and although the darkness weeps, the moon smiles. These opposites re-echo in the two invocations to the hour of union, a *coy* hour from one viewpoint, moonless 'lest eyes see their own delight' (i.e., lest each is abashed to see his own pleasure mirrored on the other's eyes: a variant of Blake), a *swift* hour from the other viewpoint, transient yet renewable like the moon – and an hour which, after all, both sides want to hasten on. The girls' opening appeal, made jointly to fairies and angels, indicates (like Shelley's word *phryghte* written playfully above the text) just how serious it all really is.

As in Catullus, the verbal dance now brings boys and girls into direct opposition. The planet Venus, whose setting as Hesperus and rising as Phosphorus symbolizes the bedding and rising of a married couple, is besought by the boys to stay hidden so as to lengthen the night, by the girls to return quickly and allow the bride to sleep. Unbarring the gates of sleep – admitting the lovers to their ultimate peace – deftly completes the ceremony whose public end was the shutting of the bedroom door. Finally, both sides drop their feigned postures to join in the traditional invocation for fruitfulness in the marriage: the lovers are to sleep only after duplicating their qualities in a child, as the 'wished starre' of love itself is mirrored in a calm sea.

The sea image enters in because it is from across the Mediterranean that 'glassy weather' is even now returning in the person of Adalette's true husband; while the meeting of 'Strength and Beauty' reminds us ironically of the unauthorieed union of Mars and Venus, caught in the act by Venus's true husband and exposed to the laughter of the assembled gods. 'Golden' gates of sleep and 'purple' mist of love sound like poeticisms, but even the make-up matches: these were the colours of the god Hymen, *croceo velatus amictu*, and 'purple' was used atmospherically, in both classical and English epithalamia, of the bliss environing a bridal.[25] The poem is concise, shapely, precisely pointed; mindful of its lineage yet perfectly attuned to its own dramatic purpose. No one would call it an important poem, least of all its author, yet it is almost faultless of its kind, a first-rate piece of craftsmanship.

The kind is not easy to define. It might be called a dramatic imitation into the spirit of which the poet enters with such deceptive wholeness that the pretence – the gap between the playfulness of the role and the absorbed gravity of the manner – constitutes an uncommon sort of poetic wit. A splendid example of this wit is the maligned *Indian Serenade*. Shelley did not publish this poem either, but the titles of all the existing versions of it stress that it is *Indian* and for *singing*. It was in fact composed to be sung by Sophia Stacey,[26] and it is a dramatic imitation of an Oriental love-song, not just in atmosphere, the potency of which has always been recognizzd, but in its entirety. A proper imitation of the mode represented by the following lines required emotional abandonment:

> My cries pierce the heavens!
> My eyes are without sleep!
> Turn to me, Sultana – let me gaze on thy beauty.
>
> Adieu! I go down to the grave.
> If you call me I return.
> My heart is hot as sulphur; – sigh, and it will flame.

> Crown of my life! fair light of my eyes!
>   My Sultana! my princess!
> I rub my face against the earth; – I am drown'd in
>   scalding tears – I rave!
> Have you no compassion? Will you not turn to look
>   upon me?[27]

It is a very physical as well as a very evocative poem (five parts of the body are named); its subject is a passionate assignation in which a dream is about to be made flesh and the languishing bodily senses are to be revived by physical love as rain revives the grass. By a hyperbole familiar also in Elizabethan poetry, wind, magnolia-blossom and birdsong, faint, fail and die respectively in contiguity with the beloved; then the singer herself capitulates with them ('As I must die on thine'). Her own person embodies the senses by which she perceives these lesser delights: touch (the wind on the stream), smell (the champaca), hearing (the nightingale); but her senses are ungratified, she is a songless nightingale, a perfume without scent, a wind without motion ('*I* die! *I* faint! *I* fail!'). Her recent love-dream is melting like the champaca's odour, with nothing substantial to take its place. Only the beloved's response will save her, as the effect of 'rain' on 'grass' lifts the cloying languor of the night; and three lines from the end the loud, anticipatory heartbeats of the lover echo and replace the low breathing of the sleeping winds three lines from the beginning.

The lover in the Turkish poem quoted was a male; Shelley's song could fit either sex, but the draft of line 11, 'the odours of my chaplet fail', shows that his singer is a girl.[28] The title on a manuscript auctioned in 1960, 'The Indian girl's song', confirms what should have been obvious.

This, too, is perfect of its kind. Its imaginative structure is taut and sound, its atmospheric versatility astonishing. Its loving exaggeration, its total absorption in a dramatic pretence, give it some of the qualities of brilliant parody, yet it is no parody. *Craftsmanship* is again the only single word to fit it. As an expression of its author's personality and feelings it is of about the same order as *Gerontion*, or *Gretchen am Spinnrade*.

A companion piece is *From the Arabic: An Imitation* (again unpublished) which according to Medwin was 'almost a translation from a translation',[29] in Terrick Hamilton's Arab romance *Antar* (1819–20). But *Antar* is male-orientated, with a hero as stupendously virile as Kilhwch in the *Mabinogion*, whereas Shelley's poem takes the Arab woman's point of view, and amounts to a critique of that novel's values. Such a capacity for adopting the female viewpoint, uncommon in male lyric poets, suggests that others among Shelley's lyrics might repay reexamination. The final stanza of *Remembrance* ('Swifter far than summer's flight') begins

> Lilies for a bridal bed –
> Roses for a matron's head –
> Violets for a maiden dead –
>   Pansies let *my* flowers be: (Hutchinson, p. 718)

Mary Shelley's remorseful letter after Shelley's death has helped to put readers on the wrong track. 'In a little poem of his are these words – *pansies let my flowers be* . . . so I would make myself a locket to wear in eternal memory with the representation of his flower . . .'[30] But in the poem the three flowers, seasons, and birds correspond to three conditions of female life, bride, wife, and spinster; the series, therefore, *cannot* culminate in a male poet. 'Pansies', plainly, are the symbol-flowers of a deserted mistress. One possible way round is to assert that in that case the deserted mistress must be Shelley, in the manner of the character in *Alice* who argued that little girls must be a kind of serpent; alternatively, that although his *personae* are distinct from their creator, their attitudes and verbal habits are not. Both arguments are unpromising. For instance, the lyric posthumously entitled *Mutability* ('The flower that smiles today Tomorrow dies') has seemed a typical expression of Shelley's disillusioned idealism:

> Whilst skies are blue and bright,
>   Whilst flowers are gay,
> Whilst eyes that change ere night
>   Make glad the day;
> Whilst yet the calm hours creep,
> Dream thou – and from thy sleep
> Then wake to weep. (Hutchinson, pp. 640–1)

'Earthly pleasures are delusive – like me, Shelley, you will have
a bitter awakening.' But the poem was evidently written for the
opening of *Hellas*,[31] to be sung by a favourite slave, who loves
him, to the literally sleeping Mahmud before he awakens to
find his imperial pleasures slipping from his grasp. This puts the
naivety of the sentiment in an unexpected light. Far from voic-
ing a self-pitying bitterness, the poem is really an ironical en-
dorsement, with qualifications, of Mahmud's reversal of fortune.
The qualifications arise from the personal loyalty of the slave
to her tyrant master, which complicates the irony of the lament
and tempers our gladness at his downfall. Something similar was
attempted in *Laon and Cythna*, where the only being who showed
any love for the deposed Othman was his child by the slave he
had violated (v xxi–xxx).

The dramatic impulse was at least as strong in Shelley as the
lyrical, and the two were often inseparable. An especially interesting puzzle is set by yet another posthumous lyric, *When the
lamp is shattered*. Besides a draft, there are two known manuscripts,
including one given to Jane Williams (now in the University
Library, Glasgow). This is the only one of the nine poems given
to her which is without title or dedication at any known stage of
its existence, and her copy has one other curious feature. Between
the first pair of stanzas and what would have been (if the final
stanza were not missing)[32] the second pair, the words 'second
part' appear, in Shelley's hand. What can this mean?

The draft throws some light. *When the lamp is shattered* was undoubtedly written for the *Unfinished Drama* of early 1822, and
is closely related to the lyric printed at the opening of that play,

in modern editions. In these editions[33] the drama opens 'before
the Cavern of the Indian Enchantress', who sings:

> He came like a dream in the dawn of life,
>   He fled like a shadow before its noon;
> He is gone, and my peace is turned to strife,
>   And I wander and wane like the weary moon.
>   O sweet Echo, wake,
>   And for my sake
> Make answer the while my heart shall break!
>
> But my heart has a music which Echo's lips,
>   Though tender and true, yet can answer not,
> And the shadow that moves in the soul's eclipse
>   Can return not the kiss by his now forgot;
>   Sweet lips! he who hath
>   On my desolate path
> Cast the darkness of absence, worse than death!

(Hutchinson, pp. 482–3)

All that is known about the *Unfinished Drama* comes from Mrs
Shelley's headnotes. Undertaken, she says, 'for the amusement
of the individuals who composed our intimate society', its plot
concerned an Enchantress on an Indian island who lures a
pirate, 'a man of savage but noble nature', away from his
mortal lover. 'A good Spirit, who watches over the Pirate's fate,
leads, in a mysterious manner, the lady of his love to the
Enchanted Isle. She is accompanied by a Youth, who loves the
lady, but whose passion she returns only with a sisterly affection.'
The text, some of which is unpublished, does imply a kind of
lovers' chain, similar to that in Moschus's Idyl VI, or in
Andromaque. Diagrammatically it seems to go: Indian girl A,
deserted by Pirate lover (or husband) B, leaves admirer E and
on a magic island meets (not accompanies) boy C, who himself
has been deserted by girl D (the Enchantress?). Presumably B
and D began this merry-go-round for the sake of each other,
and presumably all would have returned in the end to the

original truce-lines.[34] Despite the bittersweet atmosphere of *Faust* and *The Tempest* that haunts the context of *When the lamp is shattered,* and may originate in the poet's own situation, it is ludicrous to treat a song written for private theatricals as if it were the cry of Shelley to his own soul. Not the major love-poets but the minor dramatists, Lyly, Fletcher and the masque-writers, are in its line of descent.

The notation 'second part' could have been intended in a semi-musical sense, of a dialogue in which a second voice takes up and answers the first. The imagery changes abruptly in the 'second part', though both pairs of stanzas share a basic idea: in part one, lamp, cloud, lute and lips with their 'contents', the hollow heart, the empty cell, the lifeless corpse; in part two, the nest with its winged occupant, the heart as cradle, home and bier, the raftered eyrie, the naked refuge. Because of the idea common to all these, Professor Pottle's attractive defence of 'The light in the dust lies dead', as meaning that the light reflected from the physical environment (the 'light-in-the-dust') stops shining when the source goes out,[35] seems narrowly to miss the mark. Rather, the light is inseparable from the 'dust' of which the physical lamp is composed, and perishes with it; the glory of the rainbow *is* the cloud, and is 'shed' with the cloud's waterdrops; music and the lute are annihilated together.[36] The heart cannot sing – respond emotionally – when the signal to which it resonates, the spirit of love, is 'mute'; it can only echo, passively and hollowly the noises of wind and water. All these light-and-dust images are analogues of the 'good Spirit's' lodgement at the earth's centre. He is contained in the reality he energizes, as radiance in the lamp, as music in the lute, as words between the lips:

> Within the silent centre of the earth
> My mansion is; where I have lived insphered
> From the beginning, and around my sleep
> Have woven all the wondrous imagery
> Of this dim spot, which mortals call the world; (15–19)

A cancelled stage-direction hesitates whether to call this Spirit 'Love', but he was evidently to be the Prospero of the island, moving its affairs to the kindliest end.

The whole poem is about the loss of love, and if part one laments that when the physical embodiment is lacking, the essence disappears, part two seems to retort that if the essence is lacking, the physical embodiment disintegrates. It is tempting to guess that the two halves of the poem were intended for the Enchantress and the Lady respectively. This would account for the domestic imagery of the second part, while the ruined cell and the knell for the dead seaman are proper 'currency values' for an Indian Lampedusa on whose shores a pirate-lover has probably been wrecked.

The first word of part two is not 'When' but 'Where', so these two lines are a simple inversion: Love leaves the nest where hearts once mingled. It has been asked, In what form are we to imagine Love doing this? To answer, In the form of Love, seems irreverent, but the episode of Cupid and Psyche in Apuleius's *Metamorphoses*, which Shelley much admired, had clearly some influence on this poem.[37] By *first* leaving the nest, the winged form of Love suggest also a fledgling (genuine love is a result as well as a cause of 'mingling'). This stresses the contrasting images of raven and eagle, because the raven was supposed to evict its young from the nest and abandon them, whereas the eagle is famous for the care it takes of its own young. Golden eagles, as Shelley would know, mate for life, and their nest is permanent, literally cradle, home and bier.

'The weak one is singled' of course has nothing to do with the sad lot of woman; 'the weak one' is the weak heart, and applies to either sex. The paradoxes (*one* is *singled*, the *weak* one must *endure*), and the pun (*singled*, 'picked on', 'divorced'), lead to the ambiguities of 'To endure what it once possessed', which could have secondary meanings of 'to make indifferent that which it once fascinated', and 'to imprison what it once owned by right', and to the major paradox that 'Love' is now confronted with:

why does one who laments 'frailty', transience, choose to nest in 'the frailest of all things', the human heart?

The change of pronoun in the final stanza implies that the speaker has turned to address a human, or superhuman, rival. 'Its passions' (the passions of the heart) will rock 'thee', she says, and reason will only give you clarity without comfort, like the sun in winter. And the epithet 'naked' returns to the hint of the fledgling, the product of love's union, not now in voluntary flight but evicted, defenceless, and – perhaps deservedly – laughable.

The parent play is so sketchy that any detailed account of *When the lamp is shattered* can only be very conjectural. What is essential is to begin with the right questions: what *is* this poem, what was it for? Once the dramatic function is recognized, tone, imagery, emotional mode take on appropriate significances; even if the poem is moving it is not self-expression but artifice, creative play. Shelley's lyrics deserve a fresh – and a more responsible – critical look.

SOURCE: 'Shelley's Lyrics', in *The Morality of Art: Essays Presented to G. Wilson Knight by his Colleagues and Friends*, ed. D. W. Jefferson (London, 1969) pp. 195–209.

NOTES

1. *The Letters of Percy Bysshe Shelley*, ed. F. L. Jones (Oxford, 1964) II 310.
2. *Letters*, II 189.
3. D. Masson, *Wordsworth, Shelley, Keats and other Essays* (London, 1875) p. 129.
4. E. Chesser, *Shelley and Zastrozzi: self-revelation of a neurotic* (Farnborough, 1965) p. 29.
5. By 'personal' lyrics, I intend (*a*) short poems that name names ('What would cure, that would kill me, Jane'), and (*b*) poems that seem recognizably biographical ('Her voice did quiver as we parted'). (*b*) is, however, a very unsafe category.
6. D. Reiman, 'Structure, Symbol and Theme in *Lines written*

among the Euganean Hills', *PMLA*, LXXVII (September 1962) 404–13.

7. 'There is no justification for the frequent definition of the Sensitive Plant as Shelley saw himself or as a special category of man, such as the Poet . . . The Garden . . . is the total animate universe as it is experienced by man, the Sensitive Plant.' (E. R. Wassermann, *The Subtler Language* (Baltimore, 1959) pp. 257–8).

8. *Letters*, II 434.

9. *Letters*, II 246.

10. *Blackwood's Edinburgh Magazine*, II (February 1822) 238; Ollier to Mary Shelley, 17 November 1823, *Shelley and Mary*, IV 990–1.

11. *Letters*, II 306.

12. *Conversations of Lord Byron* (London, 1824; reprinted N.J.: Princeton U.P., 1966) p. 314 n.

13. *Letters*, II 396.

14. Some of the relevant stanzas are nos I–III, XII–XIV, printed on pp. 37–8, 42–3.of *Verse and Prose from the MSS*, ed. Shelley-Rolls and Ingpen (London, 1934).

15. Cold statistics are again helpful. From 1816, Shelley is known to have given one poem to Clair Clairmont, and (probably) to Emilia Viviani; two to the Hunts; three to the Gisbornes; four to his wife; six to Sophia Stacey; and ten to the Williamses – twenty-seven altogether in six years. Two of these were not lyrics, and five others were commissioned contributions to plays.

16. A. C. Swinburne, *Essays and Studies* (London, 1876) pp. 229–30.

17. D. Davie, 'Shelley's Urbanity' (1952) [reproduced in this Casebook – Ed.].

18. One experienced modern editor still maintains (*Keats–Shelley Memorial Bulletin*, XVII, 1966, pp. 20–30) that in a fully representative passage (essentially *Prometheus Unbound*, III iii 49–62) Shelley's punctuation corrupts the sense. The reader is given no chance to judge the MS. punctuation for himself (Bod. MS. Shelley e. 3, f. 21v), which in my view is careful, intelligible and better than Hutchinson's. Bridges's punctilious tinkerings make good sense too, but not quite Shelley's.

19. *The Complete Poetical Works*, ed. T. Hutchinson (Oxford, 1945) pp. 646–7.

20. 'Shelley's Urbanity' [reproduced in this Casebook – Ed.]. Professor Davie has repudiated this essay (*New Statesman*, 27 November 1964, p. 840). But the dyslogistic passages, I take it, are still part of his faith.

21. Text from Hutchinson, p. 723, with the singular 'gate' corrected in line 23.

22. P. Whigham, *The Poems of Catullus* (Penguin Classics, 1966) p. 133.

23. Herrick, *A Nuptiall Song on Sir Clipseby Crew and his Lady*, line 91.

24. Compare Herrick:

> These precious-pearly-purling tears
> But spring from ceremonious fears . . .
> O! give them [the lovers] active heat
> And moisture, both compleat:
>
> (*An Epithalamie to Sir Thomas Southwell and his Ladie*)

25. E.g., at the official wedding of Cupid and Psyche in Apuleius, *Met.* VI xxiv, 'Horae rosis et ceteris floribus purpurabant omnia'.

26. C. S. Catty, 'Shelley's *I arise from dreams of thee* and Miss Sophia Stacey', *Athenaeum*, no. 4199 (18 April 1908) 478.

27. Turkish lines translated literally in Lady Mary Wortley Montagu's letter of 1 April 1717.

28. Bod. MS. Shelley adds. e.7, f. 153.

> 'The strong aromatic scent of the gold-coloured *Champac* is thought offensive to the bees . . . but their elegant appearance on the black hair of the *Indian* women is mentioned by RUMPHIUS; and both facts have supplied the *Sanscrit* poets with elegant allusions.' (Sir William Jones, *Works*, 1807, V 129).

29. *Life of Shelley*, ed. H. B. Forman (Oxford, 1913) p. 351.

30. *The Letters of Mary W. Shelley*, ed. F. L. Jones (Univ. of Oklahoma Press, 1947) I 176–7.

31. Bod. MS. Shelley adds e.7, cover ff. 1–2, 154. Compare the song actually adopted in the play:

> . . . could my prayers avail,
> All my joy should be
> Dead, and I would live to weep,
> So thou mightst win one hour of quiet sleep. (22–6)

32. The final stanza must have existed once, as this text was the

source of Medwin's memorial piracy in his *Ahasuerus, the Wanderer* (1823).

33. Beginning with *The Poetical Works* (1839) IV 168. The *Posthumous Poems* text has no stage-direction or notes (neither has the draft from which all texts of the play are derived).

34. The rehearsals of *Lover's Vows* should warn us that the proposed casting is unlikely to have reflected real alignments, wished or existing. Working backwards from the most tactful final combination we might get: A = Jane Williams, B = Trelawny, C = Edward Williams, D = Mary Shelley, E = Shelley. Shelley, unattached, could thus take the part of the Spirit, fitting in with the role he gave himself in *With a Guitar, To Jane*.

35. F. A. Pottle, 'The Case of Shelley' (1952) [reproduced in this Casebook – Ed.].

36. 'The common observer . . . contends in vain against the persuasion of the grave, that the dead indeed cease to be. . . . The organs of sense are destroyed, and the intellectual operations dependent on them have perished with their sources. . . . When you can discover where the fresh colours of the fading flower abide, or the music of the broken lyre, seek life among the dead.' ('Essay on a Future State', *Essays, Letters from Abroad* . . . , ed. Mrs Shelley, 1840, 1234–5.)

37. Cupid and Psyche are happily married, mingling nightly in a love-nest built by Cupid himself, with ivory rafters; Psyche entertains her treacherous sisters with lute and song; a spilt lamp is the cause of Cupid's flight (in Mrs Tighe's well-known version the lamp is shattered: '. . . from her trembling hand extinguished falls the fatal lamp'); he leaves Psyche's bed as a feathered god every morning, and at last deserts it for good; Psyche is then exposed, half-naked, to Venus's mocking laughter and is tormented by the passions of Anxiety and Sorrow; but in the end the lovers are reunited – as no doubt they were in Shelley's play.

Judith Chernaik

THE MAGIC CIRCLE:
POEMS TO JANE WILLIAMS (1972)

The poems to Jane Williams were written in the winter and spring of 1822,[1] when the intimacy between Shelley and Jane and Williams was too close, perhaps, to sustain the easy friendship in which it had begun. Since October the two families had lived on separate floors of the same house on the Lung'Arno, in Pisa; in early May, Shelley and Mary moved to Casa Magni for the summer, and Jane and Williams moved in as their temporary guests[2] – a living arrangement fraught with danger when one couple is reasonably happy and the other miserable. For Mary was pregnant and ill; she loathed the isolation and discomfort of the house and hated the sea, and Shelley was unable to break through her misery. He was driven despite his sympathy for her to suspect that her coldness signified not only that she was unhappy but that she no longer loved him. The poems to Jane were to be kept from Mary's eyes (they are headed: 'For Jane and Williams alone to see'; 'Not to be opened unless you are alone' – and to Williams: 'If any of the stanzas should please you, you may read them to Jane, but to no one else');[3] and their implied or explicit subject is not only the delight the poet takes in Jane's singing, or her hand on his forehead, but his embittered 'life and love', his 'cold home'. Jane appears to have had none of Mary's intellectual or Emilia Viviani's spiritual refinement; Shelley must have been drawn to her at least in part because she and Williams were devoted to each other. This meant that she could be kind to Shelley in a disinterested way (a 'friend'), and that she could never be his – ideal circumstances, in a way, for Shelley, and thus celebrated

and lamented in the poems. By July he was in love with Jane –
guilty enough in imagination, at least, to write in the last letter
Mary was to receive from him, four days before he sailed for
Leghorn: 'You have no idea how I am hurried & occupied – I
have not a moments leisure – but will write by next post –'
(*Letters of P.B.S.*, II 444), and immediately afterward, to Jane:
'[I] shall urge [Williams] to sail with the first fair wind without
expecting me. I have thus the pleasure of contributing to your
happiness when deprived of every other – and of leaving you
no other subject of regret, but the absence of one scarcely worth
regretting . . . Adieu, my dearest friend – I only write these lines
for the pleasure of tracing what will meet your eyes . . .' (*Letters
of P.B.S.*, II 445).

The poems to Jane . . . are the most intimate as well as the
most charming of Shelley's love poems. In them he breaks away
from the brief lyric form, with its simplifications, into sustained
analysis of the themes that dominate all the late lyrics: the
perversity of human desire, its illogic and self-destructiveness,
the illusory and fragile nature of happiness and love, the conflict
between reason and desire, between desire and obligation. It is
unlikely that Shelley would ever have turned away completely
from political and prophetic poetry; but these poems, representing as they do his last work, suggest the deepening pessimism of
his vision of life. For poetry in these lyrics has nothing to do
with changing the world, nor does it impinge on the larger
world in any way; it is rather a means of cherishing the moment
of happiness, of celebrating and perhaps immortalizing 'one
moment's good' after long pain.

The social context of the poems is drawn in a letter Shelley
wrote to John Gisborne:

I like Jane more and more, and I find Williams the most amiable of
companions. She has a taste for music, and an elegance of form and
motions that compensate in some degree for the lack of literary
refinement. Mrs. Gisborne knows my gross ideas of music, and will
forgive me when I say that I listen the whole evening on our terrace
to the simple melodies with excessive delight. I have a boat here

... Williams is captain, and we drive along this delightful bay in the
evening wind, under the summer moon, until earth appears another
world. Jane brings her guitar, and if the past and future could be
obliterated, the present would content me so well that I could say
with Faust to the passing moment 'Remain, thou art so beautiful'.
(Letter of 18 June 1822, Letters of P.B.S., II 435–6)

The poet's momentary happiness, his general unhappiness, the
fact, more or less apparent to him, that he was falling in love
with Jane – these are the materials of the poems, their ostensible
occasion and subject. They analyze complicated adult relationships; above all they demonstrate the poet's insight into his own
nature, his acute sense of the personal necessities that made it
imperative for him to tame his ardor, not to 'break his chain'.
Yet the privacy of actual lives is protected, the personal details
disguised (especially those having to do with Mary), even as the
emotions they cause in the poet are analyzed. In their subtlety,
the poems reveal a quality of Shelley's mind he hints at with
reference to his strained relations with Byron: 'What is passing
in the heart of another rarely escapes the observation of one who
is a strict anatomist of his own' (*Letters of P.B.S.*, II 324).

The Magnetic Lady to her Patient is frank in its portrait of the
relationship between Jane and Shelley. Jane is made to say at
least three or four times that she pities Shelley but cannot love
him, that her role is that of friend and physician, not of
mistress. The explicitness of the poem (she reminds him at the
outset of her own happy relationship with Williams) is part of
its charm, the tone of affectionate raillery and wholly disinterested tenderness. The patient's ills are the same as those which
plague the poet of *Stanzas written in Dejection* – 'lost health',
'the world's dull scorn' – but they are validated by the fact that
it is not the poet but the Lady who names them. The cure, again,
is forgetfulness, but the self-pity of the earlier poem ('I could lie
down like a tired child') is modified by the poet's awareness of
the several players in the drama, not only Jane and himself but
Edward and Mary.

The occasion of the poem – Jane practicing hypnotism on the

ailing poet – becomes a metaphor for their relationship, both
for what Jane insists that it be, and for what he would like it to
become. The metaphor of love as a sickness, the mistress as
physician, is one of the oldest staples of love poetry, and it is a
function of the poem's wit to raise possibilities even as their
implications are denied. In hypnotism the subject is laid to
sleep and forgetfulness induced; when he is entirely receptive,
a new spirit is infused into him. In this last stage, the physician–
patient relationship is easily confused with that of mistress and
lover: 'By mine thy being is to its deep/Possest' (35–6).

The entry of the hypnotist's spirit into the subject suggests
unmistakably the spiritual or physical union of love, a thought
which no doubt the poet briefly, wistfully, entertains, before he
descends to earth:

> 'The spell is done – how feel you now?'
>   'Better, quite well' replied
>   The sleeper – 'What would do
> You good when suffering and awake,
>   What cure your head and side?'
> 'What would cure that would kill me, Jane,
> And as I must on earth abide
> Awhile yet, tempt me not to break
>   My chain.'   (37–45)

The effect of the stanza lies in the shift from Jane's concern to
the poet's oblique play on her words: 'What would cure that
would kill me, Jane.' As her frankness comes from a free heart,
his allusiveness, in the form of pun and metaphor, comes from
the knowledge of burdens he cannot shake off. The 'chain' he
must not break is the chain of life; also, undoubtedly, it is the
chain of his marriage.

The keen stars were twinkling is a poetic rendering of the experience Shelley describes in the letter to Gisborne: 'we drive along
this delightful bay in the evening wind, under the summer
moon, until earth appears another world.' The poem concen-

trates upon the presentness of the scene, even though the poet's delight has its source in something more, the yearning for 'some world far from ours'. The lyric is reminiscent of *To Constantia*, both in its occasion and in the relationship suggested between song and feeling, between the singer and the instrument. In both lyrics the erotic component is submerged; the emphasis is on the power of song to move the spirit to delight and to transport the hearer to another world. But the later lyric is more personal and circumstantial, not an extended analysis of the experience, like *To Constantia*, but a musical imitation of it.

The structure of the poem depends on the analogy between the moon, which gives splendor to the stars, and Jane's voice, which gives life to the guitar's soulless notes. Each stanza interweaves the same terms – keen stars, fair moon, sweet tones – until they are given final shape in the last lines:

> Though the sound overpowers
> Sing again, with your dear voice revealing
> A tone
> Of some world far from ours,
> Where music and moonlight and feeling
> Are one. (19–24)

The present scene, the rising moon, the stars, the guitar, Jane's life-giving presence – all are turned into an emblem of the poet's desire for love and harmony and his sense that although the elements are present, a particular human magnetism is needed to bring them into relationship. The stanza, with its ingenious verbal and metrical patterning, its rhythmical pauses, is an imitation of the song Jane might have played (as Shelley's description of it, 'words for an ariette', suggests); the syncopated rhythm approximates the pattern of a voice singing against strummed chords. The stress pattern compels one to read with 'rests' included, so that the short lines are isolated: 'Tonight'; 'Delight'; 'A tone'; 'Are one'. In the final lines, the three

stresses, which summarize the three elements of the
scene, 'music and moonlight and feeling', literally become
'one'.

The remaining three poems inscribed to Jane are essays in
light tetrameter couplets, conversational in tone, intimate,
analytic. Each poem idealizes Jane, partly as a compliment to
her peculiar grace and serenity, partly in response to the poet's
needs, to which Jane is merely an accessory. For in these poems
Jane, the 'spirit of peace in our circle of tempests', is identified
with the harmonizing and life-giving spirit described in *The Zucca*,
that which the poet, or in the allegorical framework of the poem,
the human soul, desires beyond all else. It is this spirit which the
poet or lover adores –

> In winds, and trees, and streams, and all things common,
>   In music and the sweet unconscious tone
> Of animals, and voices which are human . . .
> In the soft motions and rare smile of woman,
>   In flowers and leaves, and in the grass fresh-shown
>
>   (*The Zucca*, 33–5, 37–8)

– and whose sudden and unpreventable flight he laments, since
he cannot follow after.

With a Guitar represents the happiest side of this spring interlude. It has the overtones of social intercourse, the affectionate
nicknaming and play-acting in which the Shelley circle always
indulged (and which Shelley alludes to in the last section of
Epipsychidion). Its theme, like that of *The keen stars were twinkling*,
is the happy union of love, music, poetry, nature.

The opening section imagines the group of friends as immortal spirits temporarily imprisoned in their present bodies.
Jane and Edward are Miranda and Ferdinand (ideal love)
Shelley is Ariel (their guardian spirit, devoted servant, agent of
poetry), and Mary, one is tempted to say, is 'the silent Moon/
In her interlunar swoon', sadness personified. True to the
fiction, Miranda and Ferdinand are quite unaware of Ariel's

long service, of which he must gently remind them; this is his excuse for the long introduction, with its ingenuous declaration of 'more than ever can be spoken'.

The second part of the poem turns to the guitar itself, which, in a kind of mirror image to the opening fiction (Ariel, we remember, was imprisoned for twelve years in a pine), is seen as the second and happier life of a tree. To those who know how to question it, the guitar will reveal the secrets of nature and the oracles it conceals:

> For it had learnt all harmonies
> Of the plains and of the skies,
> Of the forests and the mountains,
> And the many-voiced fountains,
> The clearest echoes of the hills,
> The softest notes of falling rills,
> The melodies of birds and bees,
> The murmuring of summer seas,
> And pattering rain and breathing dew
> And airs of evening; – and it knew
> That seldom heard mysterious sound,
> Which, driven on its diurnal round
> As it floats through boundless day
> Our world enkindles on its way –   (65–78)

The natural world is conceived in terms of its sounds – many-voiced fountains, echoes, pattering rain; these merge naturally into the sounds of the guitar, which both echoes and interprets natural sound. The pastoral survey, like that in *Lines written among the Euganean Hills*, climaxes in the intuition of a transcendent principle of unity or harmony, a 'mysterious sound' (like the 'soul of all' or the inconstant Spirit of Intellectual Beauty), which, though seldom heard, can be divined or sensed through its analogy with that which can be heard. The poem ends with what amounts to a definition of poetry or art, lighter in tone than those in *A Defence of Poetry* but in agreement with Shelley's

general insistence on 'the wise heart' and the 'mind's imaginings' as the ultimate source of love, beauty, and truth:

> All this it knows, but will not tell
> To those who cannot question well
> The spirit that inhabits it:
> It talks according to the wit
> Of its companions; and no more
> Is heard than has been felt before
> By those who tempt it to betray
> These secrets of an elder day.   (79–86)[4]

Nature and natural mythology on the one hand, the grace and
intuitive feeling of the pure spirit on the other – these remain
Shelley's absolutes. The tribute Shelley pays them in this poem
balances the sadness of other poems of this time, the despair of
When the lamp is shattered, the recurrent lament for the loss of
love and happiness.

The companion poems *The Invitation* and *The Recollection* are
perceptibly the work of the author of *Lines written among the
Euganean Hills*. Again the poet's mood is described in relation
to a scene lovingly and accurately set down, to which he is intensely responsive and yet which serves to establish beyond all
question his isolation from nature. In the poems to Jane, unlike
Lines written among the Euganean Hills, other persons figure in the
poet's thoughts: the woman he is falling in love with, whom he
identifies with all that is happy, free and life-giving, and his
wife, who has come to be associated only with 'low-thoughted
care', past tragedy, the poet's inescapable responsibilities. While
the poet concentrates on the image of his own happiness or
grief – the day, the scene – the human relationships in the
background, barely hinted at, color all that he says. In addition
to the human quality of these lyrics, their tenderness and nos-
talgia of tone, we notice as in all the late lyrics the quiet dis-
appearance of apocalyptic hope, the ambition to change the

world. The pine forest in the Cascine and the day spent there
provide just such a 'green isle' in the sea of agony as the day the
poet spends in the Euganean Hills, but his modest joy in it –
'To-day is for itself enough' – does not radically alter his initial
pessimism; he has no hopes of permanent relief, change or
transcendence. For in these poems the poet's personal distress
takes the form of a stoicism most closely akin to that of Keats's
great Odes. From a world of care and sorrow the poet imagin-
atively enters a closed and secret and delightful world, of nature,
art or love, from which he must at last return, tolled back to his
'sole self'. The psychological and artistic movement of the poems
is similar to Keats's characteristic procedure. The poet first
holds the image of perfection in his mind – for Keats the song of
the bird, the Greek urn, for Shelley the hour spent in the forest
with Jane – then, through the process of imagining it, he appears
to be physically absorbed into its reality, which becomes exclus-
ive and absolute: 'Already with thee! tender is the night . . .' But
as the intensity of the imagined moment fades, as the song of the
nightingale recedes over the hills, the vision dissolves, and the
world's reality breaks in upon the poet with the return of his
self-consciousness.

 The Invitation is organized, like *Lines written among the Euganean
Hills*, on an extended analogy between the physical rhythms of
nature and the emotional rhythms of human life. The fair day,
unexpectedly breaking into the winter, come to smile at the
'rough Year', is sister to the fair Jane, come miraculously to
ease the poet's sorrow:

> Best and brightest, come away –
> Fairer far than this fair day
> Which like thee to those in sorrow
> Comes to bid a sweet good-morrow
> To the rough year just awake
> In its cradle on the brake.   (1–6)

The poet offers a pseudo-mythological genealogy for the sweet morning, which draws closer and closer to the thought of the ministering Magnetic Lady, until the analogy is made explicit:

> The brightest hour of unborn spring
> Through the winter wandering
> Found, it seems, the halcyon morn
> To hoar February born;
> Bending from Heaven in azure mirth
> It kissed the forehead of the earth
> And smiled upon the silent sea,
> And bade the frozen streams be free
> And waked to music all their fountains
> And breathed upon the frozen mountains
> And like a prophetess of May
> Strewed flowers upon the barren way,
> Making the wintry world appear
> Like one on whom thou smilest, dear.   (7–20)

The analogy between the frozen earth, wintry and barren, and the desolate state of the poet leads to the second analogy, between the nature of the day – a rare halcyon day in February, with winter soon closing in again – and the nature of the poet's experience, a brief moment of peace and happy forgetfulness interrupting cares to which he must return. Given this simple framework, it is easy to see why the poem should be so modest in scope compared to *Lines written among the Euganean Hills*, where the terms are on the one hand the physical vista of all Italy, its cities islanded in the fair plains, on the other a metaphor for the human condition, green isles of happiness in a sea of agony. The tone reflects the difference in scope; Shelley turns next to a confession Cowperesque in its modesty and humour, its defiance of the 'accustomed' demons. Yet the poetic sensibility is the same as that of *Stanzas written in Dejection, Invocation to Misery*, and *Song*: ('Rarely, rarely comest thou'):

Hope, in pity mock not woe
With smiles, nor follow where I go;
Long having lived on thy sweet food,
At length I find one moment's good
After long pain –   (41–5)

The Invitation ends with a brief description of the 'wild woods and the plains' reminiscent of the noon moment described in *Lines written among the Euganean Hills.* But in *The Invitation* the description is limited to the physical scene, and the felt unity is an appearance, momentary and fragile:

Where the earth and ocean meet,
And all things seem only one
In the universal Sun. –   (67–9)

The account of wintry woods and sea is the kind of natural description at which Shelley is unsurpassed, in which physical life, and the meaning it embodies and evokes, effortlessly pass one into the other. The whole of nature – land, sea and sky – seems to have a life of its own, whose secrets are bare to the eye of the poet. It is as if nature, in its multiplicity and continual process, revealed to him the secret of unity and timelessness – in the 'wild woods' where nature is not bound or limited, where day and night, winter and summer, earth and ocean, meet and appear to be merged into one. The natural scene represents innocent relationship, the more innocent, perhaps, because the elements that meet or reflect one another in love do not merge, barely touch, and bear no fruit, scent or color. Nature under such an aspect offers still another inducement to Jane to join the poet, and demonstrates the innocence of his request.

The Recollection is, as Shelley says, 'The epitaph of glory fled' and is therefore more serious, more complicated. It is an attempt to fix the exact quality of the scene and of the poet's happiness; more precisely, it seeks to find an image that can permanently stand for the day in the pine forest. Its formal introduction

sustains the tone of epistolary verse; with an inversion of rhyme
the passage ends on a sad, suspended cadence: 'A frown is on
the Heaven's brow.' The 'frown' recalls the 'smile' with which
The Invitation begins; the reader will guess that it is not only the
earth that has returned to its wintry state. And the experience
as it is now recalled, takes on more and more the character of
an interlude, a pause, marked by a silence and stillness, a pro-
found calm, which is gradually elaborated and deepened until
it takes on magical properties, like the trance of dream vision or
revelation. Land, sea and sky are drawn, each soothed to peace
and harmony by the 'smile of Heaven', the waves 'half asleep',
the clouds 'gone to play', the twisted pine stilled by the 'azure
breath' of the wind, the 'tree-tops . . . asleep/Like green waves
on the sea,/As still as in the silent deep/The Ocean woods may
be'. The universal calm is finally made to include the human
beings who perceive it; its source, imaged as the lovely day, the
'smile of Heaven', is identified more precisely as the 'Radiant
Sister of the day' of *The Invitation*.

> There seemed from the remotest seat
>   Of the white mountain-waste,
> To the soft flower beneath our feet
>   A magic circle traced,
> A spirit interfused around
>   A thrilling silent life,
> To momentary peace it bound
>   Our mortal nature's strife; –
> And still I felt the centre of
>   The magic circle there
> Was one fair form that filled with love
>   The lifeless atmosphere.   (41–52)

The 'magic circle' recalls the windless bower envisaged by the
poet at the end of *Lines written among the Euganean Hills*, its peace
made permanent by 'the love which heals all strife/Circling
like the breath of life,/All things in that sweet abode' (366–8).

But where the island paradise is an image of an Elysium, a universal source of hope, the 'magic circle' is drawn around an hour of present life, the peace is momentary, the source of love is embodied in human form, hence transient and frail. And as if the statement alone is not sufficient, Shelley draws the 'magic circle' in terms of a new circle image of sky and forest reflected in the forest pools (like the reflection of 'old palaces and towers' in 'the wave's intenser day', in *Ode to the West Wind*). The still reflection, while real, has the perfection and truth as well as the illusory character of dream or vision; it strangely approximates a Platonic absolute – 'purer', 'more boundless', 'more perfect' – to which the 'upper world', 'our world above', is but a dim shadow.

> We paused beside the pools that lie
>   Under the forest bough –
> Each seemed as 'twere, a little sky
>   Gulfed in a world below;
> A firmament of purple light
>   Which in the dark earth lay
> More boundless than the depth of night
>   And purer than the day,
> In which the lovely forests grew
>   As in the upper air,
> More perfect, both in shape and hue,
>   Than any spreading there.   (53–64)

Just as in lines 33–52 the notion of absolute peace yields imperceptibly to the idea of the love which is its source and which emanates from Jane, so in lines 53–76, as the description of the reflected Elysium continues, its perfection and truth become identified with physical love: the water's desire to receive the surrounding woods.

> Sweet views, which in our world above
>   Can never well be seen,

> Were imaged in the water's love
>   Of that fair forest green;
> And all was interfused beneath
>   With an Elysian glow,
> An atmosphere without a breath,
>   A softer day below —   (69–76)

The poem ends with a return to reality, the 'frown . . . on the Heaven's brow', the poet's melancholy; the shift is accomplished aphoristically by pun and metaphor:

> Like one beloved, the scene had lent
>   To the dark water's breast,
> Its every leaf and lineament
>   With more than truth exprest;
> Until an envious wind crept by,
>   Like an unwelcome thought
> Which from the mind's too faithful eye
>   Blots one dear image out. —
> Though thou art ever fair and kind
>   And forests ever green,
> Less oft is peace in ——'s mind,
>   Than calm in water seen.   (77–88)

To paraphrase: as a passing wind blots out from the pool the reflection of the scene (by ruffling the surface, distorting the reflection), so an 'unwelcome thought' erases Jane's image from the poet's 'too faithful' mind – 'too faithful', I think, simply as the water reflects the scene with 'more than truth', though the line is ambiguous. One might guess that the lines allude to the poet's marriage, to which he is 'too faithful'; in his relations with Mary he must have felt that patience and endurance were indicated, but there was no reason for him not to indulge his happiness in Jane's companionship. The final quatrain seems to be a frank statement of the poet's dilemma, but the meaning is still restricted to the terms of the metaphor, and one knows no more than at the beginning. As the green forest is to the water that images it in love, so is the fair Jane to Shelley; but (to return to the opening analogy of the poem) the peace of the present day is but a moment's respite from the poet's 'long pain'; the waters of his spirit are troubled indeed, and whatever beneficent effect Jane may have is bound to be merely temporary.

As *The Invitation* and *The Recollection* suggest comparison with *Lines written among the Euganean Hills, Lines written in the Bay of Lerici* suggests *Stanzas written in Dejection* in its simplicity of statement, its directness. As in the earlier poem, the poet's agitation of spirit is measured against a scene so lovely and so intensely felt that it becomes an image of the serenity from which he is excluded. The displacement of emotion in the opening lines of the poem is characteristic of Shelley's last poems. Brooding about Jane, he addresses the Moon: 'Bright wanderer, fair coquette of Heaven'; suffering the effects of her recent presence and her departure, he analyses the nature of time and the relationship of the present to past and future. Thus before turning directly to the beloved, his thoughts linger over the moment of departure, which turns into an image of suspended time. And the image of this 'silent time', when the moon hovers between its rise and its setting, 'like an albatross asleep', anticipates the thought of the moment of happiness, the 'time which is our own', suspended between past and future, which, the poet implies, possess or enchain us. It is a moment caught and imprisoned, like the noon moment of *Lines written in the Euganean Hills*, or the hour spent in the pine forest in the Cascine, when flux, process, physical reality are for a moment transcended by feeling and memory. The images that render this moment are similar to those which dominate *Music, when soft voices die*: they have to do with the analogy between the vibrations of feeling and those of sound and odor, the relation of physical cause to nonphysical effect. The effects of love are imperceptible, immeasurable, but felt by the 'enchanted heart', which is not dependent upon physical presence. But the demon reassumes his throne, despite a momentary enchantment; the poet's 'antient pilot, Pain' takes control of his 'frail bark' once more, in the image which represents Shelley's persistent vision of the solitary human life. No sooner does he mention his 'faint heart', though, than he turns again to the scene, displacing his need onto the landscape:

> . . . I dare not speak
> My thoughts; but thus disturbed and weak
> I sate and watched the vessels glide
> Along the ocean bright and wide,
> Like spirit-winged chariots sent
> O'er some serenest element
> For ministrations strange and far . . .   (35-41)

As in *Stanzas written in Dejection*, the very solitude of the poet sharpens his sensibility to the harmonies of the natural scene, as well as to its analogy with human life. The enumeration of the elements of the scene – the gliding vessels, the wind, the scent of the flowers, the coolness of dew, the sweet warmth left by day – seems to parallel the enumeration earlier in the poem of the beloved's ministrations, her tones, the 'soft vibrations of her touch', her healing presence. Both passages imply the gulf between the suffering poet and the harmony of spirit toward which he yearns, whether represented by his 'guardian angel' (who, like the moon, is bound after her brief stay for her own 'nest'), or by the natural scene in its clarity and freshness.

The poet has instinctively turned to the scene for some easing of his pain, perhaps for a continuation of the peace ministered by his beloved, who serves in all these poems as an extension of a beneficent nature. And the scene finally supplies its more than adequate image. With a sudden twist or tautening the quiet description ends with the vision of the fisherman with lamp and spear – the human figure in the landscape, the natural predator, as the fish are natural victims. And to this image the poet ap-

pends a moral, somewhat in the fashion of the wry aphorism
that ends *The Recollection*: 'Less oft is peace in [Shelley]'s mind/
Than calm in water seen':

> Too happy, they whose pleasure sought
> Extinguishes all sense and thought
> Of the regret that pleasure [   ]
> Seeking life not peace.   (55–8)

The final contrast is between not happiness and despair but the
simplicity of nature, even in the urge of natural creatures toward death, and the complexity of human life, which, subject
always to 'sense and thought', must endure the departure of
pleasure, and which survives all it loves. What the poet envies
in the luring of the fish, which otherwise seems to mirror his
own foolish pursuit of pleasure, is the singleness of animal instinct, the sureness of its consequences.

The image of the 'delusive flame' is the last variation on a
theme that runs through Shelley's poetry, the desire of every
living creature:

> . . . ever from below
> Aspiring like one who loves too fair, too far,
> To be consumed within the purest glow
>
> Of one serene and unapproached star,
> As if it were a lamp of earthly light,
> Unconscious, as some human lovers are,
>
> Itself how low, how high beyond all height
> The heaven where it would perish!
>   (*The Woodman and the Nightingale*, 25–32)

Yet the image of temptation, desire and destruction in Shelley's
last poem has a special quality entirely different from the soar-

ing affirmations of *Adonais* and *Epipsychidion*, an objective, ironic detachment. The appended moral suggests that the choice for the aspiring soul is simply between the seeking of life – i.e., of its necessity, of light, love, delight – and the sensible pursuit of peace. Life and peace are incompatible; by implication, peace is possible only in the grave. The earlier images of present peace and happiness are set in a most somber perspective. And for the first time, the image of the flame is qualified by the suggestion that it is indeed a false lure, and that the heart which follows the flame does so because it is a 'weak heart of little wit' (*Love, Hope, Desire and Fear*, 49).

These last lyrics confirm the darkening of spirit that is suggested so strongly by *The Triumph of Life*. One senses an increasing pessimism on Shelley's part, the gradual withdrawal of the poet's bright Elysium until it appears to be no more than an image of what the soul in vain desires, counter to all reason, all evidence. Yet as Shelley's hope of permanent change in society and in private life recedes and its place is taken by the notion of endurance, the ideal for which his spirit longs seems suddenly to take shape in the present moment, the beloved Italian scene, the brief presence of a woman. Hence the poignancy of these poems, which celebrate present happiness in the certainty of loss, which do not seek beyond the 'present and tangible object' but rather draw a magic circle around that which is mortal and doomed.

Even as Shelley's perspective seems to shift, his art is strengthened. In these last poems there is always a hard core of thought at the centre, whether the poem appears to be a simple description of a natural scene, an expression of nameless joy or sorrow, or an ecstatic approximation of an ideal beyond sense experience or rational inference. Though Shelley's unique qualities as a poet come from his intense sensibility to just these things, though he is pre-eminently a poet of passionate feeling and commitment, his intelligence, which is essentially abstract and logical, is always in control. The precision of his thought should never be underestimated; as it is the source of difficulty, sometimes of ambiguity, so it is what finally gives his poetry its strength.

SOURCE: Judith Chernaik, *The Lyrics of Shelley* (1972) pp. 162–79.

NOTES

[Verse-quotations from *The Zucca* and *The Woodman and the Nightingale* are from the Oxford edition; those from the 'Jane Williams' poems are from the newly edited texts in Dr Chernaik's *The Lyrics of Shelley* (1972).]

1. Only one of the poems is dated, but the others can be placed roughly. *The Recollection* is dated 'Feb. 2, 1822' (the day commemorated, according to Williams's *Journal*); *The keen stars were twinkling* can be dated by its close verbal resemblances to Shelley's letter of 18 June; *Lines written in the Bay of Lerici* must have been written in late June as well. *With a Guitar* was written sometime after 25 January (when Shelley asked Horace Smith to purchase a pedal harp for Jane) and before *The keen stars were twinkling. To Edward Williams* was sent to Williams on 26 January, according to Williams's *Journal.* The poems and their dates are discussed in N. I. White, *Shelley,* 2 vols (N.Y., 1940) II 343–7. Medwin includes among the poems to Jane *When the lamp is shattered* and *I arise from dreams of thee* (Medwin's *Life of Shelley,* ed. Forman, pp. 317–18). The relationship between Jane and Shelley is analyzed in G. M. Matthews, 'Shelley and Jane Williams', *Review of English Studies,* n.s. XII (1961) 40–8; and Donald H. Reiman, 'Shelley's *The Triumph of Life*: The Biographical Problem', *PMLA,* LXXVIII (1963) 536–50. I would agree with Reiman that it is unlikely that anything more passed between Shelley and Jane than conversation and vibrations from Jane's cool hand – at least as of the writing of *Lines written in the Bay of Lerici* ('Memory gave me all of her/That even fancy dares to claim', 26–7). But the tone of Shelley's last letter to Jane unquestionably suggests infatuation.

2. Shelley wrote to Byron: 'The Williamses, with all their furniture embarked, and no place to sleep in, have taken refuge with me for the present; and they are, in my actual situation [a reference to

Claire's presence, and the recent death of her daughter Allegra]
a great relief and consolation' (letter of 3 May 1822, *Letters of Percy
Bysshe Shelley*, ed. Frederick L. Jones (Oxford: Clarendon Press,
1964) II 416). According to Mary, no other house was to be found
nearby, and therefore the temporary arrangement was continued
(*Letters of Mary W. Shelley*, ed. Frederick L. Jones (Univ. of Oklahoma Press, 1947) II 169–70).

3. That the secret was well kept is indicated by the fact that Mary
did not publish complete texts of these poems until the second edition
of *Poetical Works* (1840).

4. As Locock points out in his note (Locock, *Poems*, II 529),
Shelley imitates his own translation of Homer's *Hymn to Mercury*,
lxxi–lxxxiii. But in *With a Guitar* Shelley puts 'perfect skill' beneath
Jane's natural feeling.

F. H. Ludlam

THE METEOROLOGY OF THE
ODE TO THE WEST WIND (1972)

Conflicting views have been expressed about the question
whether there is any scientific basis in Shelley's descriptions of
natural phenomena. At the one extreme, A. N. Whitehead (in
Science and the Modern World) was sufficiently impressed with
Shelley's enthusiasm and capacity for scientific studies to say
that if he had 'been born a hundred years later the twentieth
century would have seen a Newton of Chemistry'. On the other
hand, F. R. Leavis (in *Revaluation*) found a 'weak grasp upon
the actual' to be an 'essential trait' of Shelley; and, referring
especially to the *Ode to the West Wind*, concludes that 'no general
satisfaction could be obtained from Shelley's imagery'.

Some adverse critics have shown little understanding either
of natural phenomena or of the nature of scientific inquiry,
evidently not appreciating that the aim of both artists and
scientists is to communicate a new and valuable way of regarding the phenomena, an enterprise in which there can be no
absolute and permanent correctness. John Holloway (in his
Percy Bysshe Shelley) succeeds in making a more penetrating
analysis of the same and other verses. He warns that the poet is
likely 'to be always right as against the critic . . . the likelihood
that [the critic] will be even as well informed as the poet, on
not one but a variety of subjects which the latter exclusively has
chosen, is virtually nil.'

An example – arising in another discipline but which, like
the analyses of the *Ode to the West Wind*, concerns a meteorological interpretation – is John Constable's criticism of a painting by Ruisdael: a winter scene with snow on the ground.

Constable interprets the picture as one of an approaching thaw, not only on the basis of the appearance of the sky, but also from the recent change of wind shown by the positions of the sails of two windmills, one working and facing the present wind, and the other, with furled sails, still turned in the direction of the wind which prevailed when it was last used.

In what follows, the first line and the second stanza of the *Ode to the West Wind* are re-examined, and, contrary to the opinions of some critics, these passages are found to describe a meteorological phenomenon not only with eloquence but with an insight which was quite extraordinary for Shelley's time and which has hardly been matched since, even in the scientific literature.

Shelley wrote that his Ode was 'conceived and chiefly written' near the end of October 1819,

in a wood that skirts the Arno, near Florence, and on a day when that tempestuous wind, whose temperature is at once mild and animating, was collecting the vapours which pour down the autumnal rains. They began, as I foresaw, at sunset with a violent tempest of hail and rain, attended by that magnificent thunder and lightning peculiar to the Cisalpine regions.

The weather which he observed, and his understanding of the natural processes at work, inspired the second stanza. . . . From the last lines of this stanza –

> Vaulted with all thy congregated might
> Of vapours, from whose solid atmosphere
> Black rain, and fire, and hail will burst: oh, hear!

and from Shelley's remarks, it seems clear that 'the approaching storm' is a thunderstorm. It is recognised as such by Dr Holloway, who also identifies the 'locks' of the storm with the frayed 'anvil' of a thundercloud which will be described later. However, in D. King-Hele's *Shelley* – a study written by a professional scientist at about the same time as Dr Holloway's – the same stanza was interpreted as accurately describing two essentially different kinds of clouds, one of which is the familiar forerunner of the great cyclonic storms of temperate latitudes. This view was recently accepted by Roy Fuller (in 'The Osmotic Sap', *TLS*, 14 May 1971) as establishing in the poem 'truth to nature', apparently because it was advanced by one who could be presumed to speak for science. Nevertheless, in respect of the nature of the storm and its clouds, the interpretation is not correct, and it is instructive to consider the error.

The cyclonic storms which continually form over the North Atlantic and travel into the north and west of Europe occur throughout the year, but during the summer they are mostly not so intense as in winter, and they are confined mainly to paths lying to the north of Britain and leading into or near Scandinavia. Although they often spoil the season in Britain, they hardly disturb the placid, sunny weather which at this time of year prevails over the Mediterranean Sea and its neighbouring lands.

The first signs of the approach of the typical cyclonic storm are the wispy high cirrus clouds which progressively occupy the sky from the west, individually moving swiftly from the northwest. The leading clouds are often separate tenuous trails of ice crystals, miniature snow showers in the cold upper atmosphere, whose lower parts lag behind their fast-moving tops. Seen from one side they appear drawn out in the shape of a comma with a long and nearly horizontal tail. Mr King-Hele provides an illustration of these clouds, which he thinks Shelley sees as the locks of an approaching storm.

Although it would be reasonable to describe such clouds as 'locks', it is difficult to understand why they should be 'Like the bright hair uplifted from the head/Of some fierce Maenad', because the heart of the cyclonic storm occupies a region too extensive for it ever to be perceived by eye from the ground, regarded as an entity and likened to some wild being. Moreover, as Mr King-Hele notes, the other clouds in his picture are not of the second kind described in the Ode: those tattered fragments which are likened to 'decaying leaves . . . Shook from the tangled boughs of Heaven and Ocean'.

This is an important discrepancy, because the low clouds in his illustration – the small 'woolpack' or cauliflower-shaped heap clouds (cumulus) which have level bases and domed upper parts – are indeed characteristic of an afternoon sky overland when there is still sunshine, but the high cirrus have arrived as the harbingers of the cyclonic storm. They are quite different from the ragged low clouds of bad weather, which are discussed in more detail later. Also, at this time, on the outermost fringe of the storm, the wind near the ground is light, and backing towards *south*. As the storm advances the wind freshens but not until some hours later has it become strong, still from a southerly quarter. The cirrus have by then been succeeded by a lowering pall of thick grey cloud from which rain sets in. Not until still later, just before the rain ceases and the cloud lifts and breaks, does the wind veer into a *westerly* quarter. Had Shelley's approaching storm been a cyclonic storm, the Ode might have been to the South but not to the West wind.

> thou breath of Autumn's being
> . . .
> . . . Thou dirge
> Of the dying year

It is precisely in the central part of the Mediterranean that a wild westerly wind is so aptly described as the 'breath of Autumn's being'. Over Britain and much of the north-west of Europe fresh westerly winds, and even gales, occur from time to time throughout the summer; in particular, the westerlies are even more prevalent in June than in the three preceding months. In contrast, the Mediterranean and the lands around it have more definite winter and summer seasons in which the character of the weather is strongly influenced according to whether the sea is cooler or warmer than the land. Both sea and land are coolest in February, but the seasonal warming of the land is much more rapid, and by day it becomes distinctly warmer than the sea, during the period between about May and October.

During this season the rain-belts of the cyclonic depressions passing over the north of Europe generally fail to enter the Mediterranean, and over the sea and the coastal regions the weather there is persistently almost cloudless and rainless. Only in the more mountainous countries, and especially near the Pyrenees and the Alps, is the fine weather occasionally interrupted by short-lived thunderstorms, which are provoked by the heat of the intense sunshine and a cooling of the upper atmosphere in the fringes of the cyclones whose centres pass by much farther north.

During the winter, on the other hand, the rain-belts of cyclonic storms frequently enter the Mediterranean and even occasionally reach North Africa. Also, showers and thunderstorms often form over the warm sea when cool air from more northern latitudes intermittently invades the Mediterranean in the rear of cyclonic storms, usually through the gap between the Pyrenees and the Alps. It is a well-known feature of Mediterranean weather that these invasions are usually accompanied by a fall of barometric pressure which is greatest over the Gulf of Genoa, leading to the formation of new cyclones in the lee of the Alps. On their southern flanks the flows of cool air intensify. Over and near the Ligurian and northern Tyrrhenian Seas gusty westerly winds often reach gale force, especially near the thundery rainstorms and hailstorms which grow over the sea and are carried some distance inland from windward coasts by both day and night.

The season of disturbed weather in the Mediterranean usually begins at some stage in the month of October with the first pronounced invasion of cool air since the preceding winter. Sometimes it arrives with remarkable abruptness in the latter half of the month, suddenly breaking the prolonged summer tranquillity, and subsequently similar irruptions of cool air and bad weather are liable to recur frequently. They bring intense showers and thunderstorms which drench exposed northern coastal regions with 'autumnal rains'.

Thus in the region around Florence, the descriptions of the wild West Wind' as the 'breath of Autumn's being' is peculiarly appropriate. In no other part of Europe could it be recognised from ordinary experience as so apt. The abrupt awakening of the Mediterranean 'from his summer dreams' (the third stanza of the Ode) is part of a phenomenon sufficiently striking to have been given a special name: 'the autumn break'. It is not so regular an event that it can reliably be anticipated by a weather forecaster. Nevertheless it is prominent in some climatological statistics. The records for a number of places in and around the Mediterranean show a rather steady and high average level of the barometer during the summer season, a sudden fall on about 20 October, and afterwards and throughout winter a comparatively irregular trace which implies unsettled weather. In these statistics the fall of the barometer in late October, corresponding to the autumn break, is remarkably large at Genoa, and can still be detected as far away as Gibraltar and, a little later, even at Cairo.

At the time of the autumn break, the days are shortening rapidly and the sun sets already at about five o'clock in the afternoon, so that, after the long bright days of summer, a West wind with dense clouds shadowing the sky and obscuring the sun may well seem to have brought darkness too and the threat of winter, and to be sounding the 'dirge of the dying year'.

> Loose clouds . . .
> Shook from the tangled boughs of Heaven and Ocean

The second stanza of the Ode begins by likening 'loose clouds' to the wind-scattered leaves of the first stanza. These clouds Mr King-Hele currently identifies as fractostratus (broken layer-cloud), better called fractocumulus (torn cumulus), and still better by their popular name of 'scud'.

Scud occur in and near the rain areas of cyclones, especially in strong winds, and near the advancing sides of the dense columns of rain and hail which fall from thunderclouds. They almost always lean forward, so that they can readily be imagined to be fleeing from the storm centre, 'like ghosts from an enchanter'. Their texture is ragged, with clear spaces between irregular strands, so that they have a skeletal or ghostly appearance; and they tend to cluster, rather like wind-driven dead leaves, which are also withered, crumpled and torn. The 'loose' or frayed structure of scud makes them quite different from their fair-weather counterparts, the compact and domed cumulus. In the shadow of the more massive or extensive storm clouds the scud appear dark and sinister, whereas in the mind's eye the cumulus are clouds of tranquil afternoons, brightly lit by sunshine.

The concept of the incessant circulation of water between the earth and the sky, now so familiar, had barely been formulated in Shelley's time, but that he understood it well is clear from his writing. It appears, for example, in *The Cloud*:

> I am the daughter of Earth and Water,
> And the nursling of the Sky;
> I pass through the pores of the ocean and shores;
> I change, but I cannot die.

Evidently the scud which Shelley sees driven by the West wind are clouds running beside thunderstorms, which can be seen discharging water into the sea but which themselves are composed of water evaporated from the sea. These opposing streams of liquid and of vapour, partly condensed into cloud, are 'the tangled boughs of Heaven and Ocean'. In technical language they would now commonly be called 'branches of the circulation of atmospheric water'.

It is the mountainous thunderheads and the lesser but towering cumulus elsewhere in the sky whose tall flanks prompt the description of the sky as 'steep', and whose boiling outlines, combined with the presence of rain shafts and the fleeing scud, give the true impression of the atmosphere in 'commotion'. Not only is the air stream rushing with 'skiey speed' across the sea and inland as a wild wind, which sets the wood ringing with its tempestuous strength, but it has within it the upheaval of the powerful ascending currents which swell the growing thunder-clouds, and the descending cataracts of rain-chilled air which strike the sea and whip across it in blustery squalls. The atmosphere is in an uproar, but only superficially in chaotic disarray: to the perceptive mind the commotion becomes an interplay of tremendous organised forces, the sky and the tumult expression of the 'mighty harmonies' of the West wind.

The locks of the approaching storm . . .

The barometric depression accompanying the storm which causes the autumn break does not travel from the Atlantic, but forms in the Gulf of Genoa, and the weather in the storm is not like that experienced during the passage of the middle-latitude cyclones. In particular, the rains are not the prolonged, rather steady, rains which fall from the widespread cloud-sheets of these cyclones, but the more local downpours of scattered thunderstorms. The locks of the kind of storm which Shelley sees approaching are not the tenuous curl clouds of the edges of the cyclonic storm; they represent the equally high but denser plume of fibrous cloud which reaches far ahead of the towering cloud columns at the heart of a thunderstorm.

The plume consists of cloud particles too small to reach the ground as rain or hail; they remain suspended in the air which ascends in the storm and which, on reaching into the high atmosphere (several miles above the ground), spreads outwards and forwards. The plume is especially well developed in the more severe kind of thunderstorm which characteristically travels across a great tract of land or sea at a regular speed of some thirty or forty knots. It extends up to some 100 miles in front of the storm, and so, when it reaches into the zenith, it is a warning of the arrival of the storm an hour or two later. When the observer looks westward before sunset, and the fringes of the plume are lit golden in the rays of the sinking sun, it is apparently 'uplifted' from the menacing thunderheads just discernible above a horizon dimmed with the spume of breaking waves. It is much more like the bright hair of some 'fierce Maenad' than the delicate tresses of the curl clouds.

> . . . congregated might
> Of vapours . . .

On the closer approach of the thunderheads, with their crenellated towers, the neighbouring thickest parts of the plumes begin to cover over completely the previously mainly clear and blue sky. The sky becomes 'vaulted over' by the overhanging arches formed by the adjoining plumes. There is little time to watch the 'congregated might' of the beetling craggy thunderheads before their advancing inky bases hasten on the darkness of night, leaving the impression of an atmosphere filled with such substantial and opaque clouds as to seem 'solid'.

'Black rain, and fire, and hail will burst', writes Shelley; and, indeed, when the downpour of rain and hail finally arrives, it is flung forward in a *burst* by the storm wind, which rises to gale force in a succession of violent gusts. The first drops come winging invisibly out of the night, stinging the face or spattering windowpanes: 'black rain', accompanied by the intermittent blinding 'fire' of lightning and blasts of small wet 'hail'.

As a concise statement of the form and nature of the travelling thunderstorm, one of Nature's most complicated and still imperfectly understood phenomena, Shelley's description is unrivalled in English literature – even, until very recently, in scientific accounts. By comparison, Luke Howard's, published widely at about the same time, was rather vague and caused some confusion among meteorologists. He called the thundercloud 'cumulostratus' (now known as 'cumulonimbus'), writing that, when cumulus grows rapidly, a layer of cirrus frequently forms around the summit, which speedily becomes denser and spreads until a large cloud is formed which may be compared with a mushroom with a very thick short stem. However, only in calm weather is this cap symmetrical: generally it spreads mainly on one side (in temperate latitudes, ahead of the weather) to form the plume described above.

Shelley's verse has an immediate appeal, even to the reader who is no expert student of the weather. This is not only because of the inspired way in which it is used to develop the theme of the Ode, but because it is based on an acute awareness of the nature of the scene before him, and of its relation to a dramatic event of an even grander scale: the sudden onset of the Mediterranean winter, a phenomenon even now hardly mentioned, still less examined, in meteorological texts.

SOURCE: 'The Meteorology of Shelley's Ode', *Times Literary Supplement*, 1 September 1972.

Patrick Swinden

THE *ODE TO THE WEST WIND*
(1973)

Nothing is more typical of the romantic consciousness than the movement of the wind. For Swift, at the opening of the eighteenth century, wind was an image of irresponsible inspiration. When a man took upon himself the power of the wind, he belched. Inspired speech was therefore a sort of belching. Inspired makers of speeches were wind-bags. It took a massive shift in the way people looked at the world for Shelley to be able to address the West Wind as 'The trumpet of a prophecy'. In doing so, however, he shows no sign of the vagueness, the lack of sense, that Swift suggests automatically accompanies inspiration. Shelley doesn't merely pick on the West Wind as a stock symbol of inspiration lying ready to hand. He looks at it more closely and more carefully than any poet had done before. His 'picture' of the West Wind is more accurately painted than it had been in the seventeenth and eighteenth centuries when, as Zephyrus or Favonius, it had blown, usually gently, through the nooks and crannies of several admirable poems. Milton in *Comus* has 'West-Winds, with musky wing,/About the cedar'd alleys fling/Nard and cassia's balmy smells'. The same 'Western Winds' blew on the 'breathing Roses' of Pope's *Spring* pastoral. And again, 'Cool Zephyrs thro' the clear blue sky/Their gather'd fragrance fling' in Gray's *Ode on the Spring*. Each poet is happy to forgo the difficult problem of describing the wind, which cannot be seen, in favour of the easier one of describing the scents of the herbs and flowers it conveys to the senses. But to what senses does the wind address itself? No one before Shelley had thought to ask.

Shelley was being original in addressing his *Ode to the West Wind* in Autumn.[1] In a note he describes the poem's conception in a wood near Florence on a day of tempestuous autumnal wind. [See quotation in preceding essay, page 218 above.] Shelley had been living in Italy since the beginning of 1818. Towards the end of 1819 he moved with his family to Pisa, near Florence, and wrote the poem shortly afterwards. It is the fruit, therefore, of much observation of the weather and scenery of the Italian littoral. Especially of the weather. Shelley is one of the very few English poets who were interested in and competent at science. He was fascinated by the movement of clouds, their formation and dissolution in rain. Descriptions of weather conditions abound in his poems. Sometimes they are painstakingly scientific – too much so for many of his modern readers, who fail to make allowances for the progress of meteorological science over the past hundred and fifty years. The most celebrated instance of this is his description of *The Cloud* (a poem included, with *Ode to the West Wind*, in the *Prometheus Unbound* volume of 1820) as a natural phenomenon directed by electric charges ('Sublime on the towers of my skiey bowers,/Lightning my pilot sits'; etc.). There was a very respectably scientific support for this view in 1819 – Shelley's science teacher, Dr Adam Walker, advanced it in his *Analysis of a Course of Lectures on Experimental Philosophy* [see John Holloway's essay, page 137 above] – and Shelley is being intellectually alert and 'contemporary' in incorporating the theory in a poem. He may not have been very tactful in the way he did it, but that is another matter.

Elsewhere Shelley is content to look carefully at the weather he is describing. The poems to Jane Williams are full of such accurate descriptions ('. . . the pools of winter rains/Image all their roof or leaves' or 'How calm it is! – the silence there/ By such a chain was bound/That even the busy woodpecker/ Made stiller by her sound/The inviolable quietness'). *Prometheus Unbound* is as good as the ode *To a Skylark* on the movements of heavenly bodies, particularly on the way stars impress themselves on the senses. *Prometheus* has this, for example, as a description of a star reflected in still water, at a distance, as parts of several cloud formations drift across it:

> The point of one white star is quivering still
> Deep in the orange light of widening morn
> Beyond the purple mountains: through a chasm
> Of wind-divided mist the darker lake
> Reflects it: now it wains: it gleams again
> As the waves fade, and as the burning threads
> Of woven cloud unravel in pale air.

In the middle of a description like this, 'purple mountains' cease to be an embarrassment.[2] So does the whole progress of the imagery of the following stanza from the ode *To a Skylark* once we have understood, as Donald Davie has pointed out [see page 79 above],[3] that the silver sphere is not the moon but Venus, the evening star:

> Keen as are the arrows
>   Of that silver sphere,
> Whose intense lamp narrows
>   In the white dawn clear
> Until we hardly see – we feel that it is there.

The dwindling points of the star contract to a pinpoint and draw into the star, as it were, the silver-white atmosphere of dawn. Silver star and white space almost fuse. The lamp is intense and we are intent on apprehending it as a discrete object – but by this time apprehension is hardly a matter for the senses, we hardly *see*, we *feel* that it is there. More common, but no less difficult to render, are the uncertain movements of a summer evening breeze, the kind of thing Shelley manages with such clarity and poise in the unfinished (not quite finished) *Evening: Ponte Al Mare, Pisa*:

There is no dew on the dry grass to-night,
   Nor damp within the shadow of the trees;
The wind is intermitting, dry and light;
   And in the inconstant motion of the breeze
The dust and straws are driven up and down,
And whirled about the pavement of the town.

Three examples, then, of Shelley's sensitivity to the appearance of atmospheric conditions – wind, starlight, the movement
of clouds, the look of dawn in a cloudless sky. They had to be
given to disabuse those who have read some of the attacks on
Shelley in the present century of the notions that Shelley was,
in Dr Leavis's words, 'peculiarly weak in his hold on objects –
peculiarly unable to realize them as existing in their own
natures and their own right'. For myself I do not know how you
get hold of an object like the fading of the evening star at dawn,
or the motion of wind through dry grass, but in so far as it is
possible I should say that Shelley has done it better than any
other English poet I have read.

In the *Ode to the West Wind*, however, there is much more than
the accurate transcription of sense impressions. Shelley has
impregnated his subject with philosophical speculations which
are interesting and of great importance to himself. The skill
with which he has fused the visible subject with the invisible
thought, so that it can scarcely be said that the one is simply an
image or metaphor of the other, accounts for much of the beauty
and the complexity of the poem.

In spite of its rapid movement, the impression it gives of
inspired improvisation, the Ode is constructed with the utmost
rigour. Each of its five parts is shaped rather like a sonnet,
fourteen decasyllabic lines ending with a couplet (in the
Shakespearean manner). Unlike the sonnet, though, there is no
division into octave and sestet. The momentum of the stanza
(as I shall call each of the five parts) continues unchecked to the
opening of the couplet or even beyond this to the last line. This
means that the first line gives a powerful thrust to the stanza,

shifting the rhythms that follow with a remarkable energy.
Sometimes more than one heave is required, and the heavily
stressed opening of the first line is augmented with something of
the same sort in the second:

O wild West Wind, thou breath of Autumn's being

Four stressed syllables are followed by a pause at the comma,
then perhaps 'thou' takes a half stress, followed by the stress on
'breath' – after which there is a release of momentum along
with the stresses on the first syllable of 'Autumn' and 'being'.
But to make sure sufficient energy is conserved to carry the rest
of the stanza, 'Thou' at the opening of the second line receives
another heavy stress, and a pause after. Then it is allowed to
take off, with that halting and careering movement that is so
hard to define, so easy to hear. It is typically Shelleyan, and we
shall have to return to it at a later stage. The other stanzas vary
in the amount of 'thrust' they need from the start to carry them
through the twelve or thirteen lines before the invocation. The
fifth is most like the first, in the rhythmical terms I have been
describing.

The vigour and rapidity of movement throughout the poem
have a great deal to do with Shelley's manipulation of the
terza rima verse form. He uses this with an apparent ease that
has been achieved by no other English poet. Shelley adapted it
from his reading of Dante, and used it to fine effect also in his
late unfinished poem, *The Triumph of Life*.[4] The difficulty of the
form in English, with its paucity of rhyme words compared
with the Italian, can be gauged by looking at two other poems.
One of these, Dorothy Sayers's translation of the *Divina Commedia*
into English *terza rima*, shows the intolerable strain imposed on
an English translator of Dante, for this reason among others.
The other, the 'fire watcher' section of T. S. Eliot's *Little Gidding*,
shows how another English poet, and admirer of Dante, had
recourse to a variation of blank verse to get at all close to the
lucidity, plangency, force and ease of the Italian. No other poet

in English has extracted such a variety of music out of *terza rima* as Shelley. Indeed no other poet in English has come near to him in this respect.

So, Shelley's use of *terza rima* accounts in large part for the fact that none of the five stanzas of the Ode reads like a sonnet. The division between the two parts of the sonnet is counteracted by the impetus of the rhythms, driving the poem forward from the thrust of the opening lines, across the interlinking rhythms of the verse form, to the solemn halt at or within the couplet.

Nevertheless the poem as a whole does reveal the division into two slightly unequal parts that we associate with the sonnet. The first three stanzas are a single unit. Each one of them describes the power of the wind over one of the elements – the earth, the sky and the sea. The last two are also a unit, emphasising the relation between the wind and the poet. The first three stanzas connect with one another at a number of sensitive points, making them a single source of power, not merely three separate descriptions of different 'landscapes' dominated by the tendentiously unifying force of the wind. And the last two overlap into a single statement or address to the wind through the invocation which is prepared in the first three sections of the fourth stanza, released at the fourth section (at 'Oh, lift me . . .'), and thrust over the couplet to fuse with the imperatives at the opening of the fifth stanza – 'Make me thy lyre, . . .'. So what is lost in the single stanzas (with what gain in terms of energy, speed and rhythmic vitality!) is retrieved in the design of the poem as a whole. How secure is the over-all gain to the poem will depend on Shelley's success in binding the constituents of the two parts together, and then again in fusing the two parts *after* they have made their proper separate impact.

I

O wild West Wind, thou breath of Autumn's being,
Thou, from whose unseen presence the leaves dead
Are driven, like ghosts from an enchanter fleeing,

Yellow, and black, and pale, and hectic red,
Pestilence-stricken multitudes: O thou,
Who chariotest to their dark wintry bed

The wingèd seeds, where they lie cold and low,
Each like a corpse within its grave, until
Thine azure sister of the Spring shall blow

Her clarion o'er the dreaming earth, and fill
(Driving sweet buds like flocks to feed in air)
With living hues and odours plain and hill:

Wild Spirit, which art moving everywhere;
Destroyer and preserver; hear, oh, hear!

The first two stanzas describe the West Wind primarily in its character as a destroyer rather than as a preserver. The wind cannot be seen. It must be felt by witnessing its effect on things which can be seen, and which are the objects or the agents of its power. In stanza one these are the leaves, like ghosts (they are thin and frail) fleeing from an enchanter; and the winged seeds blown to the ground and buried like corpses in a grave, but in fact resting in cradles to be reborn with the coming of Spring. The images in this stanza strike me as being incidentally felicitous. Holloway suggests that in the paraphrases for line 11 we are looking at flocks of sheep 'spreading across a whole landscape, being slowly driven up to their mountain pastures'. Probably this is so, but I fail to see how the image of buds being driven into flower by the breeze is made more impressive by the comparison. The line evinces more power than appropriateness – often a defect in Shelley – though it is true that it reinforces the impression of a spring landscape to which the unfolding buds also belong. The force of the stanza is created more through its rhythms than through its imagery. I think it is worth pointing out that at this stage the imagery is all of a piece in one respect – it suggests throughout the presence of the earth and

growing things. There is no hint of the presence of sky and sea
that is the subject of the following stanzas. But whilst in this
sense the stanza is discrete, in a retrospective sense it will be
discovered to have been a preparation for what follows. That
is to say, the stanza offers no positive links with what is to come
(other than the presence of the West Wind itself). But what is
to come, we shall find, provides many links with what it has
come from. Words and groups of words that are to be used in
the next two stanzas will suggest very strongly a link backwards
to what appeared to be discrete and unconnected in the first
stanza.

II

Thou on whose streams, mid the steep sky's commotion,
Loose clouds like earth's decaying leaves are shed,
Shook from the tangled boughs of Heaven and Ocean,

Angels of rain and lightning: there are spread
On the blue surface of thine aëry surge,
Like the bright hair uplifted from the head

Of some fierce Maenad, even from the dim verge
Of the horizon to the zenith's height,
The locks of the approaching storm. Thou dirge

Of the dying year, to which this closing night
Will be the dome of a vast sepulchre,
Vaulted with all thy congregated might

Of vapours, from whose solid atmosphere
Black rain, and fire, and hail will burst: oh, hear!

The second stanza has provided the occasion for a good deal of
adverse (because ill-informed) criticism. Dr Leavis, for example,
spent a great deal of time insisting that the cloud formations
here are inaccurately visualised, that the phrases used to describe them are unintelligible and self-contradictory. But recent

studies of the Ode and of cyclonic storms in the Mediterranean have tended to vindicate Shelley. The clouds Shelley saw were probably those described in modern meteorological terms by F. H. Ludlam [see preceding essay] and as thunderclouds in anvil formations by Holloway (taking the phrase from H. Duncan Grant's *Cloud and Weather Atlas*). I do not think Holloway's paraphrase of this stanza can be improved upon, and so I offer it verbatim from his note to lines 15–28:

A large 'anvil' thunderstorm cloud is mounting in the western sky ('steep sky', l.15, rightly suggests that such a cloud seems to rise vertically). The wind is high, and the two arms of the anvil are fraying out forwards into long, fibrous cirrus clouds like the hair of a Maenad blown forwards from her head by the wind (l.21). The base of the anvil is dissolving in streams of small clouds ('found at the base, or even more often on the lower surface of anvil projections', Grant). Finally, the sun ('this closing night' l.24) is setting in the west, and the whole cloud is thus partly in deep shadow, partly a rich ruddy colour. Here, in fact, is the crucial point of the whole passage. Coloured in this way, the storm-cloud looks like a gigantic tree, with the loose, flying lower clouds streaming from it like autumn leaves (l.16) and the upper cirrus clouds looking like its branches.

So Shelley is using his eyes to register very precisely the appearance and movement of clouds in the formations Holloway describes. At the same time he brings forward the imagery of trees and leaves from the first stanza; and he projects forward into the nest the imagery of stream and 'aëry *surge*'. This suggests that the power of the wind operates in essentially the same way in the air as it does on land and sea. It is indifferent to the variety of the phenomena it works upon.

III

Thou who didst waken from his summer dreams
The blue Mediterranean, where he lay,
Lulled by the coil of his crystalline streams,

Beside a pumice isle in Baiae's bay,
And saw in sleep old palaces and towers
Quivering within the wave's intenser day,

All overgrown with azure moss and flowers
So sweet, the sense faints picturing them! Thou
For whose path the Atlantic's level powers

Cleave themselves into chasms, while far below
The sea-blooms and the oozy woods which wear
The sapless foliage of the ocean, know

Thy voice, and suddenly grow gray with fear,
And tremble and despoil themselves: oh, hear!

The third stanza reverts to the West Wind as a preserver, at any
rate as a power that enlivens and invigorates rather than one
that buries and entombs. There are two 'pictures': one of the
Mediterranean, the other of the Atlantic. Shelley can usually
be counted on to reproduce accurately the effect of light on
water, or indeed of light striking objects reflected in water and
then thrown back from the surface of the water (I am thinking
of The Question in which water lilies, floating near the edge of a
river, 'lit the oak that overhung the hedge/With moonlight
beams of their own watery light'). In the part of the Ode we are
looking at, the Mediterranean is lulled to sleep by the sound of
streams flowing into it. These produce the effect of currents
observed on the surface as coils, gently binding as well as lulling
the recumbent inland sea. As the sunlight beats on the surface
(the proximity of 'wave' and 'day', along with the emphasis on
blueness, intensity and quivering, releases the hidden word
'ray' as a ray of light creating that quivering effect on the
water) the submerged palaces and towers at Baiae seem to
float and move under the wave. Presumably the moss and
sea flowers can be seen to quiver as the light strikes down
to them and the motions of the water rock them. The

impression of clear light, in both air and sea, is intense – not merely blue, but azure and crystal producing this effect of calm brilliance.

With the appearance of the Atlantic the passive acceptance of light and of the coils of those streams, which the West Wind disturbed when it awakened the Mediterranean, gives way to an energetic activity. The Atlantic has powers of its own. Responding to the wind, not merely being acted upon by it, the outer sea cleaves itself into chasms. The woods and foliage at the bottom of the ocean 'despoil themselves'. The initiative has passed from the wind to the objects in nature that respond to it. They have, as it were, anticipated the will of the wind and have made themselves the vehicles of its power. In doing so they anticipate the demands of the poet in the last two stanzas, in which he too strives towards the condition he has described in the forms of leaf, cloud and wave in the earlier stanzas. But as well as anticipating the demands of the poet, the images in stanza three also cast back reflections on stanzas one and two, much as stanza two 'read back' its leaves and boughs to stanza one. Here the Mediterranean half hides the earth of palaces and towers sunk beneath it; its moss and flowers, together with the 'sea blooms' and 'oozy woods' of the Atlantic, carry back to the leaves and seeds and buds of stanza one. I have already commented on the projection of the stream and the 'Blue surface of thine aëry surge' across stanza two to merge with the water imagery of this third stanza.

IV

If I were a dead leaf thou mightest bear;
If I were a swift cloud to fly with thee;
A wave to pant beneath thy power, and share

The impulse of thy strength, only less free
Than thou, O uncontrollable! If even
I were as in my boyhood, and could be

The comrade of thy wandering over Heaven,
As then, when to outstrip thy skiey speed
Scarce seemed a vision; I would ne'er have striven

As thus with thee in prayer in my sore need.
Oh, lift me as a wave, a leaf, a cloud!
I fall upon the thorns of life! I bleed!

A heavy weight of hours has chained and bowed
One too like thee: tameless, and swift, and proud.

v

Make me thy lyre, even as the forest is:
What if my leaves are falling like its own!
The tumult of thy mighty harmonies

Will take from both a deep, autumnal tone,
Sweet though in sadness. Be thou, Spirit fierce,
My spirit! Be thou me, impetuous one!

Drive my dead thoughts over the universe
Like withered leaves to quicken a new birth!
And, by the incantation of this verse,

Scatter, as from an unextinguished hearth
Ashes and sparks, my words among mankind!
Be through my lips to unawakened earth

The trumpet of a prophecy! O, Wind,
If Winter comes, can Spring be far behind?

By the end of stanza three the energy of the poem is unabated, but its direction has changed. What began as the onslaught of the wind upon passive will-less attributes of nature – dead leaves, seeds, clouds, a lulled Mediterranean – has been transformed into the active, if fearful, co-operation of the Atlantic with the terrifying power of the wind. When Shelley turns to himself, in these last stanzas, it is the example of the Atlantic that is at the forefront of his mind. First he turns back to the whole of the poem so far to gather together the dominant images – to be borne on the back of the wind like a leaf; to fly with the wind as a cloud; and then, at the same time as panting beneath the power of the wind, to 'share/The impulse of thy strength'. The poet wants to subdue himself to the purposes of whatever power is represented by the wind; at the same time he sees himself as the wind's competitor, sharing its strength, striving with it in prayer. He is 'chained' and 'bowed' by precisely those attributes that belong to the wind – he is 'tameless', and 'swift', and 'proud'. But he needs to be tamed by the wind so that he is a fit instrument for it to blow through, so that he will fulfil his function in the world as the leaves and clouds and waves do – passively, co-operatively. His invocation to the wind to make him its lyre recalls his comments in the *Essay on Christianity*: 'There is a Power by which we are surrounded, like the atmosphere in which some motionless lyre is suspended, which visits with its breath our silent chords, at will.' The will is that of the Power, not of the lyre of human consciousness upon which it breathes. To receive the power the poet must use his will to harmonise his own identity with what he calls an 'exquisite consentaneity of powers'. This is what Shelley is recommending to himself to the last stanza. But he recognises that the recommendation is couched in what may be unfittingly imperative terms: 'Be thou, Spirit fierce,/My spirit! Be thou me, impetuous one!'.

Earl Wasserman refers disparagingly to a 'persistent critical tradition' according to which the poet in this part of the Ode is represented as being objectionably weak and praying for strength. This, he says, is incorrect:

> If to be strong means to have a rbitrary choice and self-assertiveness, then the poem presents that kind of 'strength' as the poet's flaw; what he is in need of is the difficult, strenuous 'weakness' that will make him available to the laws of the Power.[5]

I believe this to be a serious misreading of the poem and that
the critical tradition referred to is quite right. A paraphrase of
the fourth and fifth stanzas would probably support Wasserman's point of view, and his reference to the Spirits' Song to
Asia in *Prometheus* ('Such strength is in meekness') shows the
appropriateness of the sentiment contained in it to Shelley's
conception of the relationship between the World Power and
the individual soul. But we are reading a poem, not a précis of
the philosophical content of a poem; and the poem says, quite
emphatically, that the poet has been 'chained and bowed' and
suggests that the reason for this is he has not been 'tameless, and
swift, and proud' enough. The return to imperatives, very
urgent imperatives, in the middle of stanza five, testifies to his
recovery from the abject self-pity of 'I fall upon the thorns of
life! I bleed!' – surely a blotch on the poem; it is tonally quite
out of key with the rest. But the terms of the poem do not really
permit this kind of self-pity to exist at all. It does exist, and that
is why I think Wasserman's interpretation of the lines is wrong.
He wants the poem to justify itself line by line as a description
of a metaphysical system, and I don't think this is possible. I
want to respond to it line by line as a poem expressing
Shelley's feelings about his place in a world which can be
described in terms of that same system, and I think this
is possible but that it reveals unresolved tensions in the poet's
attitudes.

To my mind the poem's tone begins to falter at the fifth line
of stanza four: 'If even/I were as in my boyhood . . .'. In spite
of the presence of the peculiar and obviously Shelleyan word
'skiey' at line 8, these middle lines are strongly reminiscent of
the Wordsworth of *Tintern Abbey* and *The Excursion*. They take
us back to the Shelley of three or four years before, the Shelley
of *Alastor* and *Mont Blanc* with their crude Wordsworthian
borrowings[6] of both style and substance. At line 10 he falls into
the self-pitying manner to which I have already referred. Then,
with the substitution of 'one' for 'I' in the couplet, the poem
returns to the proper, imperative and not merely imprecatory,

mood that has characterised the first three stanzas. It continues
to express this mood throughout the fifth, and last, of its
stanzas.

I want to draw attention to the clause that bridges the
'Wordsworthian' and the 'bad Shelleyan' divisions of the stanza.
This forms the two half lines: 'I would ne'er have striven/As
thus with thee in prayer . . .'. The past tense we owe to the
preceding 'boyhood' reflections, but the point is that Shelley is
acknowledging that the prayer is not just a prayer but a
striving. He is simultaneously beseeching and commanding the
wind. It is the felt presence of this double mood that makes the
rest of the poem so powerful and the absence of it here that
weakens the verse disastrously. It is not difficult to see why
Shelley should have responded in this complex and irrational
way to the Power represented by the wind. The freedom he
refers to at line 4 is perfect service to the Power. At the same
time freedom involves a sharing of strength, 'the impulse of thy
strength'. Strength is felt primarily through conflict. But the
only thing in the poem that provokes conflict is the wind, which
embodies the Power. So Shelley can't help himself 'striving . . .
as thus' with the wind which, according to the system, and the
logic, should contain and channel that strength in the interest
of its own Necessitarian authority. So, being what he is, and the
wind representing what it does represent, Shelley is committed
to what I have called an irrational double attitude, of beseeching and commanding, of praying to and competing with the Spirit
of the universe as he understands it. His idealism is thwarted by
its own strength and assertiveness. It recognises the need for
submission to a higher authority. But because submission requires the poet to become like that authority and because the
authority is characterised by a competitive energy and remorse-
less power, submission itself becomes a kind of conflict.[7] In these
circumstances Shelley cannot be expected to identify strength,
the strength that is expressed through submission, with the
petulant weakness represented in stanza four; and that is the
only kind of weakness to which he seems able to give (albeit

unsatisfactory) poetic expression. That is why he is stuck in the double attitude I have described; and that is why any movement away from that attitude, towards a past and spurious Wordsworthian satisfaction or a present maudlin complaint, is a movement towards insincerity, towards a dishonest simplification of the central experience of the poem.

As for the strength, the power of Shelley's expression, it is present in almost every other part of the Ode: in its commanding structure, the binding force of its imagery, the precision of each separate image, and the driving energy and speed of the rhythms. Most of all it is in the rhythms. It is well known that the great Romantics of both the first and the second generation fell, in their different ways, under the influence of Milton; and that they adopted different strategies to cope with that influence – with greater or lesser success. Shelley's best poetry is quite free from this influence. It is less well known (though Eliot seems to have covertly recognised it) that Shakespeare's influence has been even more widespread and sometimes more insidiously damaging – a source of weakness as well as strength. Shelley's poetry seems to me to be as far as English poetry can get from Shakespeare's influence. His handling of imagery, his own variant of Romantic diction, above all the rapid, headlong movement of his rhythms, are at the furthest remove from Shakespeare's.

Perhaps, in so far as imagery is concerned, Dr Davie comes nearest to the truth when he writes that the sensuousness of some of Shelley's poetry 'is of a peculiar sort which makes the familiar remote. (He takes a common object such as a rose or a boat, and the more he describes it, the less we remember what it is.)' This is quite different from saying, with Leavis, that Shelley was 'peculiarly weak in his hold on objects'. After all, in *To a Skylark* Shelley describes the bird, and by implication the poet, as an '*unbodied* joy'. The poet is 'hidden/In the light of thought'. The more powerful the light, the more intense the feeling, the more likely it is that the solid object the poet contemplates loses its solidity and gives place to an almost abstract intensity of experience. This must be why in Shelley's world so much is shifting, why light fails to mould objects into solid, weighty things that can be turned around and touched like Keats's urn or Wordsworth's stones and pitchers. Instead light splits up, refracts, floats objects, catches them as they catch something of the intensity and abstraction of light. That is why, in spite of the uncanny vision of moving things Shelley produces in the Ode, the final impression we take away with us is of an intense transparency. The 'thought' of the poem is self-consciously stuck in a trap of its own devising. But that very self-consciousness, refracted through the imagery of leaves, clouds and waves, bound together by the darting rhythms of the *terza rima*, is profoundly liberating. It is that liberty, the quality of that unencumbered aspiration, we go to Shelley for. In this poem, he does not disappoint.

SOURCE: Essay originally published in *The Critical Survey*, vol. 6, nos 1 and 2 (Summer 1973) 52–8, and revised for this Casebook.

NOTES

1. Though he had already done so himself in *The Revolt of Islam*, IX 3649–93.

2. Though the anonymous reviewer of the poem for the *Literary Gazette* (1820) objected to the colouring of this description. In doing so, he provides the earliest specific example I can find of the critics' disbelief in what Shelley saw. [See page 37 above.]

3. An earlier and more detailed explanation of the image is provided in A. Eiloart, 'Shelley's *Skylark*: the "silver sphere" ', *Notes and Queries*, VI (4 July 1931) 4–8.

4. Shelley had translated the first canzone of the *Convito* by 1820, and translations of a section of the *Purgatorio* (XXVIII 1–51) and of the *Inferno* (XXXIII 22–75), both in *terza rima*, followed. None of these translations was published in Shelley's lifetime. Almost certainly all of them were written after the Ode.

5. Earl Wasserman, *Shelley: A Critical Reading* (Baltimore and London, 1971) p. 247

6. See John Piper, *The Active Universe* (London, 1962) pp. 164–73.

7. Kapstein's essay on *Mont Blanc* [included in this volume] also emphasises Shelley's ambivalent or irrational attitude to the 'act of submission' to Necessity.

SELECT BIBLIOGRAPHY

The following books and articles are, in the editor's opinion, of particular interest as contributions to the criticism of Shelley's shorter poems, though for various reasons (such as limitations of space) it was not possible to represent them in the main body of this book.

Carlos Baker, *Shelley's Major Poetry* (Princeton N.J.: Princeton University Press, 1948). The most sensible and lucid full-length study of Shelley's poetry, but, as its title suggests, it is mainly concerned with the longer poems.

James E. Barcus, ed., *Shelley: The Critical Heritage* (London: Routledge, 1975). Reproduces the most important essays and reviews on Shelley's poetry between 1810 and 1868.

F. W. Bateson, 'The Quickest Way out of Manchester: Four Romantic Odes', *English Poetry* (London: Longman's 1950). A study of the *Ode to the West Wind* as evidence of Shelley's 'retreat from politics' – the point at which he discovered that 'Romanticism and politics are inherently incompatible'.

Colin Clarke, 'Shelley's "Tangled Boughs" ', *Durham University Journal*, LIV (1961). A discriminating survey of the critical history of a single image from the second stanza of the *Ode to the West Wind*, concluding that the image 'provides clear proof that allegory is not adequate to the rendering of the subtle processes of nature'.

R. H. Fogle, *The Imagery of Keats and Shelley* (Chapel Hill, N.C.: North Carolina University Press, 1949). Contains four long chapters of comparison and contrast between Keats and Shelley in their use of imagery (sensitive, synaesthetic, empathic and abstract). A little schematic and dull, but sometimes helpful on the detail of the poetry.

Herbert Grierson, *Lyrical Poetry from Blake to Hardy* (London: Hogarth Press, 1928) pp. 46–54. Contains a brief sub-chapter on Shelley which has been unaccountably praised by some critics.

D. W. Harding, 'Shelley's Poetry', *Pelican Guide to English Literature*, v (London, 1957) pp. 207–19. A good essay, with a great deal of reference to the shorter poems; takes a similar line to Leavis in his *Revaluation* essay (on 'self-absorption or narcissism'), but this does not prevent him from offering sensitive readings of the *West Wind* and *Adonais*.

Graham Hough, 'Shelley as Lyricist', *The Romantic Poets* (London: Hutchinson, 1953) pp. 140–50. Does not add significantly to our knowledge of Shelley's lyrical poems, but is a sensible and modest account of the subject.

D. J. Hughes, 'Coherence and Collapse in Shelley', *English Literary History*, xxviii (1961) 260–83. Incidental references to the lyrics, some of which are thought-provoking, but the principal interest is in the narrative poems.

D. J. Hughes, 'Kindling and Dwindling: the Poetic Process in Shelley', *Keats–Shelley Journal*, xiii (1964). As above.

C. S. Lewis, 'Shelley, Dryden and Mr. Eliot', *Rehabilitations and Other Essays* (London: O.U.P., 1939). One of the most celebrated rejoinders to Eliot's criticism of Shelley (reprinted in this Casebook); but most of the useful material is on *Prometheus*.

E. B. Murray, '*Mont Blanc*'s Unfurled Veil', *Keats–Shelley Journal*, xviii (1969). A good essay on *Mont Blanc* which would have been included in the present volume if space had permitted and if the editor had not thought two essays on the poem excessive.

Neville Rogers, *Shelley at Work: A Critical Inquiry* (Oxford: O.U.P., 1967). Of great interest to anyone studying Shelley's composition of the poems; separate chapters on the *Skylark* and *West Wind*.

Earl R. Wasserman, *Shelley: A Critical Reading* (Baltimore and London: Johns Hopkins University Press, 1971). A very difficult book, not least because of its occasionally turgid and pretentious expression; has some information on certain of the shorter poems, but its distinction lies overwhelmingly in its lengthy and often brilliant exposition of *Prometheus Unbound*.

N. I. White, *The Unextinguished Hearth: Shelley and his Contemporary Critics* (Durham, N.C.: Duke University Press, 1938 and 1968). A history of Shelley criticism during the poet's lifetime; overlaps with the Barcus volume, but contains more explanation and less contemporary critical material.

S. C. Wilcox, 'Sources, Symbolism, and Unity of Shelley's *Skylark*',
Studies in Philology, XLVI (1949) 560–76. A close reading of the
Skylark with a great deal of material on the sources, principally
Platonic.

NOTES ON CONTRIBUTORS

JUDITH CHERNAIK, critic and novelist, has taught at several American and British universities, including Columbia and London. Her publications include *The Lyrics of Shelley* (1972).

DONALD DAVIE, poet and critic, has taught at Stanford University and the Universities of Cambridge and Essex; in 1978 he became Mellon Professor of the Humanities, Vanderbilt University, Nashville, Tenn. His publications include his *Collected Poems* (1972) and subsequent verse collections, *Purity of Diction in English Verse* (1952, new edn 1967), *The Language of Science and the Language of Literature, 1700-1740* (1963), *Thomas Hardy and English Poetry* (1972), *The Poet in the Imaginary Museum: Essays* (1976), *A Gathered Cloud: The Literature of the English Dissenting Interest, 1700-1930* (1978) and *Trying to Explain* (1979).

T. S. ELIOT (1888-1965), poet, dramatist and critic. His most important works of criticism are *The Sacred Wood* (1920) and *The Use of Poetry and the Use of Criticism* (1933).

DAVID V. ERDMAN taught English literature in the State University of New York at Stony Brook. His publications include works on Blake, the most recent of which is *The Illuminated Blake*.

JOHN HOLLOWAY, poet and critic, has taught in several universities and in 1972 was appointed Professor of Modern English in the University of Cambridge. His publications include collections of his verse, and *Language and Intelligence* (1951), *Selected Poems, by P.B. Shelley* (1960), *Widening Horizons in English Verse* (1966), and *Narrative and Structure* (1979).

RALPH HOUSTON, American writer, is the author of *White Jade* (1950).

EDWARD B. HUNGERFORD taught English literature at Northwestern University, Illinois. His publications include *Shores of Darkness* (1941) and *Recovering the Rhythms of Poetry* (1966).

I. J. KAPSTEIN taught English literature at Brown University, Rhode Island.

F. H. LUDLUM (died 1977) was Professor of Meteorology in Imperial College, London.

G. M. MATTHEWS is Reader in English Literature in the University of Reading. He is the editor of the 'Critical Heritage' volume on Keats, and has written widely on Keats and Shelley.

WILLIAM MILGATE is Professor of English in the Australian National University. He has edited Donne's *Satires, Epigrams and Verse Letters* (1967).

VALERIE PITT is Head of the School of Humanities at Thames Polytechnic London.

FREDERICK J. POTTLE was Professor of English in the University of Yale. His publications – in addition to authoritative studies on James Boswell – include *Idiom of Poetry* (1963) and *Shelley and Browning: A Myth and Some Facts* (1965).

PATRICK SWINDEN lectures in English Literature in the University of Manchester. His publications include *Unofficial Selves: Character in the Novel from Dickens to the Present Day* (1973), *An Introduction to Shakespeare's Comedies* (1973), *Paul Scott: Images of India* (1980) and the Casebook on George Eliot's *Middlemarch*.

ALLEN TATE, poet and novelist, taught at several universities and latterly at Minnesota. His *Collected Poems* were published in 1978; his publications on criticism include *On the Limits of Poetry* (1948), *The Man of Letters in the Modern World* (1956) and *Essays of Four Decades* (1969).

INDEX